T. R. (Thomas Rawson) Birks

First Principles of Moral Science

A Course of Lectures Delivered in the University of Cambridge

T. R. (Thomas Rawson) Birks

First Principles of Moral Science
A Course of Lectures Delivered in the University of Cambridge

ISBN/EAN: 9783742815897

Manufactured in Europe, USA, Canada, Australia, Japa

Cover: Foto ©Thomas Meinert / pixelio.de

Manufactured and distributed by brebook publishing software
(www.brebook.com)

T. R. (Thomas Rawson) Birks

First Principles of Moral Science

FIRST PRINCIPLES

OF

MORAL SCIENCE.

Cambridge:
PRINTED BY C. J. CLAY, M.A.
AT THE UNIVERSITY PRESS.

FIRST PRINCIPLES

OF

MORAL SCIENCE,

A COURSE OF LECTURES

DELIVERED IN

The University of Cambridge

BY

THOMAS RAWSON BIRKS,

KNIGHTBRIDGE PROFESSOR OF MORAL PHILOSOPHY.

London:

MACMILLAN AND CO.

1873.

PREFACE.

THIS small volume contains the substance of a first course of Lectures, delivered in October and November 1872, in partial fulfilment of the honourable trust a few months earlier confided to me, after the lamented death of Professor Maurice.

The subjects formally assigned to the Knightbridge Professor are Moral Philosophy, Casuistry, and Moral Theology. The first and third of these scarcely need any exposition of their meaning. The second was viewed by Dr Whewell as an historical term, now superseded by the more general and comprehensive phrase, Moral Philosophy. On the other hand Professor Maurice, while he looks on the solution of cases of conscience as impossible, applies the name of Casuistry to that subjective side of Moral Science, which enforces the claims of the personal "I," the individual conscience. This subject, though highly important in itself, does not seem to me, whether in history or by etymology, to answer to the name. But I think it may be transferred, by a moderate license, from doubtful

and disputed questions in the details of Moral Duty, to
Controversial Ethics, or the attempt to gain clear and
firm convictions on those great questions, which give birth
to rival schools of ethical teaching, and have perplexed
and divided the judgments of moralists for thousands of
years.

The present work treats of three topics, all preliminary
to the direct exposition of the first of these three main
subjects, Moral Philosophy. These are the Certainty and
Dignity of Moral Science, its Spiritual Geography, or
relation to other main subjects of human thought, and
its Formative Principles, or some elementary truths on
which its whole development must depend. In the coming
year I propose to myself to enter on the second subject,
or Controversial Ethics; by a review, first, of Modern
Utilitarianism, as expounded by Paley and Bentham, and
recast by Mr Mill into a different form; and next, of modern Cambridge Ethics, represented by the Discourse of
Professor Sedgwick, and the writings of my three eminent
predecessors. In Mr Mill's review of Professor Sedgwick
these two schools came first into direct collision, almost
forty years ago; and now in the present year, within a
few months, these distinguished writers have both passed
away. The harsher sounds of controversy should be
stilled, and only its grave and gentle utterances be
heard, over the recent graves of the dead.

I have ventured to append to these Lectures a college
essay or declamation, delivered in Trinity College Chapel

in December 1833, or just forty years ago. I believe that the thoughts it contains, however youthful the style, are seasonable and important at the present hour. They secured at the time a favourable notice from Dr Chalmers and some other distinguished men. But I reproduce them here for a double reason. They are a pledge that the views held in the present volume, and others which may follow, are no hasty product of recent study, but convictions early formed, and deepened by all the study and reflection of so many years. Its date is just one year after Professor Sedgwick's Discourse, and a few months after its publication. It may thus be taken as one further sign of a reaction against the selfish and utilitarian school of ethical teaching, which had then set in, alike among older and younger members of the university, and which has continued to the present day.

I commit this work, as a small sheaf of first-fruits, to the candid and forbearing perusal of learned readers; but still more to the blessing of Him, without whom nothing is strong, nothing is holy, the only Fountain of moral insight and true wisdom, the uncreated and eternal Goodness, in whom all truth dwells in its perfect fulness, from whom its streams proceed, and to whom they return, after watering the wide universe of moral being through which they flow.

TRINITY PARSONAGE,
CAMBRIDGE,
        September, 1873.

LECTURE I.

THE TRUE PLACE OF MORAL SCIENCE.

In entering on the duties of the Knightbridge Professorship, I have endeavoured, in my Inaugural Lecture, to point out the great importance of the systematic study of Moral Science in the days in which we live. It is natural to begin this first course of Lectures with some remarks on the main outlines of the subject, and the order of treatment I hope to pursue. This seems doubly needful, when I succeed to writers so eminent as Dr Whewell and Professor Maurice. They have left behind them, besides four volumes of published Lectures, a full and detailed History of Moral Philosophy, ancient and modern, and a systematic treatise on the Elements of Morality. And still they vary considerably from each other in their construction of the titles by which this Professorship is defined, and in their methods of ethical exposition.

The original subject, by the deed of the founder, Dr Knightbridge, is "Moral Theology, or Casuistical Divinity." But when Dr Whewell, on his election in June 1838, revived the office from a long and deep slumber, he introduced in his first Lecture the name

"Moral Philosophy", as well adapted, in his view, to
express "the substitution of a newer form of science, full
of life, hope, interest, and solid truth, for older and more
imperfect speculations." "I shall reckon," he says, "on
the implied sanction of the University, in considering
myself as Professor of Moral Philosophy, a branch of study
of which a Professorship exists, I believe, in every University
but our own." The sanction implied at first, was
afterwards expressly and publicly given, when the University
made a later addition to the original endowment.

Dr Whewell began with a course of Lectures on the
English Moralists from Hobbes to Paley, Gisborne, and
Price, at the close of last century. To these, when published,
six others were added on Bentham's works; and in
a second edition, in 1862, fourteen others, which began
with Plato and ended with Coleridge. His second and
main work, published in 1846, was the "Elements of
Morality," a full and systematic treatise on Moral Science.
It was followed, the same year, by eight "Lectures on
Systematic Morality," and appeared anew in 1864, shortly
before his death, in an enlarged and revised edition.

The Third Book of the Elements includes a full treatment
of Ethics in their religious aspect, or Moral Theology.
But Casuistry, in Dr Whewell's view, holds quite a
secondary place in Christian Morals. It refers, he says,
to "questions of human conduct, in which conflicting
duties, or obscurity in the application of moral rules,
perplex and distort the faculty which judges of right and
wrong." It is thus "neither the main part" of the general
subject, "nor that from which it can with propriety derive
its name."

Prof. Maurice, on the other hand, in his opening
Lecture, seems to regard Casuistry, Moral Philosophy, and

Moral Theology, as three distinct and successive stages of Moral Science, which fitly express its personal, social, and religious elements. He appears further to assume that these titles of the office are a guiding light, which the University itself has supplied, to fix the limitations of the main subject, and the due and proper order of its exposition. He had published, twenty years before his election, an instructive treatise on the history of Mental and Moral Philosophy, and it has since appeared, in a revised and enlarged form, as his latest work. It was natural for him, then, to abstain in his Lectures from this branch of the main subject, and to confine himself to a more direct treatment of moral questions. His first course, accordingly, was on the Conscience, under the title of "Lectures on Casuistry," and his second on Social Morality. Had his life been spared, we may assume that a third would have followed on Moral Theology. But he remarks that he had found it impracticable to maintain entire distinctness, and that Moral Theology had really intruded into both. "It must be so," he observes, "for any one who discovers, beneath the conscience which testifies of our personal existence, and beneath all the order of human society, a Divine foundation."

Dr Whewell, then, has unfolded Ethical Science mainly on its objective side, as a connected and very extensive scheme of thought, under the heads of Springs of Action, Morality, Religion, Rights and Obligations, Polity and International Law. But in such an outline, however ably filled, there may be some danger of the conscience finding itself oppressed, like David in Saul's armour, by a panoply of solid and laborious thought, too heavy for its weakness to sustain. A treatment less complete and exhaustive, but appealing more directly to the spontaneous emotions of the heart, like arrows from the bow, or stones from the sling, must therefore have been desirable at least as a supplement for common minds.

Prof. Maurice, accordingly, took up in his first course the subjective side of Ethics. He sought earnestly to bring out into full relief the "I ought" of conscience, to protest against theories which would resolve it into the mere dread of human punishment, and to summon it, by a direct appeal to the consciousness of its own supremacy, to the pursuit of high and noble aims. An awakened conscience, fully alive to the claims of duty, which looks up with reverence to a law it cannot alter and is bound to obey, is the first essential of true morality, the only genuine passport to the temple of ethical science. Where this is absent, learned speculations on moral theories, and on schools of ancient and modern thought, become immoral trifling, bewildering to the reason, and deadening to the heart.

But while the subject of these Lectures is, I conceive, a most suitable and needful supplement to Dr Whewell's more systematic work, I do not think that they are "Lectures on Casuistry," either in the sense of the founder, or in the well-known and historical meaning of the name. The earnest inculcation of thorough conscientiousness in all cases, and under all sacrifices, is indeed of vital and almost supreme importance to the moral student. It is the starting-point of genuine progress, the living sap in the tree of Ethical Science. But Casuistry in its proper sense, or the provision of rules for the guidance of such a conscience in doubtful and obscure cases, is widely different. One is like the root of the fruitful olive-tree, the other is the gleaning berries on its outmost branches, when the harvest has already been gathered in.

The threefold title of the Professorship may be adopted, I think, with less violence to the real distinctions of the subject, in another way, without disturbing their order, or using Casuistry in a sense wholly diverse from its historical meaning. Moral Theology, instead of being included, as in Dr Whewell's work, midway in the course, should be reserved, as the highest division, for the crown and climax of the whole. Philosophy deals with the conclusions of human reason, aided and enlightened by Revelation, but acting still within the limits of that Divine appeal—"Yea, and why even of yourselves judge ye not that which is right?" Theology deals with the character and works of God, as made known to us more clearly and fully by Divine revelation. And thus Moral Theology is the meeting-place and border province of these two kingdoms of thought. It deals with the religious aspect of Moral Philosophy, and the ethical aspect of Revealed Religion. It binds these together in a higher synthesis, where reason is ennobled and purified by faith in a Divine message; while faith itself, cleansed from mere superstition, offers to God a reasonable service, and sees light in the light of heaven.

Moral Philosophy, thus defined, must include the subjective and objective side of Ethics, the enforcement of the claims and supremacy of conscience, and the whole range of social morality; or, in one word, all the direct and positive teaching of Moral Science. What place, then, is left for Casuistry? In the strict and proper sense, Dr Whewell justly regards it as a very subordinate branch of the general subject. The difficulties, also, to which it relates are more likely to seek and find their solution from the pastor or the friend than from academical lectures. And Professor Maurice, even while he retains the term,

seems wholly to abolish the science or art itself, since he
holds that attempts to lay down rules for cases of conscience "only leave those cases more unsettled than ever."
But if doubts and questionings, in the present day, are
mainly transferred from curious and involved cases, where
the path of duty is obscure, to the very foundations of
morality, we may come near to the true design of the
founder by retaining the title in a somewhat varied sense.
Casuistry will thus refer to the polemical aspect of moral
questions, and deal with those controversies and disputes
which tend to cloud and perplex the minds of students,
and are constant attendants on every imperfect stage of a
progressive science.

I propose, then, to arrange the general subject under these
three main divisions: 1st, Direct Ethics, or Moral Science
in its relation to other sciences, its fundamental principles,
and the wide range of personal and social obligations, including some first lessons of religious faith and duty; 2ndly,
Controversial Ethics, answering nearly to Casuistry, or the
inquiry into the debateable ground of Morals, and the discussion of rival and conflicting systems; and, 3rdly, Moral
Theology, a wide and interesting, as well as difficult, field
of thought.   For here an awakened conscience and intelligent Christian faith act and react on each other.   The conscience tests pretended revelations by laws of its own,
while it submits reverently to the authority of a Divine
message.   It can thus learn new facts and lessons of God's
moral government, grow more fully instructed as to its
own nature and the duties and hopes of man, as responsible to his Maker, and walk in the light of a teaching
higher and even purer than its own.   Here, also, an intelligent, but sober and reverent, faith brings its unsolved and
perplexing problems, in messages that claim a Divine

origin, to be examined in the light of a purified reason,
and to be solved even here, when the answer is possible, for
our present comfort, and the due strengthening of its own
powers. But when such a solution is too hard for present
attainment, it is the further office of Moral Theology to
remind us of the limitations of our moral insight, while
we see "as in a mirror, darkly"; and to encourage us
to wait hopefully, and not impatiently, for clearer light;
whether the blessing may be given in the world's eventide,
or only in that brighter morning, when the day shall break
on the immortal spirit, and the shadows of the night shall
flee away.

These few remarks on the conflicting definitions of
Casuistry by the two most eminent of my predecessors,
and their differing arrangements of the whole subject,
seemed needful to explain and justify the order I propose
to follow. My purpose, in the present course, is to treat of
some first principles of Direct Ethics, or Moral Philosophy
in its narrower sense, under these two heads: its relation,
as in a moral geography, to other branches of human
knowledge, and its fundamental principles, or the courses
of solid masonry on which it rests below. And my first
subject will be the True Place and real dignity of Moral
Science.

There is a school of thought, in our own days, which,
under the boasted name of Scientific Progress, would wholly
abolish all Theology, and reduce Morals to a dependent
and precarious existence, in which it becomes the vassal
and slave of Physics or Human Anatomy. And its
strength, in popular esteem, has been derived, in no small
measure, from its attempted classification of every department of human science. The instinctive craving after
unity, never wholly asleep, has been wakened into new

and more intense activity by the discoveries of the last
hundred years. Many run to and fro. The bonds of
commercial intercourse are interlaced and strengthened.
Nations learn thus to look beyond themselves, and recognize dimly a wider and larger brotherhood of all mankind. The same influence extends to the mutual relations
of the sciences themselves. The various branches of intellectual speculation and thought borrow from each other,
and melt into each other, more and more. Thus Astronomy
borrows from Mechanics, Optics, Electricity and Magnetism, and even of late from Chemistry, the means
for its further and wider progress. Geographical research becomes more exhaustive, and geological inquiry
deeper, more profound, and more various than before.
Both of these alike borrow largely from Zoology and
Botany, and lend to these sciences rich and copious
materials in return. Heat is identified with motion, and
becomes a subtler branch of Mechanics. The magnetism of the earth has its changes linked with solar phenomena. Deep ocean soundings, made by new refine-
ments of instrumental skill, modify geological theories.
The same craving for comprehensiveness and unity reveals
itself in antiquarian pursuits, and modern researches into
the history of language and of race. It seems as if the
limbs of Science, torn asunder by ignorance, and violently
scattered, were striving to come together, and clothe
themselves with sinews and flesh once more, and thus to
form one living, united, and harmonious system.

In such a period of thought, any school which professes to exhibit all the sciences in their orderly succession,
and to ground on that arrangement special theories and
deductions of its own, wields an engine of aggression on
all rival systems of no common power. The combat is

like that between a regular army with its well-disciplined battalions, and guerrillas or volunteers without discipline or concert, spread out in loose array.

Such a theory has arisen, it is well known, in French Positivism, and, variously modified, has many disciples or admirers among the cultivated classes of our own land. But such a doctrinal system, which destroys and proscribes all religious faith, and degrades morality into a cerebral secretion, a blind necessity, or a pleasure-seeking prudence, can only be met and overthrown by one better and nobler; by a system which retains whatever is true and sound in the lower fields of thought, but includes in its larger geography those sacred heights and mountain-tops of human science, which deal with moral and spiritual objects, and pierce into the skies above, while they command the widest and most comprehensive views of the peaceful valleys below.

Let us begin, then, by endeavouring to fix clearly the true place of Ethics in the wide range of human science. And here the scheme of Lord Bacon, in his *De Augmentis*, supplies a basis, capable indeed of no slight improvement, but from which the remarks of Locke, and the fuller system of Comte, are really a retrogression and decline, rather than an advance to clearer insight, and a more perfect and comprehensive arrangement.

The first division of human knowledge, Bacon has well observed, must be drawn from the threefold powers of the rational soul, which is the seat of knowledge. History belongs to the memory, Poetry to the fancy or imagination, and Philosophy to the reason. But here two further remarks naturally arise. First, this division is common alike to every branch of human thought, just as breadth, in Geometry, coexists with the other dimensions of space. It seems thus more natural and convenient, instead of separating History and Poetry altogether from the kindred branches of Philosophy, as Bacon has done, to make this distinction subordinate to the main objective divisions of Human Science. And next, in the case of Natural Philosophy, the registration of natural phenomena, which answers to history, and the invention of hypotheses and development of their consequences, which correspond to poetry, are properly quite subordinate to the branch of science to which those phenomena and hypotheses belong. They form its materials, and supply the means for its further progress. Tables of observations, records of observed facts, registered stellar phenomena, and the successive theories of Ptolemy and Copernicus, of Kepler and Herschel, are thus the inseparable adjuncts of astronomical science.

Science or Philosophy, as Bacon has well observed, receives its primary and fundamental division from its threefold object, " Deus, natura, homo." "It is convenient," he adds, "that Philosophy be divided into three sciences, concerning God, nature, and man." But when he has laid this clear and simple foundation, he proceeds at once, rather strangely, to deviate from the only true and natural arrangement. He distinguishes inspired Theology wholly from Philosophy, and reserves it for the last place at the close of his treatise, as "the haven and sabbath of all human contemplation." And yet he places Natural Theology, as a separate branch, first in the three main divisions of Human Philosophy.

Such a scheme has plainly a double fault. It severs Natural and Revealed Theology as widely as possible, making them form the two extremes of the whole system. But they are plainly mere subdivisions of the same grand

subject. The contrast implied in the names does not
extend to the truths themselves, but refers wholly to the
different means by which our knowledge of them is supposed to be attained. And next, his plan involves a disturbed order of the three divisions themselves, which are not
allowed to form either an ascending or a descending scale.

The truer plan of arrangement, in this respect, which
M. Comte has justly followed, is that of an ascending
series. Natural Theology, in Lord Bacon's outline of
sciences, should plainly be reserved for the third place,
near the close; so as to prepare the way, by a gradual
ascent, for the fuller and higher teaching of Divine
Revelation. Nor should this be excluded from Philosophy.
It ought rather to be included in it as its highest and
noblest portion. For the genuine pursuit of wisdom, which
is the meaning of philosophy, can never rest short of the
vision of the Only Wise, or that " knowledge of the Holy"
(Prov. xxx. 3), which alone is true understanding and "life
eternal."

Again, that "prima philosophia," which Lord Bacon
places as the common stem of the three main divisions,
seems to have no real claim to this high position. So
far as it is real, and not a mere play on words, or on
the analogies and ambiguities of human language, it belongs to some aspect or other of Natural Theology, and
the relations between the First Cause, the Creator, and the
whole universe of created things.

The first and main division, then, of Philosophy or
Science is threefold. Its first and lowest portion is Natural Philosophy; its second, Humanity; its last and
highest, Theology, both Natural and Revealed. This, too,
is the very order implied in the system of our ancient
universities. It is far more full, harmonious, and complete,

than the maimed and imperfect substitutes which have
been proposed or invented in modern times.

Natural Philosophy is divided by Lord Bacon into
Speculative and Operative, and the Speculative into
Physical and Metaphysical. The former of these is said
to deal with the efficient cause and matter,¦ the other
with the final cause and form. Again, the Physical is
divided into three subjects, the Principles of things, the
World, and the Variety of things. It is further divided
into a doctrine of Concretes and Abstracts, the first
having the same divisions as Natural History. The Metaphysical is divided into the doctrine of Forms and of
Final Causes.

Operative Physics, again, are parted into Mechanics,
and Magic in a revised sense of the term. This, in Bacon's
view of it, seems nearly to agree with the modern science
of Imponderables, since he defines it to be "a practical
knowledge of the more secret powers and subtle influences
of the natural world." Last of all, Mathematics, both
pure and mixed, are made a separate appendix of the
whole.

Such an arrangement of Natural Science, it can hardly
be denied, leaves on the mind a vague and confused impression. From the objective principle, clearly laid down
at first, we are thrown back on subjective divisions of a
wholly different kind, which are made to depend, in
part, on the abstractions of Greek philosophy. What
is called Operative Natural Philosophy really consists
in the application of natural knowledge to the wants of
mankind, and thus properly forms a part of the higher
subject of Humanity. Lord Bacon seems to have known
little of Mathematics, and, like Sir W. Hamilton, held
them in light esteem. Instead of being made an accidental

appendix of Physics, they ought rather to come first, as the
intellectual starting-point and basis of the whole scheme.
They are lowest, indeed, in dignity, though first in order of
ascent, but still claim a very high importance, because their
truths underlie every branch of Material Physics, and may
thus be justly held to be the foundation of the whole.

Mathematics, or the Science of Number, Space, Motion
and Force, will thus hold the first place in the natural
arrangement of the Physical Sciences. Next will come
Uranology, or the knowledge of the heavens, and all the
worlds they contain, whether suns, stars, planets, satellites,
or meteors, star-dust, and nebulous matter, spread through
the depths of space. Third in order will be Ecumeno-
logy, or the knowledge of the habitable world, a subject
in outward extent far more limited than the last, but also
far more accessible, and thus capable, practically, of a
fuller development, and of more various subdivision. It
includes three main classes of objects—lifeless matter,
plants, and animals or living things. The first may be
called Hylology, and is either analytic or synthetic. Physics, or Analytical Hylology, will include Solid Mechanics,
Hydrodynamics, Pneumatics, the doctrine of the Imponderables—Heat, Light, Electricity, and Magnetism—and
analytical Chemistry, or the determination of the laws
which distinguish the main classes of lifeless things. Geo-
gnosy, or Synthetic Hylology, will include Physical Geography, Hydrography, Meteorology, and Geology; with
two appendices of Palæontology, or the determination of
past changes, and the probable state of the Earth in every
former age; and a corresponding science, still nameless,
and beyond the range of present human foresight, which
would include the prediction of all future changes in
distant ages still to come.

Passing over the two higher divisions of Natural Philosophy, Botany and Zoology, we come to a higher subject, which holds the middle place in the ascending series, and to which the words of Pope will apply—

The proper study of mankind is Man.

The leading division in the *De Augmentis* of Lord Bacon has here been reproduced by M. Comte under different names. The Philosophy of Humanity and Civil Science, in the former, answer very closely to Biology and Sociology. The first is parted by Bacon into a science of the Body and of the Soul. A third division is added, on the State of Man, or his Personality, and the union of body and soul. This, again, is made to include two parts, a doctrine of the Miseries, and one of the Prerogatives of Man. The Science of the Body is parted into four divisions, relating to health, beauty, exercise and pleasure, or a science of Medicine, Cosmetics, Athletics, and Hedonics. The Science of the Soul is parted into one of the Substance and Faculties, and another on the use and objects of those faculties. This latter is divided into Logic and Ethics. Ethical Science is parted into a doctrine on the Standard of Good, and another on the Culture and Guidance of the Mind; and this last into three portions, on Character, on the Affections, and on Moral Remedies.

Civil Science, again, is ranked under three main divisions. The first is the Science of Conversation, or Social Intercourse; the second, of Business or Occupation; and the third, on the Republic or Empire. To this brief outline are added two supplements, on the fountain of social right, and on enlargement of the bounds of empire.

A simpler arrangement, I conceive, may be based on the ascending scale of human faculties or powers, and will thus be in closer harmony with the main objective division of all science into Natural Philosophy, Humanity, and Theology.

Humanity, or the Science of Man, in its widest sense will include the knowledge of Human Action, Speech, and Thought. Human Action will admit a fourfold distinction, with reference to the individual, the outer world, the family, and the state. These might perhaps be conveniently styled Autonomics, or the discipline and culture of man's own person and bodily frame; Geonomics, including agriculture, horticulture, zoonomy, or the culture of animals, and navigation; Economics, or the science of domestic and family life; and External Politics, or the science of human action, when men are gathered in civil societies of various kinds. The Science of Speech will include Grammar, Lexicography, Oral and Written Language, Semeiology, or various modifications, used as signs of thought, such as Hieroglyphics, Stenography, Secret Writing and Telegraphy; and the higher branches of Logic, Rhetoric, Dialectics, Education, Jurisprudence, Literature, and Public Worship. The Science of Thought will include Mental Philosophy in all its various aspects, and is either Analytic or Synthetic. The first refers to the different faculties and powers in each individual, and includes a doctrine of Perception and Sensation, or the relations of the mind to outward nature; of Reflection or Self-knowledge, of Sympathy and human fellowship, and of Religious Faith, aspiring to things unseen and eternal. The Synthetic Science of Human Thought is that which deals with the various characters and classes of mankind, and all the diversities of sex, age, race, intelligence, culture, and the countless varieties of human life and feeling, of social and religious thought.

But a Science of Humanity, when pursued within these limits, does not satisfy the conditions of scientific completeness. For it deals wholly with the actual, and not the ideal. It contemplates Man as he has been or now is, and not as he might be or ought to be. But Man is conscious of powers of choice, on the use or abuse of which his happiness very mainly depends. He is not a mere tool or engine, set in motion by external powers, over which he has no control. He has a knowledge of good and evil, of evil which he seeks to avoid, and of good which he dimly seeks after, and longs to attain. He feels himself capable of progress and improvement, or of degeneracy and decline. Herein he feels himself to differ widely from lifeless matter, with its laws which it must obey, and even from all the lower animals, though these are gifted with wonderful instincts and powers of spontaneous motion. And thus there remains a higher field, beyond and above all those branches of Human Science which have now been briefly indicated, and coextensive with their whole range. Man's nature is twofold. It includes the consciousness of actual powers and capacities, and the dim perception of a high and noble ideal, attainable, but not yet attained. This is well expressed in the often-quoted lines—

> Except above himself he can
> Erect himself, how mean a thing is Man!

Humanity, then, since it refers to a being far higher in its powers than lifeless matter, or mere animal instinct, and still far below Divine perfection, resolves itself necessarily into two main divisions. The first is Actual Humanity, or the knowledge of Man such as experience proves him to be, in his various relations to nature, to his fellow-men, and to the Unseen Power on whom his being depends.

The second is Ethics or Ideal Humanity, the knowledge of that high standard of perfect action, speech and thought, below which men may fall continually, and too often with a deplorable and melancholy contrast, but towards which they are bound ever to aspire; and, aspiring towards it with earnest desire and effort, may hope for its fuller and fuller attainment.

Ethics, then, in one word is the Science of Ideal Humanity. It sets before us Man, not as he is, but as he ought to be. It implies a standard of right and wrong, which does not depend on the actual state and conduct of mankind, and is not fixed by past experience, but which shines out amidst the storm-clouds of human passions and vices like a rainbow of hope and promise, pointing onward to something bright, excellent and glorious, not yet attained. This science of Ideal Humanity is the true mainspring of all human progress, which really deserves the name. And it forms also the natural transition to the best and highest field of human thought, Divine Theology. The connection is no mere result of fancy, or philosophical reasoning. It is inwoven into the very texture of Christian faith. For this is the grand "mystery of godliness," on which the whole fabric of the Christian revelation depends, that the ideal Man is no other than the Incarnate Son of God.

A clear view of the main outlines of human knowledge, and of their mutual relation, will thus enable us not only to ascertain the true place, but to maintain the dignity, of Moral Science. The arrangement of Lord Bacon is in this respect very faulty and imperfect. It would lead us to suppose that Ethics are a mere subdivision of one subdivided branch of the doctrine of Humanity; that they come nearly midway in its course,

8/   B. L.   2 and form hardly one-tenth of the whole. But this is wholly different from the real truth. They constitute a vast and wide field of thought, conterminous with the whole range of actual human knowledge. Throughout all the wide expanse of human interests they prescribe a standard of perfection to the actions, words, and thoughts of men, towards which they are bound unceasingly to aspire.

Ethical Science is no mere product and corollary of man's past experience. It is rather its needful antidote. Its motto is evermore "Excelsior." It never permits this standard to be torn from the staff, and trailed in the mire of human corruption. It calls unceasingly on the corrupt and the impure to awake and arise. Amidst the strife of parties, the speculations of false philosophy, and the seductions of sensual vice, its clear and solemn voices are heard continually in such utterances as these : "Thou shalt not follow a multitude to do evil." "Speak to the children of Israel that they go forward." "Whatsoever things are lovely, whatsoever things are of good report, if there be any virtue, and if there be any praise, think on these things."

This view of the true place and correct definition of Ethics as the Science of Ideal Humanity agrees closely with some striking remarks in Professor Grote's *Examination*, a posthumous work, full of careful and suggestive thought.

"There is no moral logic which will teach us to conclude what should be, in the great features of it, from what has been, and what is. If we do so conclude, it is in a manner which destroys all our moral being. Man has improved as he has, because certain portions of his race have had in them the ideal element, have been unsatisfied with what to them at the time has been the positive,

tho matter of fact, the immediately utilitarian ; have risen
above the cares of self and of the day, have been imaginative in thought, enterprising in action, deep and earnest
in feeling....If what Man's experience teaches him is to
give up the imaginative, the deep and unsatisfied thoughtfulness, the desire to penetrate to the reason of things,
tho hopefulness of becoming a worthier and higher creature; if it teaches him to be content with the idea of
knowledge as the registering of facts, and as what, rightly
used, may benefit his material condition—he will, I think,
cease to improve. If ho had acted on this principle from
the first, he would never even have begun to improve."

Two distinct charges may be brought against Ethical
Science, as thus defined. The first, that it must bo unpractical, dreamy, and Utopian. The second, that it is
barren and inoperative, confined to a few popular truths,
and incapable of real progress.

Professor Maurice has remarked, in the opening of his
first lecture,—" If the moral teacher adopts the distinction
which is sanctioned by one of the ablest and most accomplished of his class—that his business is with what ought
to be, that of other students with what is, can there be a
clearer or fuller confession that he means to leave the
actual world for some other world which he has imagined ?"
And again, in the third lecture, after naming Sir J.
Mackintosh as the source of the quotation, he resumes,
" The distinction was plausible in itself, even without considering the authority from which it proceeded. Yet if
we accepted it, Ethics seemed transferred from tho real
world in which we dwell to some other imaginary
world. In this case I am sure we should get no serious
attention for them in this busy, practical age. Dismiss-
ing, therefore, this opinion, without examining what might

2—2

be the arguments for it, we asked whether there was no
other difference between this study and those with which
we are engaged elsewhere....The Moralist cannot be less
immediately occupied with that which is, with existing
facts, than any physical student.   His business cannot be
carried on in some distant Atlantis, nor can he be en-
grossed in the search for one."

In passages of this kind it is not always easy to know
whether my predecessor merely describes the probable
feelings and impressions of others, or adopts them for
his own.   But it seems a cause for regret that there
should be no formal censure of an inference, which, if
actually drawn, would be one of the most inexcusable
follies into which this busy, practical age could possibly
fall.   Ethical Science may be safely neglected, and in
such an age is sure to be neglected, if it deals, not with
what is, but with what ought to be!   Now the true sense
of the definition is plain.   Neither Sir J. Mackintosh nor
any other moralist of common sense could ever be supposed to mean that the business of Moral Science is to
quarrel with God's constitution of the universe, or to copy
the traditional blasphemy of Alphonso of Castile, who said
that he could have taught the Creator how to frame a much
better and more perfect world.   Moral Science, it simply
affirms, teaches us how men ought to act, not how they
have acted in time past, are acting now, or may, with
more or less likelihood, be expected to act in time to
come.   It deals, of course, with the actual conditions and
circumstances of human life.   But still its proper work is
to teach what human actions ought to be, not what they
have been or are, in all the countless relations they fulfil
to each other, and to the great Author of their being.

Such is plainly the meaning of Sir J. Mackintosh, in the

words of his brief definition. They involve no confession, whether clear or obscure, of a purpose to forsake realities, and to speculate principally on some distant and imaginary world. Should a busy, practical age turn away from them, and justify its conduct by such a plea, our first duty, as moralists, is to expose the misconception, and point out the mischievous folly of the practical result to which it leads. It is just in proportion as any age is really practical, that the maxim has the highest claim on their notice and their reverence. For it reminds these busy, practical men, that the world in which their lot is cast is not as it ought to be, because they themselves, the moral agents by whom it is peopled, are not doing as they ought to do.

There is a certain sense, it is true, in which the maxim does labour to transport men from the actual to an imaginary world. Only that other world is no fabled Atlantis, no unknown planet, governed by laws which human fancy has devised, and forming a part of some unknown system. It is our own world, changed and transfigured by a moral renovation, when a pure and noble ideal of thought, speech, and action, shall once have been deeply and abidingly implanted in the hearts of men. Its nature has been well and clearly expounded by our Christian poet,—

> O for a world, in principle as chaste
> As this is gross and selfish! one in which
> Custom and prejudice shall bear no sway;
> That govern all things here, shouldering aside
> The pure and modest Truth, and forcing her
> To seek a refuge from the tongues of strife
> In nooks obscure, far from the ways of men!

Morality is thus an intensely practical science, and

claims the most eager and earnest attention in a practical age of busy men, for this very reason, that it exhibits before their eyes a lofty ideal of right conduct in all the relations of life, which it is our bounden duty, every day and every hour, to strive more nearly to attain. It admits, in accomplished facts, or in the voice of numbers and the clamours of a multitude, no excuse whatever for selfishness, vice, and crime, but reminds men solemnly what they ought to be, and the high standard they ought to keep ever full in view.

But ethical study, if it escapes the charge of being dreamy, unreal, and Utopian, is exposed to a kindred reproach, that it is barren in all results, stationary and unprogressive. Thus we read as follows in a work of some reputation :

"Though moral excellence is to most persons more attractive than intellectual, it is far less active, less productive of real good. The efforts of the most active philanthropy, the most disinterested kindness, are short-lived, and rarely survive the generation which witnessed their commencement....There is nothing to be found in the world which has undergone so little change as the great dogmas of which moral systems are composed. To do good to others, to love your neighbours as yourself, to forgive your enemies, to restrain your passions, to honour your parents, to respect those who are set over you— these, and a few others, are the sole essentials of morals. But they have been known for thousands of years, and not one jot or tittle has been added to them by all the sermons, homilies, and text-books, which moralists and theologians have been able to produce."

Moral Science, if these strictures are just, consists of little more than half a dozen sentences, known for thou-

sands of years, and containing maxims which very few
have cared to practise. These maxims are incapable of
any real addition, and have also exercised a very slight
influence on the welfare and happiness of mankind.
Physical Science, it is affirmed on the other hand, consists
of an immense body of truth. It is cumulative and progressive in its nature, and has grown constantly from
age to age. And thus we may reasonably hope that it will
conduct mankind by a surer path than mere moral teaching, and with a more effectual guidance, to some distant
goal of social happiness and well-being.

Now if it be meant simply to affirm that the first
principles of Moral Truth have been known long ago, the
same is clearly true of arithmetic, mechanics, and geometry. Yet their progress has been as real, and almost as
conspicuous, as that of the Physical Sciences which depend
upon them. On the other hand, if it be affirmed that
simplicity and permanence, in general laws, forbid any
development of the various results to which they lead, the
facts of modern astronomy offer the paradox a decisive
refutation. The moral law, which enjoins the love of
our neighbour, is hardly more brief, and certainly not
much more simple, than the law of gravitation. Yet the
ablest analysts and geometers, for two hundred years,
have tasked their powers to the utmost in tracing out
the results of Newton's great discovery. And still they
are very far from having exhausted the mine of its
intellectual treasures. In binary stars, in asteroids and
planets once unknown, in comets and meteorolites, in
lunar disturbances, and tidal retardation, new discoveries
reward their efforts from age to age. And after all
their labour, the problem of three bodies, one of the
simplest that can be proposed, defies their attempts at

a perfect answer, and can be solved only under favourable conditions, and by gradual and successive approximation.

Why, then, should Moral Axioms be less fertile than the Laws of Physics in the results to which they lead? The field is higher and nobler, and the capability of large development, on every ground of reason, is just the same. If mankind at large were half as zealous in the pursuit of moral excellence, as astronomers have been, since the days of Newton, in their calculation of attractive forces, and their practical study of the heavens, a thousand years would not suffice to exhaust the various development of the great laws of social duty, or bring to a close their progress in moral insight, and their successful labours of thought, and practical endeavours in this higher field.

Once let us see clearly the true place of Morals in the grand series of the sciences, and these censures aimed against them by authors who may be clever in their own pursuits, but are sorely wanting in moral discernment and true wisdom, will drop away like withered leaves, and disappear. A science, of which the very aim and purpose is to discover and enforce the true ideal of right feeling and right action for every moral agent, and for each individual of mankind, cannot possibly be barren and worthless, or devoid of practical power. It must be, from its very nature, of high and inestimable worth. Spurious counterfeits, indeed, may be not only unprofitable, but most mischievous. But surely a lofty and pure ideal of thought and action can never be set before the eyes of men, even in the most corrupt age, and the most degraded state of society, wholly in vain. If such truths, plainly taught, and such high aims, held up before their eyes, were to be barren of all results, then assuredly, in the words of Milton,—

> The pillared firmament is rottenness,
> And earth's base built on stubble!

It is quite conceivable, however, that the mode of operation of such truths, and the amount of influence they exercise, may wholly elude the notice of keen-eyed worldly men, or even of clever essayists and philosophers, intent on physical research, or buried in the strife of parties in the political world. There are tens of thousands who feel the steep ascent of a hill-side, or even the weight of some slight burden they carry in their hand. But who has felt, or feels at this hour, that mighty force of solar attraction, which has been unceasingly at work, on the largest scale of dynamical energy, through successive ages? Yet this alone has kept our earth stedfast in its orbit, and hindered it from losing itself long ago, with all its inhabitants, in outer darkness.

When the stern and grand old prophet stood on Horeb, on the mount of the law, it was not in the earthquake and the fire, the wind and the storm, that he recognized the special signs of the Divine presence. It might have been known and felt there also, but it was found and felt chiefly in the still small voice alone. In nature those influences are the most penetrating and powerful which escape the gaze of the superficial observer. There can be no doubt, either to calm students of human history, or to firm believers in Christianity, that the practical influence of great moral truths, in all past ages, has been grievously hindered, and often neutralized, by the moral dulness, or the vicious and sinful perverseness, of the greater part of mankind. They have been too often like dews alighting

on the rock, or seeds that are sown on a barren and un-
grateful soil. But it would be a fatal and immense error,
on this account, to imagine that their publication, their
ceaseless iteration, and earnest enforcement, whether by
moralists or divines, have been wholly in vain. Whenever the thoughts are turned to them, the dullest conscience is in some degree stirred and aroused. The coldest
heart is either touched with a secret pang of remorse,
or kindled into dim and secret longing after a higher life.
The weak and irresolute are awakened from the sleep of
useless indolence, and nerved for conflict with temptation.
The trance and stupor of sensuality is disturbed or
broken. A voice—What meanest thou, O sleeper? awake
and arise! startles the truant conscience in its guilty
wanderings. A breath of heavenly life seems to visit and
breathe on the moral being, like the change which comes
on all the face of nature in the first days of spring.
Such emotions, indeed, when left to themselves, may
quickly expire, and the coldness become greater, the darkness deeper than before. Some higher power is needed
to sustain the awakened spirit, to keep it from relapsing
into double apathy, and to guide its steps along the steep
hill-side of heavenly truth. When the brightness and
beauty of a high moral standard has dawned on the feeble
and tempted spirit, the first impulses of awakened thought
need to be sustained by prayer for Divine help, and the
hand to be stretched out eagerly, to meet the proffered
succour of heavenly grace. The parting words of Milton
in Comus will then be found to be no mere utterance of
a sportive fancy, but the veiled expression of the deepest
philosophy, and of the highest lesson of Christian faith
—a faith and a philosophy far more profound than
modern theories for manufacturing some miserable sem-

blance of a conscience out of the transmuted instincts of the ape or baboon :—

> Mortals, who would follow me,
> Love Virtue, she alone is free:
> She will teach you how to climb
> Higher than the sphery clime:
> Or, if Virtue feeble were,
> Heaven itself would stoop to her!

LECTURE II.

THE CERTAINTY OF MORAL TRUTH.

ETHICS is the Science of Ideal Humanity. It is no mere subdivision of one secondary and limited province in the wide domain of human thought. It is rather like that blue firmament, which is above us and around us wherever we go, and encompasses the lofty mountain summits and the lowly valleys of earth on every side. Its aim is to teach men, in every various field of thought and action, what they ought to be, how they ought to live, and what they ought to do. It claims to preside over all their converse with the world of nature, and the conduct of their inner life, their relations to their fellow-creatures, and their duties of prayer, praise, trust and worship, towards the Supreme Creator.

In width of range it must thus be coextensive with all the various and countless fields of human thought, speech, and action. In dignity it rises above them, and surmounts them all. They set before us man as he is; Ethics, man as he ought to be. They unfold his actual powers, habits, tendencies and dispositions. The science of Ethics sets before him a pure and lofty ideal, of good which he ought to seek, of moral beauty and perfection which he should ever strive to attain. Its lessons, when fully learned, show him how far he has come short of this high standard, which his own conscience, when thoroughly awakened, is compelled to approve. And thus it leads him by the hand to that footstool of revealed mercy, where heaven stoops to the feebleness of human virtue, or even to the degradation of human vice and folly, and with sovereign power raises up the lost and guilty to holy blessedness without measure and without end.

But here, at the entrance of our inquiry, a great stumblingblock lies in our way, and needs to be removed. Have Ethics any just claim to be a genuine science? Is certainty, on moral questions, possible or attainable? Do we not rather enter here on a dark path, a thorny jungle of barren strifes of words, and tedious disputations "never ending, still beginning," and renewed with a wearisome and fruitless pertinacity from age to age?

The past history of mankind at large, and the known course and cycles of moral speculation, tend to strengthen these doubts, either of the reality, or else of the attainableness and practical worth, of ethical science. The fact is undeniable, which Locke has made so prominent in his reasoning against innate ideas (Bk. I. ch. 3, § 9), that a low and corrupt, sometimes a most repulsive rule of conduct and practice, has often prevailed in whole tribes and families of mankind. Again, warm and earnest debates on the foundations of morality, and its primary laws, were transmitted from the clearest and keenest intellects of Greece to those of Rome. They remained still under ceaseless discussion for five centuries, until Christianity replaced them by other questions of a still deeper kind.

At the revival of learning after the middle ages, the flames of these ethical controversies, which had smouldered so long, broke out anew. And now, for more than three centuries, moralists and divines have rivalled the ancients in the zeal with which they have espoused conflicting theories. The strife, almost as keen and eager as in the days of Zeno and Epicurus, has lasted even to the present hour.

How is it, again, that when Physics have advanced with such giant strides, the students of morals, by the confession of some of its ablest writers, should hardly change their ground? Are they not still renewing the same questions, which occupied youthful disputes in the days of Socrates and Plato, more than two thousand years ago?

"There is no study," says Professor Grote, "more universal than Moral Philosophy. And yet, as a science, it cannot be said to have a high reputation at present in our own country. Nobody expects to learn much from what professes to be Moral Philosophy, or seems to think that much can come of it. This carelessness arises from a sort of notion that it is very likely to be mere words, or else a sort of quackery, very likely not to take hold of human nature, but to rest in useless generalities... Others are jealous of it, on account of its supposed tendency to level, regulate, and square human character, destroying its nativeness and variety; while those who are disposed to levelling and regulation are not in general interested in human philosophy of any kind."

These prejudices against the study, from the moral diseases and confusions of the world, the endless disputes of moralists, and the seeming absence of real progress, gain double strength from causes peculiar to these times. The wide spread of a school of thought, which denounces Theology as an impossible science, casts its dark shadow over Ethics also. It tends to degrade it into a secondary branch of physiology, dependent for its very being on the growth and progress of anatomical science. The advance

of Physics in all its branches, and the many inventions
with which it has enriched and adorned human life, bring
out into greater prominence the seeming absence of similar
progress in what claims to be a higher and nobler field
of thought. The restless activity of a bustling age spreads
around men a close and stifling atmosphere, like the fog
and smoke which settle down on our crowded cities. High
and lofty truths from the upper regions of thought seem
often to strive, almost in vain, to penetrate this thick
gloom. There can be no wonder that, in such an age,
ethical science should often be exposed to silent neglect
or open scorn.

In a Christian church and nation it might naturally
be supposed that the clearer light of moral truth, found
in the pages of a Divine message, would more than
compensate for other causes of neglect and decay; and
would secure for morals their due place in the intellectual
culture of the age. And this is doubtless true within
certain limits. The Decalogue and the Sermon on the
Mount, with their popular expositions, have kept before
the eyes of our people a standard which heathen nations
never attained, and have secured a very wide acceptance
for the simplest and plainest elements of Christian morality. But even this great gain, through human infirmity,
has not been free from some attendant loss. The higher
doctrines or deeper messages of Christian faith have not
seldom been so abused as to deaden the general interest
in the great lessons of Christian and revealed morality.
Nay, even the fact that great moral precepts have been
plainly revealed, and have been received in name by every
Christian, may turn to a hindrance of all activity of moral
thought. It may quench, instead of quickening, the thirst
for a fuller knowledge of the grounds on which those

precepts are based, of their various harmonies, their countless developments, and innumerable applications.

There is still another way in which the evidence of
moral truth may have been clouded and obscured by its
connection with the cause of Christian orthodoxy. Some
of our ablest Divines, in maintaining revealed religion
against assailants, have insisted strongly on the duty, in
matters obscure and uncertain, of resting satisfied to act
on probabilities alone. Thus Butler begins his Analogy
with a laboured argument, to show that even a slight
excess of evidence, in questions highly uncertain, may
determine practically what course it is *right* to pursue.
But however true in the abstract it may be, such a line
of defence must needs exercise a depressing influence on
minds really athirst for truth. It is very apt to give
them the impression, that the being of God, the person
and work of Christ, the atonement, the resurrection, and
the life to come, are looked upon as having only a slight
excess of evidence, if any, over opposite falsehoods. They
may thus be tempted to infer that the scales of faith and
no-faith tremble in an almost even balance, so that confident faith is only just one degree less foolish than confident unbelief.

Such an opinion must act like a palsy on all the
nobler instincts of the Christian heart. It must surely
have been a firm, deep, and hearty conviction, far unlike
this timorous, hesitating, moonlight faith, by which the
Apostles turned the world upside down, and overcame the
might of the heathen empire, and martyrs poured out
their very life-blood in defence of the truth.

This cautious, defensive line of thought, which Butler
and other writers have employed in their advocacy of
revealed religion, has naturally affected the kindred

subject of morals. They insist strongly on the practical obligation of being guided by the slightest excess of seeming probability. The want of fuller evidence is said to afford scope and opportunity for a virtuous exercise of the understanding, and to dispose the mind to rest satisfied with any evidence that is real.

In such remarks there is a dangerous tendency to canonize doubt and uncertainty, and consecrate dimness of moral vision, as if they formed a useful moral discipline for Christian men. To seek and long for clear light in moral inquiries has sometimes been even discountenanced and condemned, as the mark of a sceptical spirit. But this is a dangerous inversion of the real truth. Such a desire, there can be no doubt, needs to be tempered with modesty and patience. There ought to be a willingness to be guided by moonlight, or even by starlight, until a clearer day-break shall arise. But still "light is sweet, and a pleasant thing it is for the eyes to behold the sun." The desire in itself is the healthy, inseparable instinct of an earnest mind and a Christian heart. It must be owls and bats of the moral world, and not the sons of light, who find it easy and natural, in the high matters of faith and conscience, to rest content with the dim twilight alone.

Let us now inquire whether these four difficulties, which seem to beset the approaches of Moral Science, will not disappear on a closer view.

First of all, the objection from the low standards of moral feeling and practice in savage tribes, from the revolting usages which have sometimes prevailed, and the great amount of vice and immorality even in Christian lands, can have little or no real weight with thoughtful men. No sensible person, certainly no Christian be-

liever, can suppose for a moment that a perfect science
of morals can issue forth, like Minerva from the head
of Jupiter, complete, full-grown, and fully armed, from
the mind and heart of the ignorant, the sensual, and the
profane.

Every science, however sure in its principles, or fertile
in its results, needs first of all to be learned. To learn
requires not only some natural capacity, but attention,
seriousness, and diligence. Ethics are a law of duty.
How can it be learned by those who are reckless of
duty, and care chiefly or only for animal pleasure? They
are a light shining from above. How can it be seen by
those whose eyes, like those of Mammon, are "always downward bent" upon the pavement below?

In the field of moral inquiry more is required of the
willing learner than in the walks of physical research.
Moral, as well as intellectual conditions, need here to be
fulfilled. There must be a serious desire to learn and
know the truth, however humbling to our pride, and however unwelcome to our indolence its lessons may be. Yet
even in Physics, and in an age mentally so active as our
own, how small is the number of those who obtain real
scientific insight, compared with those who receive with
implicit confidence the conclusions in vogue, from time to
time, among scientific men. Let some feud arise amongst
the known students and leaders in any science, and nearly
all the seeming knowledge of these multitudes, being
nothing more than opinions taken on trust from others,
would quickly disappear.

Moral Truth, to be received and held firmly, needs an
upward eye, and an open heart. Such is the voice
even of natural reason alone. But Christianity lays a
double stress on these necessary and indispensable con-

ditions of all moral insight. "If any one be willing to do
His will, he shall know of the doctrine, whether it be of
God." "If thine eye be single, thy whole body," i.e. thy
whole intellectual being, "shall be full of light." Once let us
read the history of the moral aberrations in the world by
the light of these true sayings of Scripture, and neither the
parricide, infanticide, and cannibalism, of heathen tribes,
nor the licentious vices, the drunken intemperance, which
defile and dishonour Christian nations, will lead us to
question the certain attainableness of moral truth. The
proverb of Solomon will supply a brief and full answer to
such causeless doubts: "Evil men understand not judgment, but they that seek the Lord understand all things."
Humility, joined with earnestness and diligence, is the
portress which alone can unlock the gates, and open our
way to the temple of Moral Science.

The disputes and controversies among moralists themselves are a far more specious objection to the claim of
Ethics to be deemed a genuine science. How can certain
truth be attainable, where there seems to be neither
harvest-field nor vineyard of ingathering, but only a
battle-field of ceaseless debate?

The triangular duel of the Academician, the Stoic,
and the Epicurean, has lasted for twenty-two centuries.
Slightly varied in form, it continues to the present hour.
The morality of sentiment stands opposed to the moralities
of reason. A morality, apart from consequences, the cate-
gorical imperative of pure reason, fights with a morality
reasoned out from consequences and results alone. How
shall the disciples attain certain truth, when the leaders of
thought, from age to age, seem to be in hopeless discord?
It is the saying of Professor Grote, that "when we come to
morals and ethics, the dust and smoke" common to other

parts of philosophy "become tenfold worse." How should we look for peaceful certainties amidst the confused war-cries of a battle-field? *Silent inter arma leges.* The reproaches of unbelief against the various sects and divi-sions of Christianity seem applicable, with equal force, to impeach and annul the claim of Ethics to be a real science.

The answer to this objection, with a little patient thought, is not hard to discover. In every science there are some first principles, which are the starting-point or the foundation of all its other truths. These later truths form the pathway to which it leads, the building reared on that foundation. Now in every case these first principles, because they are the first, border on mystery, and lose themselves in the unknown.

"On what does the earth rest? On the back of a huge elephant. On what does the elephant rest? On the back of a huge tortoise. On what does the tortoise rest? Ah! that, said the Indian, I cannot tell." This Eastern tale or parable may be applied to the foundations of every science. A well-known and able writer has laboured to show, in the opening of one of his chief works, that the Ultimate Religious Ideas and the Ultimate Scientific Ideas are alike "unthinkable." By what strange leger-demain of thought the conclusion is reached, that Religion alone is mystery and nescience, and Physical Science a field of knowledge and progress, it is hard to understand. The difficulty is plainly common to both subjects, the natural on one side, the moral and religious on the other. The solution, so far as a solution is possible here, must be exactly the same for both. The striking words of Hooker apply here in all their force and beauty. "The goodliness of houses, the stateliness of trees, when we

behold them, delighteth the eye. But that foundation, which beareth up the one,—that root, which minis-
tereth life and nourishment to the other, is in the
bosom of the earth concealed. And if at any time it be
needful to search them out, yet is the search more profitable than pleasant, both to them that undertake it, and
also to the lookers on."

Geometry has its half-solved or unsolved and perplexing problems, no less than Ethical Science or Religious
Faith. It deals with the relations and properties of space.
But what is space? Is it a substance, an accident, or a
relation? Is it fixed and absolute, or relative only? Is it
finite or infinite? Is Infinite Space a real something,
or a mere expression for the "imbecility of human
thought"? Can there be empty space, or must there be
a plenum? Is it infinitely divisible? Can there be a
surface without depth, a line without breadth, a point
without length, breadth, or thickness? Velocity is the
speed or rate of motion, or space divided by time. How
can this vary from moment to moment, when both the
space and the time, for any one rate of motion, wholly
vanish and disappear? These questions, and a host of the
same kind, furnish large materials for controversy and
metaphysical debate. Had geometers forborne their labours till a perfect and clear solution of all these had been
found, the science would be still unborn. Pythagoras
would never have slain a hecatomb for his immortal discovery, the *Elements* of Euclid never have been written;
the tomb of Archimedes, re-discovered by Cicero with
natural triumph, would never have borne the trophies of
his skill, the cone, the cylinder, and the sphere. The later
triumphs of modern analysis would have been still more
impossible. But they laboured on, and built still on the

old foundations. They did not pause to grope beneath them in that region of mystery, on which all first principles must repose. For there our finite reason strives in vain to search out the unsearchable, or to attain that full insight and perfect knowledge, which the Omniscient God, the Only Wise, seems to reserve for Himself alone.

The course pursued in moral inquiries has not been altogether the same. There have been repeated attempts, it is true, and never wholly fruitless, to develop the consequences of the first principles of Ethics, and unfold them in systematic harmony. Dr Whewell's *Elements* are one example of this kind, well worthy of high praise and patient study. But, in general, more pains have been taken in re-examining the grounds of Ethics, or in exploring its debated border lands, than in tilling the soil, and reaping peaceful harvests. Or else systems have been reared on a doubtful basis, maintained by some, and by others stoutly denied. Thus an air of instability has often been given to the whole structure. Systematic Moralists are thus joined at various points in their progress, like troops in full march by stragglers, by many who dispute or deny some of their premises; and who, in the words of Jeremy Taylor, are "sure of the thing, even when they are by no means sure of the argument." But conclusions, however true and sound, when reached independently of the premises, or even in spite of their rejection, are wanting in all the main features of exact, well defined scientific truth.

But a third objection to the claim of Ethics, even more serious and vital than the discords and disputes of moralists, has been drawn from their supposed barrenness, and entire want of real progress. The contrast between the stationary aspect of moral, and the pro-

gressive aspect of intellectual truths, is said to be
startling. "All the great moral systems which have exercised much influence have been fundamentally the same.
All the great intellectual systems have been fundamentally
different."

These statements of Mr Buckle, on the face of them,
are excessive and untrue. The teaching of the Stoics
differed widely from that of the Epicureans in ancient
times, and both of them diverge widely from the ethics of
the gospel. The contrast between Hobbes and Mandeville
on the one side, and Cudworth and Clarke on the other,
is not less in modern days. On the other hand, close
resemblances may be found between some of the latest
novelties of modern scepticism, with its pantheism, fatalism, and nescience, and the oldest forms of Eastern speculation. Still, when all abatements are made, there is a
contrast not to be denied, between the rapid progress of
Physics in these two last centuries, and the seeming want
of growth in the field of ethical inquiry. What answer
can be given to this reproach, while claiming for Ethics
to be the highest and noblest part of all purely human
science ?

Now scientific progress may be of four different kinds.
These may be styled briefly, ascensive, expansive, descensive, and diffusive. A science may climb higher towards those simple laws which rule over all its complex
phenomena. It may range over a wider landscape, by
unfolding these laws into a rich and large variety of
secondary axioms. It may stoop down, to apply its discoveries more frequently and largely to the uses of daily
life. It may gather around it a wider and wider circle of
disciples, and may thus spread its light further and further
in successive generations.

To begin with the last. The diffusion of Ethical Truth has been greater, not less, than that of modern Physics. Its first maxims, indeed, are so simple as to be easily mistaken for truisms, and excite the contempt of those who cultivate the intellect and neglect the heart. They may thus be decried as too commonplace to form the basis of any science worthy of the name. So to eyes accustomed only to gaslights and chandeliers, a fixed star at midnight may seem a worthless thing. It has always been there in the sky for ages, and its light is very small and feeble. And yet this simplicity of moral maxims favours their wide diffusion, and helps to secure their spread throughout the family of mankind. "There is no speech nor language, where their voices are not heard." The great law of truth, the voice which condemns treachery and falsehood, appeals to millions who never heard of, much less received, the Copernican and Newtonian theories. The law of kindness and goodwill has vibrated through myriad hearts, which never dreamed of the undulations of light, and to whom spectrum-analysis and polarization are mysteries unheard of and unknown. The law of self-sacrifice for the good of others, whether presented in word only, or embodied in the life and death of martyrs, or enshrined in the deepest mystery of our faith, has touched and stirred the deepest waves of thought in countless hearts, to whom nearly all the terms of modern science are sounds without a meaning.

The moral science of the past may perhaps be elementary in the extreme. But even in its weakness, and amidst its ceaseless struggle with prevailing vice and passion, it has exerted a far deeper power over millions of hearts and lives, than Physics have attained in the hour of their noblest triumphs, or can ever hope to attain.

Let us next compare Physics with Ethics in their descensive progress, or their practical application to the uses of human life. Natural Philosophy, since the days of Newton, has doubtless enriched society with a great multitude of new inventions. It has supplied comforts to the artisan and cottager, as well as multiplied luxuries and triumphs of art for the homes of wealth and the palaces of kings. But this kind of progress is no less real, no less extensive, in Christian Morals than in Physical Science. The virtuous man, the sincere and upright Christian, finds occasion every day and every hour to practise anew, and unfold in some fresh application, the great and simple precepts of Christian morality. The liberal man will continually be devising liberal things. The virtuous woman "opens her lips with wisdom, and in her tongue is the law of kindness." A pure fountain will hourly be sending forth pleasant streams. The quiet, ceaseless activity of great moral truths, once received into the understanding and heart of Christian men, may easily be overlooked by busy workers on the ant-hill of science, or else may be forgotten in the glare of some brilliant invention or new discovery. But it is not on that account the less real and important. In the words of Cowper,

> Silliest streams
> Oft water fairest meadows, and the bird
> That flutters least is longest on the wing.

I come now to that double progress of science, in ascent and in expansion, where Physics may seem at first sight to have a real superiority. Even here, I think, the claim will appear groundless on a closer view.

"There is nothing in the world," Mr Buckle says, "which has undergone so little change as the great dogmas of which moral systems are composed." On the other hand, those highest laws, which embody the clearest results of modern physical discovery, the law of attraction, the undulations of light, the correlation of force in various forms, have been reached by a slow and painful ascent in the course of ages. When once attained, they work a mighty revolution in our knowledge of the material world, and in our power to control its manifold changes.

Is this a proof that Ethics are lower than Physics in the scale of science, and moral truths more uncertain and inferior in practical value? Far from it. What is cheap and procured without labour is apt indeed to be despised. But even in the natural world, the air, the sunshine and light of heaven, the rains and dews that fertilize the earth, are gifts freely bestowed on men, and require no human labour. If the Divine wisdom has secured to all men, whether by the voice of conscience, or by supernatural revelation, direct access to the vital elements of moral truth, and has left the answering laws or principles of the outward world to reward the study of the philosopher, and to be explored by human toil, ought tho free gift, on this account, to be despised, or consigned with contempt to the list of useless and barren truisms?

The law of gravitation is a noble triumph of human sagacity and persevering labour. After long ages of preparation, by Ptolemy, Copernicus, and Kepler, the profound study of Newton deciphered the handwriting of that Divine law, and expounded it clearly for the admiration of mankind. But the great law of duty—"Thou shalt love thy neighbour as thyself," however early or clearly revealed, is higher and nobler still. We may apply to it the verses of Sophocles, not in disparagement, but in praise;—

Οὐ γάρ τι νῦν τε κἀχθές, ἀλλ' ἀεί ποτε
Ζῇ ταῦτα, κοὐδεὶς οἶδεν ἐξ ὅτου 'φάνη.

What, then, is the main feature of that progress of
astronomy, during the two last centuries, which is the
chief boast of Physical Philosophy, and holds an undisputed primacy among its many signs of vitality and
growing power? It is the unchanged recognition of one
great law, and increasing faith in its perfect truth, amidst
the immense complexity, the mathematical difficulties,
and the ever-enlarging variety, of its results and applications. It forms thus a sublime example of permanence
amidst ceaseless progress.

Other branches of Physics have not reached this goal,
and their ultimate laws still elude research. There is
change and uncertainty in the first principles themselves.
The hypothesis of emission, even though sustained by
Newton's authority, retires and gives place to a theory
of undulations. This theory, again, in its first form of
direct, is replaced by another of transverse vibrations.
Caloric, the fictitious fluid of heat, disappears, and atomic
motion comes in its stead. The old elements, as elements, pass away. Phlogiston is born, and has an early
death. Forty or fifty new elements occupy the fore-
ground. But they hold their place by a precarious tenure,
till chemistry takes a further stride. The simplest elements, oxygen and hydrogen, now represent in their names
the ghost of a departed theory. Magnetic and electric
fluids come like shadows, and like shadows they depart.
Here science is still only on the steep and slippery mountain side. Though it may wield its ice-axe with steady
skill, it mounts slowly and with labour. And not seldom
it slips backward, when some hasty, seductive hypotheses,
like a crevasse thinly covered with new-fallen snow,

betrays its insecure foothold. But astronomy, since the days of Newton, seems to stand firm on the mountain-top, and gazes calmly on an ever-widening range of peaceful scientific victories.

Now whence arises this manifest superiority over other branches of physical study? The reason is plain. Astronomy has attained a comprehensive simplicity in its primary law, and fountain truth, such as Ethics, with the aid of a Divine message, had attained long ages ago. For what is the second great commandment? It is a higher law than that of universal gravitation, binding together the whole universe of moral agents. And it has been revealed, more dimly by natural conscience, but in plain and express terms by the great and divine Author of man's moral being.

The simplicity and terseness, then, of the first principles of Morals, is not, as the modern historian falsely conceives, their shame and weakness. It forms rather, as the great tragedian of Athens more truly saw, their strength and their glory. The roads and pathways of earth change continually with the revolutions of human society. Mule-tracks are replaced by turnpikes or Roman causeys, and these, in course of time, by iron railroads. But in the blue sky there are no such fashions of the age. The courses of the stars are silent and unchangeable.

Moral truths are the stars of the intellectual world. They differ from those lights, useful and yet earthly, which men dig up from the mine, distil in their retorts, conduct through pipes, and transmit to burners, all of them the laborious products of human skill. They shine by their own native light. They look down upon us calmly from above, unless when fogs and mists of earth intercept their brilliance. They are waymarks for the benighted, and also dim heralds of the coming day-break. "Men may come, and men may go,"—their mines may be exhausted, their pipes burst, their candles flicker and waste away,—but these stars are immortal, and shine on for ever.

But has not experience at least proved an immense contrast between moral maxims and the laws of Physics in their power of expansion and development? The first are stationary and barren. Nothing has been added to them, it is said, by the sermons, homilies, and text-books of a thousand moralists and divines. The others are fertile, active, and progressive, and receive from year to year a more full and large development.

The contrast, though greatly exaggerated in the remarks to which I refer, has doubtless a partial truth. The development of the great truths of Ethics, in modern times, has been far less apparent to common observers than the growth and progress of Physical Science. A fuller knowledge of the best moralists and divines than physical students, and especially positive philosophers, usually care to attain, will mitigate the sharpness of the alleged contrast, but cannot wholly remove it. When, however, we look below the surface, the seeming defect will be found to have its source, partly in the moral evil which interferes with and clogs all ethical study, but partly in the superiority and higher dignity of Moral Science.

In Physics the development of theory, and its application to the practical uses of life, are to a great extent independent of each other. The theory of magnetism might still advance to new discoveries, though timorous navigators were to abandon the use of the compass, and to creep, as in early times, timidly along the shore. Art may grow by happy accidents, and the increase of practical cleverness, while the answering science remains stationary. Science may take immense strides in advance, before its discoveries begin to be applied in new inventions, and yield fruit in the service of daily life.

In Morals the case is wholly different. Its true aim, as Aristotle observes, is "not that we may know what virtue is, but that we may become good men; for else it would be useless." It is thus essentially a practical science. It teaches men what they ought to be, what they ought to do. Its theory, when wholly divorced from practice, is not only useless, but even mischievous. It aggravates and redoubles guilt. "To him that knoweth to do good, and doeth it not, to him it is sin."

Thus in Moral Science theory and practice are not capable, as they are in lower sciences, of a wholly separate development. Corrupt, selfish, vicious practice, must cloud the eye of the soul, and impair or destroy the faculty of moral discernment. Knowledge of the truth cannot grow, unless the truth already known be received into the heart, and applied in the life. In Physics speculation is like an engine with no train attached, which can thus move more freely, and advance at a swifter pace. In Moral Science it is so closely linked with the whole moral being, that the mind, heart, and life, the conscience, intellect, and affections, must advance or recede, must rise or fall together. In a world, then, where moral evil plainly abounds, it is no wonder that Ethics, even as a science, should make only a slow, intermittent, and faltering progress. Its standard, raised higher here and there for a moment, must fall again whenever luxury and selfishness abound. Progress made by the calm and patient meditations, or the heroic virtues of a few, may be lost, to all outward appearance, by the empty folly or fierce and angry passions of the many. The fires of some scorching judg-

ment may be needed from time to time, before conscience
can burst the chains of reigning sensuality, shake itself
from the dust, escape from its cave of shadows, stand erect
in the freedom of a new life, and gaze with clear vision
and open eye on the grand realities of the spiritual world.

There is no reason, then, from the limited progress of
Ethical Science in time past, to depreciate its worth, or to
doubt its capacity for vast and large expansion in days
more favourable to its development. In the sacred words
of its Lord and Master, "its hour is not yet come." It
has now to struggle onward and upward under the burden
of a host of sluggish or perverse disciples, ready to turn
aside into seductive by-paths, or to sink lower and lower
in vice and folly. These load with a heavy weight, and
weaken with a stifling atmosphere of moral impurity,
even those willing learners who lend themselves to nobler
impulses, and strive to rise. The allegory in *Comus* well
describes, side by side with its real worth and divine
effects, the contempt with which it has thus come too
often to be regarded by some physical students:

> The leaf was darkish, and had prickles on it,
> But in another country, as he said,
> Bore a bright, golden flower, but not in this soil:
> Unknown, and like esteemed, and the dull swain
> Treads on it daily with his clouted shoon;
> And yet more medicinal is it than that moly
> Which Hermes once to wise Ulysses gave.

In a happier age, assured to us by Divine promise, that
bright, golden flower will appear. Or rather, in the sacred
words of Scripture, it will become "a tree of life, yielding
its fruit every month," and its leaves will be for the healing of the nations.

I must reserve for another Lecture the fourth and last
hindrance to the claims of Moral Science in the doctrine

of probability, and some direct enforcement of the certainty of moral truths. But before I close I must add a few words on the vast importance of a full confidence in their authority, reality, and unchangeableness, to meet and overcome the special dangers of the time in which we live.

Amidst the busy activity of commerce, the excitement of political strife and change, the progress of physical inquiry, and all the feverish, impatient movements of modern thought, careful observers must observe one symptom full of danger. Multitudes, in every Christian land, seem to be more and more uncertain on every subject that rises above man's animal wants and desires, and which touches on the unseen and eternal. The Christian Church, the domain of Theology, is vexed with endless controversy and division. Rival bodies of Christians seem often more jealous of each other than zealous for common truth. Political life is in danger of sinking into a mere strife of parties, ranged under doubtful banners, ill deciphered and guessed at by their own followers,—a battle without generals and without discipline. One tide-wave of popular impulse follows another in swift succession. All old landmarks are ready to disappear beneath the shifting flood. But where shall certainty be found? Where can the toil-worn spirit of man find solid footing, and attain a sabbath of rest? He can never be content to find it in the properties of numbers, in squares, triangles, and polygons alone. A secret instinct whispers to him, even when most debased by folly, that his true portion must be sought, and can only be found, in a higher and nobler field. Tell him that morals and religious faith are a Hyperborean region, buried in fog and mist and perpetual darkness, where endless uncertainty reigns, and doubt, sometimes honest, but more frequently dishonest, is the highest attainment, and some slight excess of the chances in its favour the only reason for a virtuous life, and what results will follow? Such a view will palsy the arm of the Christian, when uplifted for noble action, and strike an icy coldness to his heart.

Can we, who inherit the transmitted wealth of thought of so many ages, not from heathen philosophers alone, but from prophets and apostles, and the great lights of the Church of Christ in all past ages, have fallen back, in these last times, into disgraceful contentment with more than heathen darkness? Are we ready to accept, as the teaching of advanced philosophy, a creed of pure nihilism, that Theology is a dream, religion pure nescience, covered thinly with a crust of decaying dogmas and idle fancies,— conscience a strange function of nervous tissues, or at best the acquired instinct of slaves, who crouch sullenly under the lash of masters stronger or more numerous than themselves? Then indeed our boasted light can only be paralleled by the state of Elymas the stricken sorcerer, when there fell upon him "mist and darkness," and he groped about for some one to lead him by the hand.

Such a view of Moral Science, as a field of mere uncertainties, is gloomy in itself, and disheartening and melancholy in the results to which it must lead. Our duty as Christians, and even as students in this great university, doubly adorned by the greatest lights in Physics and Theology, is to hold firmly a more hopeful and far nobler view.

Ethics is the Science of Ideal Humanity. It deals with that lofty standard of the good, the right, the true, the noble, towards which all of us, from the least to the greatest, are bound continually to aspire. And this can

bo no land of mist and shadow. Even in times of heathen
darkness it had a starlight of its own. The Gentiles,
who had no direct revelation, were a law unto themselves. And now, in the times of the Gospel, it has a
light as of the daybreak, which shines more and more, in
honest and loving hearts, unto the perfect day. Its lowest
regions, indeed, must partake largely of the uncertainties
and complexities of that human life with which it has to
deal, with its manifold conditions of bodily faculties,
mental powers, diverse tastes, and different social relations.
But above and beyond these there is a higher region,
where it rises above the complex and ever varying applications of its own laws, and deals with the inward
motives, affections, and desires alone. And here it breathes
a purer air, it eats angels' food, and walks in the light
of heaven. The firmness of its deep foundations below is
only rivalled by the pureness and clearness of the light
that shines upon its higher summits from above.

To such an Ethical Science, so firmly rooted in essential
truth, and rising to such a lofty elevation above the mists
and clouds of sceptical uncertainty, which vex and obscure
the minds of busy multitudes in this present age, we may
apply the description of one who is supposed to have
practised its high lessons, and to have taught them to his
simple flock, the pastor of the *Deserted Village:*

> As some tall cliff that lifts its awful form,
> Swells from the vale, and midway meets the storm;
> Though round its breast the rolling clouds are spread,
> Eternal sunshine settles on its head!

LECTURE III.

THE CERTAINTY OF MORAL TRUTH.

EXPERIENCE AND REASON.

THE doctrine that in all moral subjects probability is the highest attainment, is a part of the wider theory of the ancient Academy, and has been held by many moralists in later times. Aristotle remarks that "it is the duty of one well instructed to seek for accuracy in every kind of subject, only so far as its nature allows;" and that "it is much the same error to be content with mere persuasion from a mathematician, and to require demonstrations from the rhetorician." "Every discourse," he adds further, "about things to be done must be in outline, and not exact." He seems here to contrast geometry with ethics, and to impute inexactness and uncertainty to the latter, but to practical or applied ethics alone. The later Academy held the principle more widely, that in all things probability was the utmost limit of the human mind, from the fallibility of the senses, and the difficulties and seeming contradictions in every field of thought.

Bp. Butler, again, is led to insist often on the responsibility which results, in moral and religious subjects, from even probable evidence and imperfect half-knowledge.

But this line of thought is often carried so far, as at least to verge on a dangerous extreme. The doubtfulness of the evidence, in such cases, is sometimes assigned to Divine appointment, in order to vary and enlarge the field of moral discipline and probation. The strict discharge of duty, he says, with less sensible evidence, does imply a better character than the same diligence in the discharge of it on more sensible evidence. "And men are bound," he observes, "to act on what appears to them, to the best of their judgment, to be for their happiness, as really as on what they certainly know to be so." It is plain, however, that mere guesses and probabilities, even when they involve a practical duty to act upon the more likely of two alternatives, can never form the materials of a genuine science.

"Physical and Moral Studies have a common ground; science, and not probability, is the aim of both." Such is one of the latest words of Professor Maurice in his Lectures on Social Morality. The principle thus affirmed is one of high importance. It might almost claim to be the foundation of Morals as a Science. I do not think that it is to be viewed as the consequence and result of worship. It is rather the indispensable condition that worship may be a reasonable service, and not sink into a blind superstition. It is a conviction by no means limited to those writers who lean to a mystic or transcendental school of thought. The judgment of Locke in its favour has double force; since it might have seemed natural for him, from the general tone of his famous treatise, to rest content with a lower view. He writes as follows:—

"The ideas of quantity are not those which alone are capable of demonstration and knowledge. Other, and perhaps more useful parts of contemplation would afford us certainty, if vices, passions, and domineering interests did not oppose or menace the endeavour."

"The idea of a Supreme Being, infinite in power, wisdom, and goodness, whose workmanship we are, and on whom we depend; and the idea of ourselves, as understanding, rational beings, being such as are clear in us, would, if duly considered, afford such foundations of our duty, and rules of action, as might place Morality among the sciences capable of demonstration. I doubt not but, from self-evident propositions, by necessary consequences, as incontestable as those of Mathematics, the measures of right and wrong might be made out, to any one that will apply himself with the same attention and indifferency to the one, as he does to the other, of these sciences."

"Two things," he continues, "have made moral ideas thought incapable of demonstration, their complexness, and their want of sensible representation." "Confident I am, that if men would, in the same method, and with the same indifferency, search after Moral as they do after Mathematical truths, they would find them have a stronger connection one with another, and a more necessary consequence, and to come nearer perfect demonstration, than is commonly imagined. But much of this is not to be expected, while the desire of esteem, riches, or power makes men espouse the opinions in fashion, and then seek for arguments either to make good their beauty, or to cover their deformity. For nothing is so beautiful to the eye as truth is to the mind; nothing so deformed, and irreconcilable to the understanding, as a lie."

This view of Locke, Dr Whewell, and Professor Maurice is exposed, no doubt, to plausible objections, and beset with seeming perplexities, but still it must commend itself spontaneously to thoughtful and generous minds.

"There is no reason," I have said, "in the nature of its first principles, why the evidence of Morals should be placed on a lower footing, or regarded as less demonstrative, than that of Geometry....It is as easy to conceive the laws of space inverted as those of conscience, and to grant that the properties of the circle might change, as that treachery should become a virtue, and compassion a crime....The spirit of man has its own self evidence, conscience its own definitions. And these are not cold and silent, as in Geometry, but vocal with strong emotion, and endued with a living power. Its truths are in their own nature as prolific. The opening for deduction is the same. Why should it not lead to certainties as sure, and conclusions as various and manifold in this higher and nobler field?"

Here, at the outset, two admissions have to be made. And first, if the doctrine of consequences is the only test of right and wrong, and such actions only are to be esteemed morally good, as can be proved in their result to secure "the greatest happiness of the greatest number," Morals can never be raised to the level of a genuine science. It must reduce itself to a loose heap of uncertain probabilities alone. A strictly utilitarian science of Morals would require for its construction nothing short of Omniscience. To compare the moral character of two alternatives, we should then have to construct two future worlds of thought and action, composed of moral agents living and unborn, reaching on through the most distant ages, and then to decide to which of these possible future worlds the greater sum of collective happiness would belong. The problem is plainly impossible in itself for human knowledge. But the impossibility is multiplied a hundred fold. For we should have to treat all the

future actions and feelings of these countless moral agents
as fixed terms, except so far as they depend on this one
alternative choice of one agent alone. Now, in reality,
each of them is unfixed and variable in the highest
degree. The attempt to found anything worthy the
name of science on such a basis must be a deception
and a failure. The seeming solution can only be gained
by the arbitrary selection of a few elements of an impossible problem, and omitting a thousand others, equally
required for a genuine solution. Loose guesses, in which
nearly all the data are wanting, must be confounded with
strict demonstration, and a power of just and true fore-
cast be claimed for human ignorance, which belongs to the
All-seeing Wisdom alone.

Again, the claim of a strictly scientific character, however justly made on behalf of pure Ethics, or the great
rules and principles of personal, social, and religious duty,
cannot be extended without serious error to its practical
applications. It may be a clear and certain truth that we
are bound to seek the good of our neighbour. It must
be a complex and doubtful inference, that we shall best
promote his welfare by this or that particular act or
mode of action. There is a time to give, and a time
to refrain from giving; a time to speak, and a time to
keep silence.

Moral principles, however firm and sure in themselves,
can only be reduced to practice by joining them with the
lessons of a wise expediency. And this expediency cannot
rise higher than the level of its source, which is the
defective knowledge of human nature and all outward
circumstances, and the imperfect foresight, which belongs to
fallible men. This contrast between pure science, and the
elements of uncertainty in its applications, is conspicuous

in Arithmetic and Geometry. Actual enumeration in many cases, and actual measurement in all, is approximate only. It can be no matter for surprise, and no proof of inferiority, that the same remark belongs equally to the practical applications of Moral Science.

How far, then, within these needful limits, may we claim for Morals a strictly scientific character, closely resembling that which belongs to Arithmetic and Geometry, and Pure Mathematical Science ?

Knowledge, in every subject, may be of two kinds. It includes the actual and the necessary, what simply is, and what must be. In the highest object of thought alone the two conceptions meet together, and melt into one. The great I AM, is at once the Supreme Reality, and the necessary, self-existing Being, He who is, and cannot but be. But in every other case, in all the objects of sense, and the varieties of created and dependent life, the two kinds of knowledge are distinct. They are the separable objects of observation and reasoning.

We observe things and persons, and thus know that they exist. But we are conscious, all the time, that it might have been otherwise, that they might not have existed, such as they are. We can conceive of others in their place, wholly different. On the other hand, we frame an hypothesis, and deduce from it by reasoning certain results. But we may still be uncertain whether the premises and their results alike have any home in the world of actual realities.

The separation of these two elements is never total. The progress of science consists mainly in successive attempts for their more complete reunion. Phenomena cannot even be registered without the aid of memory. Now memory implies some thinking agent, to whom its

successive acts belong. On the other side, the formation
of an hypothesis also presupposes such a thinking agent,
and the existence of some real objects, to supply needful
materials for the exercise of imaginative power.

Experience and reason thus approach every subject of
human thought from opposite sides. One directly observes what is, and might have been different. The other
traces the necessary connections between things which
either are, or might possibly be. Complete, full-grown
science consists in their perfect reunion. Reason, as we
approach this limit, becomes more and more practical;
till at length its hypotheses are merged and lose themselves in the real laws of the universe. In this way
they become the source of mastery over nature, by
genuine foresight of all future change. Experience, again,
travels upward, from transient phenomena to things and
persons; and from things and persons, seen as capricious
and uncertain in all their actings, to the double supremacy of physical laws, and moral, intelligent design; till
the real and actual loses itself in the ideal. All transient
phenomena are then seen to belong to one vast scheme of
Providence, firmly bound together by laws, natural, moral,
and spiritual, some of them discovered by man, others
reserved in the depths of Omniscient Wisdom, but all
alike leading upward, and meeting at the footstool of His
eternal throne.

In Pure Science the elements borrowed from experience are of the simplest and most general kind. Hence
they almost disappear from view, and our attention is
fixed on the reasoning process alone. Here, then, probability has no place. The facts which need to be silently
assumed are so clear and simple, that they may almost be
called self-evident. The reasoning, drawn from few and

simple premises, is demonstrative and exact. The opposite of its conclusions is discerned, not simply as untrue,
but as an impossible contradiction. The sum of two odd
numbers cannot be an odd number. The diagonals of a
square cannot be unequal. Two right lines, which meet
in one direction, cannot meet in the other also. You
cannot, in showing kindness to others, show more kindness to each of them than to all the rest. You cannot
inscribe a hexagon in a circle with sides greater or less
than the radius. But with experimental knowledge the
case is widely different. The evidence on which it rests
may vary from the plainest and fullest to the most uncertain and obscure. Its materials are of unequal value.
They include present, direct observation, our own memories of the past, in some cases full and clear, in others
obscure and doubtful; and also the observation and the
memory, clear or obscure, of other witnesses, who vary
most widely in veracity, caution, and intelligence.

The Applied Sciences consist either of empirical laws
and secondary axioms, derived immediately from observation and experiment; or else in the combination of pure
science with experimental data, varying in their degrees
of accuracy and completeness. They must therefore share,
more or less, in the uncertainty which belongs to human
experience. There are doubts which may arise directly
from the nature of the materials, as when the astronomer
has to put aside faulty sets of observations. But there are
others which depend on their own scientific imperfection.
They may contain empirical laws, derived from an induction too fragmentary and imperfect. They may strive to
account for one class of known facts by inventing another
and larger class, which may possibly be true, but for
which there is no direct evidence whatever. Their axioms

may often be drawn from popular notions. They will thus be vague, elastic, and variable in sense, and infect with uncertainty and vagueness the whole course of reasoning. The tendency of the homogeneous to become heterogeneous, and the persistency of force, when force is made to mean half a dozen different things, are signal examples of vague, unscientific, deceptive substitutes for the certainties of science. Assumptions may be separately made, and reasonings founded on them, which do not agree, but really exclude each other. Or finally, their complexity, usually greater than in pure science, which abstracts the most needful elements in its problems, may be so great, as to place exact reasoning on them almost beyond the reach of a merely human intelligence.

There are two main reasons which may be offered, to throw doubt on the attainableness of moral truth, and to reduce its evidence to the class of uncertain probabilities alone. The first is drawn from its place in the scale of human thought, and the second, from the freedom and variety which seem implied in the actings of voluntary moral agents.

When we rise in the scale of being, from Nature to Man, from lifeless matter to plants, from plants to animals, and amongst living animals from the lowest to the highest, the complexity of the materials of science increases at every stage. The first principles themselves, so far as they have been discovered, are more complicated; and they shroud themselves more and more in a mysterious darkness, which it is hard for the students of science to explore. It might seem, then, at first sight, that Morals, the highest part of Human Science, must partake above all the rest in the uncertainties of observation and experience, and be removed the farthest from that character of certain, definite, demonstrable truth, which belongs fully to the Pure Sciences alone.

The first answer to this doubt may be found in the important fact that Morals are an ideal science. They propose to define, not what men have done, or may do, but what they ought to do. Truth is one, falsehood is manifold. The right in morals, as the name implies, has a close analogy with the straight line in geometry, in contrast with curves of single or double curvature. The properties of triangles and squares are far simpler and easier to investigate than those of circles, ellipses, and other figures of still higher orders and more complex definition.

Now this ideal character of Morals tends greatly to diminish the complexity of the problems of ethical science. The rules of right and wrong may be comparatively simple, when the question, how such and such persons are likely to act, is difficult and uncertain in the highest degree. The complex relations between the body and the soul, between man and the series of lower animals, the varieties of personal taste and disposition, the countless combinations of varying circumstances, may, in the higher regions of pure Ethics, be left almost wholly out of view. They belong essentially to the secondary results and applications of moral principles, and to these alone. There is thus a compensation, highly important, to that extreme complexity which might else be inferred from the place of Ethics in the scale of science.

There is also another principle to be kept in view, which conspires to the same result. In the ascending scale of science we rise, it is true, from the contemplation of simpler and lower powers to others of a more complex and higher kind. But we rise also from multiplicity towards unity, from a region of seeming confusion, and

changes without visible purpose, to one of light, order,
harmony and design.   Chaos, or unformed, lifeless, multi-
tudinous matter, comes first and lowest in the scale of
being, and the well-ordered Cosmos stands higher.   In
the Cosmos itself, Man stands high above the brute creation; and highest in those characters which they do not
share, in which he is contrasted with all the rest, and distinct from them, as created at first in the image of God.

All creatures, it has been said, strive to ascend, and
ascend in their striving.   And so far as this effort really
exists, it includes a striving after unity, such as when a
regiment of soldiers, parted in the smoke and confusion of
a battle-field, seek to range themselves once more under
the standard to which they belong.   Man himself is one
order, one genus, and one species, in contrast with the vast
number of orders, genera, and species, by which he is surrounded in the animal world.   But the Creator himself is
One, in contrast to all the innumerable millions of mankind.

It follows naturally from this truth, that when we leave
the simplest conceptions or abstractions of number and
space, and mount higher in the scale of being, that complexity which renders scientific treatment almost impossible, and throws us back on mere experience and
observation, is greatest in the middle stages of our progress.   The mist, even in the intellectual world, often lies
thickest on the sides of the mountain.   When we climb
still higher, there is a growing amplitude and grandeur in
the wide firmament on which we gaze, and often in the
earthward prospect, but we may also discern increasing
signs and tokens of a Divine simplicity.

Astronomy, in the extent of space with which it deals,
has a far wider range than Geology.   And yet there is a

grand simplicity and unity in the celestial motions, which
make them far more accessible to scientific treatment than
the waves of the ocean, or the solid strata of the earth.
And so, when we rise to the highest part of men's nature,
and from action to speech, from speech to thought, feeling,
and desire, we reach at length that highest field of Human
Science, where it borders on Theology. Here, even in his
weakness, Man rises into communion with things unseen
and divine. And here also tokens of a simplicity, adapted
for the deductions of science, and difficult to discover midway in the long and steep ascent, meet us once more.

The great chain of thought and being seems thus to
be firmly anchored, and fixed in scientific certainty, at both
extremes. It is fastened firmly below to the truths of
arithmetic and geometry and mathematical reason, which
underlie the whole material creation. It is fastened
above, no less firmly, to the throne of God. But its middle
portion seems to hang more freely in space, and to oscillate
amidst the endless obscurities and uncertainties of creature
volition. It is only when, in the study of man, we leave
behind us all lower elements, and confine our thoughts
to the distinctive features of human reason and will, that
the chaos of blind, ceaseless, purposeless change begins to
recede from view, and the light of scientific certainty,
growing out of a Divine unity, slowly dawns upon us once
more.

It may be objected, further, to the doctrine of the
fixedness and certainty of Moral Science, that it is opposed
to the freedom of the human will, and would tend to
mechanize and freeze down to a cold, bare, and heartless
uniformity, the whole course of personal and social life.
Is the law of right too complex to be capable of discovery? Then it must be practically worthless, and of

no avail. Is it capable of discovery? Is there one line
of action, which it prescribes, excluding every other as
vicious, defective, and unholy? Must it not, then,
condemn all who obey it to a dull monotony of action?
Will not moral agents thus become only like material
atoms, which obey the impulses of surrounding bodies,
and have no power to deviate one hair's breadth from
the path which inexorable laws have prescribed? Will
not men thus be tempted to think of virtue as another
name for tameness and dull monotony, and associate
vice itself, breaking through these irksome rules, with the
ideas of variety, life, activity and freedom?

If we accept the notion which Mr. Mill ascribes to
most utilitarian thinkers, that morality deals exclusively
with actions themselves, and not at all with the motives
by which they are guided, and on which they depend, it
will be hard indeed to rescue it from this serious indict-
ment. It will then prescribe in every case some precise
line of action, deduced from a calculation of consequences,
and thus reduce all virtue to the level of a precise, in-
elastic, and cold routine.

This view involves, however, a great misconception of
the real aim of Moral Science. Its true lessons seem to me
very different. It lays down principles and motives, which
ought to be the living fountains and sources whence our
actions are to flow. It discloses, also, limits on the right
hand and on the left, which they are bound not to
transgress, and within which they ought to move. But
when these conditions are fulfilled, it still leaves a wide
and various range for the exercise of voluntary choice and
human freedom. Its aim and purpose is not to annul and
destroy, but to redeem from a fatal bondage, and apply
to its noblest uses, that freedom of will and choice, on

which its own existence, as a science, wholly depends. Its true type and keynote is found in the earliest Divine command revealed in the word of God; where, side by side with one special prohibition, there was expressly conceded a wide and large latitude for the free choice of the human will. "Of every tree that is in the garden thou mayest freely eat."

True morality is fixed and definite in its principles, and in the laws and limits of action it enjoins; but free, large, and various in its application to the complex economy of human life. It is not meant to extinguish, but to develop to the utmost, that genuine freedom on which its own authority depends. It is a law, but in the truest sense a law of liberty. It is firmly rooted in the soil below. But above it drinks in the free sunlight, ramifies into a thousand branches and branchlets, and effloresces freely amidst the play of the breeze, and under the light of heaven.

Two things seem chiefly required to vindicate the claim of Morals to be a genuine and certain science— simplicity and clearness in its axioms and first principles, and a capacity, in those axioms, for various and exact development. Let us briefly examine each of these points in succession.

The principle which lies at the basis of all geometry is the consciousness, gained through our senses, of the existence of an outward world. Moral Science rests upon a truth not less simple, and not less deep in its intuitive certainty—Man's inward consciousness of will, and of a power of choice, dependent on the inward activity of the mind and heart. It is a primary law of thought, one of the intuitions of the soul. "The mind is led by its very nature and constitution to perceive that there is an in-

delible distinction between good and evil, just as there
is between truth and falsehood." "It embodies itself in
the pronouns of every language, breathes in every desire
of the soul, and lives both in the memories of the
past, and the hopes of the future." It is the grand
fundamental keynote, ever sounding anew in the daily
voices of life, and the whole history of the world.

Pure Ethics deal immediately with the tempers,
desires, and affections of men, viewed in the light of
this one simple truth, that they are beings endowed with
choice, reason, and will. Applied Ethics deal with the
outward results of these same feelings, tempers, and
desires, when carried out in speech and action, and ramified
into union with all the physical conditions of man's
complex being, and all the immense and manifold
varieties of his social life. Thus Applied Ethics belong to
mankind alone. But Pure Ethics must extend to every
conceivable race of moral agents, or beings endowed with
choice and reason, however various their other characters
may be. It includes angels, as well as men. And if our
fancy chooses to people distant planets with rational animals, widely differing from ourselves in shape, sense, and
physical structure, the great laws of moral obligation must
include these also. They do not depend on the specialities
of man's animal nature, but on that gift of a reasonable
will, which marks him out as higher than the whole brute
creation.

Thus Pure Ethics, in the subject with which it deals,
has a simplicity which rivals the science of number and
of space. It deals with moral units alone. It leaves out
of sight the secondary features of human nature. It
looks on man simply as a moral agent, gifted with the
power of voluntary choice, and thus capable of right and

wrong desires, of good and evil actions. This view of his
nature gives birth at once, by an instinct invincible in
itself, and present even when most obscured, to a deep
sense of moral obligation. Such a being is not under the
constraint of a mere physical law, which he must obey.
Yet he cannot be altogether lawless. His conscience owns
a higher law, which he *may* break, but *ought* to obey.

The relations of such moral agents, the monads or atoms
of the moral world, to the sentient beings around them,
are in their own nature simple and uniform, like those of
the points which form the triangle or the square. To the
awakened conscience they are fixed, clear, and certain, like
the truths of geometry. Only they are far higher in
kind. Their voice speaks not only to the understanding,
but to the heart. And hence there is no reason, from the
nature of its first principles, why Pure Ethics should not
form a clear and definite science.

But a science cannot be formed of a few axioms alone,
unless these are capable of a real expansion and development. Are moral axioms, then, sterile in their own
nature? Are they ice-bound as in an arctic frost, where
life and growth can find no place? Such is the view, as
we have seen, in the "History of Civilization." Nothing,
its author tells us, has undergone so little change as moral
axioms. They have been known for thousands of years,
and moralists and divines, with all their labour, have not
added one jot or tittle to their amount. Morality admits
of no discoveries. It is cursed with perfect immobility
and barrenness, while Physics pursue a triumphant course
of never-ending discovery.

Now so far as a contrast may have arisen from the
vicious habits of men, or their moral dulness or perverseness,
it can have no weight to bar the claim of Ethics to be

a genuine science. It must be shown the difference depends on the very nature of moral truths, and not on the backwardness and reluctance of men to receive them simply, to search them out honestly, and to explore patiently the results to which they lead. Is the contrast then real, or is its seat to be found in a diseased judgment alone?

Let us consider the great maxim of the Divine law— Thou shalt love thy neighbour as thyself. Its simplicity is extreme. But the law of gravitation is also very simple. "Every part of matter attracts every other with a force inversely as the square of their distance." And still, simple as it appears, the most profound geometers and analysts, for more than two hundred years, have tasked their powers to the utmost in tracing out and exploring its necessary consequences. The results of their labours are embodied in treatises and essays without end, in lunar, planetary, and cometary theories, in theories of tidal motion and the figure of the earth, in essays on variation of constants, nutation, precession, in the discovery of fresh terms of lunar and planetary correction, of growing minuteness, in the orbits, periods, and inclination of double stars, and in the triumphant addition of two new planets to the solar system. And they are still far from having reached the limit of possible discovery, or exhausting all its treasures of hidden truth.

Why should the Divine rule of duty, revealed in the Law and the Gospel, and confirmed by the voice of natural conscience, be less fertile and various in the deductions that flow from it, and the results to which it leads? It resolves itself at once into the double enquiry—Who is my neighbour?—How ought I to love myself? This latter enquiry divides itself next into the twofold obligation, to seek

5—2

health of body, and health of mind, in intellectual and moral well-being.

The pursuit of bodily health includes many plain lessons of duty, in temperance, soberness, and chastity, active exertion and reasonable rest. But it also includes others less plain and self-evident, the duty of growing attention to sanitary laws, the due and proper use of medical skill and science, and watchfulness against the occasions, inlets, and provocatives, of dangerous disease. The duty has also many varieties and special forms, according to differences of occupation, and varieties of temperament, habit, and personal constitution. Thus it tends to absorb and incorporate all the successive discoveries of medical learning or practical experience. It condemns, as immoral and guilty, the careless ignorance, the blind improvidence and headstrong folly, which are like a partial suicide, and whereby so many not only endanger or shorten their own lives, but expose their fellows to the ravages of infectious and fatal disease.

The duty of self-love, when applied to the mind itself, opens a still wider field of thought. It parts at once into two main divisions. It includes the pursuit of all truth and light in the understanding, and of all pure and noble affections in the heart.

The pursuit of truth, again, is threefold, in an ascending climax of worthy objects of desire. It includes natural, moral, and spiritual truth. And each of these is vast and large in dimension and variety. The truths to be sought after, and eagerly prized and retained, become larger, nobler, and loftier, the higher we rise in the scale of being. Like the chambers in the temple of Ezekiel " there is an enlarging, and a winding still upward." The knowledge of nature is a wide field. The knowledge of Man, the free

and moral agent, the lord of nature, is wider and nobler.
And highest and noblest of all must be the knowledge of
Man's Creator, of God the Only Wise, the Eternal Foun-
tain of all wisdom, goodness, and love.

That province of self-love, which prescribes the
culture of the affections, and the control of the desires,
is no less wide and various. For these affections admit
of being doubly classified, by their internal characters,
and their outward objects. When each of these is once
submitted to a distinct inquiry, the field of thought it
discloses will grow wider and wider continually. It
includes faith, hope, love, patience, meekness, zeal, courage, prudence, humility, nobleness of mind and heart. It
views each and all of these, in their reference to all the
varied relationships of human life, parent and child,
husband and wife, brother and sister, master and servant,
neighbour and friend, subject and sovereign. Everywhere,
as we advance, new vistas of light and beauty will open
before us. The beautiful words of Milton on the benefits
and pleasures of education will apply still more fully to
these researches of moral science:—" We will conduct you
to a hill-side, laborious indeed in the first ascent; but
afterwards so smooth, so green, so full of goodly prospect,
and melodious sound on every side, that the harp of
Orpheus was not more charming." And we may sum up
the scope and compass of its teaching in the more sacred
words of the Apostolic command : " Whatsoever things are
true, whatsoever things are honest, whatsoever things are
just, whatsoever things are pure, whatsoever things are
lovely, whatsoever things are of good report—if there be any
virtue, and if there be any praise, think on these things !"

But the other question—Who is my neighbour?
implied in the same command, opens another wide and

ample field for ethical study and meditation. For it
leads us to reflect on the definition of moral neighbour-
ship, and on all those special circumstances of opportunity, kindred, sex, age, and social position, which
modify the general duty imposed by the great law itself,
and diversify it into a thousand forms. It extends, in its
widest range, to the whole human race, and even to
beings of other races, whenever their existence has been
clearly revealed. But it does not extend to all alike,
however remote. The element of nearness or opportunity enters into the very essence of the command. In
the law of gravitation we find one simple rule of insensible graduation. But here, in the great law of moral
duty, there is a gradation of a far more complicated
and various kind. All the relationships of human life,
the laws and usages of social order, the conditions of
time and place, and the sacred ordinances and bonds of
religion, supply various elements, by which the love of
our neighbour is more and more diversified; till it is
enriched with colouring as various and beautiful as the
hues and shades of light in the bow of heaven.

But it may be objected, finally, that even if moral
truth in its own nature, from the definite character of
its first axioms, and their capability of expansion,
admits of scientific treatment, its immense complexity
forbids the hope of any real success, when we pass beyond
a few precepts, which sound like truisms, and attempt to
unfold it in forms available for the conduct of life.
What is most wanted in the present stage of Moral
Philosophy, according to Professor Grote, is "not definiteness of system, but largeness of view." "Of course,"
he adds, "this renunciation of system, so far as it goes,
lowers moral philosophy from its scientific rank, and

alters it from the character of a single science to that of a group of sciences, whose relation to each other is not easy to determine." These remarks have doubtless an element of truth. They would be wholly true, if narrowness and definiteness were the same thing. He who looks, in clear sunlight, on a field shut in by high walls, has only a narrow view, but what he sees he sees clearly. He who tries to look on a wide, unbounded landscape, when a thick mist and fog is on every side, has a view, not exactly narrow, but indefinite and confused. The vision, practically, may be more confined and partial than before. The true system, in every field of science, is that which discerns clearly the relation of central truths, and traces them out towards the distant horizon; but also recognizes how dimly the more remote are seen, and how much lies beyond the horizon, and remains unknown.

In Moral Science, as in mathematical and physical study, it is thus of high importance to distinguish between principles and their application, the firmness and certainty of primary and fundamental laws, and the complex elements of man's earthly life, which diffract their pure light, and force on us the recollection of the weakness of our faculties, and our need of dependence on a higher wisdom than our own. The contrast in the words I have quoted needs thus to receive an important modification. In Pure Ethics our first and main want is clearness and definiteness of system. In Applied Ethics the great want is largeness and comprehensiveness of view. By the first we claim the privilege of moral eyesight. We escape from fog and mist and darkness, and gaze on a landscape, where we see, and know that we see, moral truths, sure and certain, which cannot deceive. By the second, we throw down the walls which would confine our view within too narrow limits, and see vistas of moral consequences, reaching out far and wide in all directions, which we see dimly and imperfectly at the best, and which lose themselves in the unknown.

It is common, in these days, to speak with exultation of the progress of science, and to boast of the many discoveries of physical students, by which we have far outstripped the attainments of every previous age. And no doubt this progress, in itself, deserves notice and admiration. But if Physics only advance, while Moral Science recedes and goes backward, our loss, we should find out ere long, would immensely exceed our gain. There can be scarcely, I conceive, a sadder spectacle, than an age of great intellectual activity, and of moral torpor and sloth ; when men trace out busily and eagerly the laws of matter, and at the same time grow deaf to the claims of conscience, and blind to the supreme authority of the great law of love. It was the honour of Socrates to recall the thoughts of the Athenian youth from doubtful speculations in physics to questions affecting the moral duties of daily life. May not the like lesson still be needful, even in our Christian nation, and when Physics has risen out of doubtful and loose speculation into the real and progressive discovery of natural laws ? Men may be eager to trace with prism and spectroscope the most subtle phenomena of light, and still be content to remain in moral darkness. They may search out, with line and dredge, the depths of ocean, and care little about the moral depths of sin and want in the human heart. They may infer, from subtle combinations of theory and experiment, the lessening distance of Sirius, and wholly neglect the revealed doctrine, echoed by natural conscience, of the sure ap-

proach of death, resurrection, and a life to come. They
may be confident of the latest guess of theory on the fossil
shells or moving glaciers of some distant, unknown age;
and be satisfied to remain in doubt whether there is a God
who made them, a law of right which they have broken,
a moral pathway of hope and recovery open before them,
and the solemn reality of a coming judgment. But to be
positive about truths of the lowest class, and contentedly
ignorant of the highest, to preach up science in the mere
heel of the body corporate of truth, and canonize ignorance
and endless doubt on those subjects which are the head and
crown of the whole, can be no mark or sign of intellectual
progress. It is rather the proof of growing anomaly and
dangerous disease. He who formed the spirit of man within him has never made him capable of finding certainty
in numbers and triangles, circles and polygons, and
wholly incapable of knowing himself, and his own duties,
hopes, and prospects, as a being made in the image of
God, far nobler and higher than the fowls of the air
or the beasts of the field. The maxim, γνῶθι σεαυτόν,
which heathens recognized as a Divine gift, is far too precious to be thrown to the moles and bats by Christian
men, under the vain fancy that sure truth is to be found
in Physics alone. It may be hard and difficult to climb
the hill-side, and we may sometimes, amidst the mists that
surround us, be ready to abandon even the effort to rise.
But to those who persevere the promise is sure, that
clearer and clearer light will dawn around them. The
scales of sense will pass from their eyes, and the mists
will slowly disappear. That grand, comprehensive Moral
Law, which it is the object of Ethics to discover and unfold, the true ideal of human thought and action, is no
child of night and darkness. It finds its proper home

> In regions bright of calm and serene air,
> Above the smoke and stir of this dim spot,
> Which men call earth,—

those regions which are the native home of all truth and
certainty, of light and love.

To this law, far more than those of physics, the noble
words of Hooker will apply. "Her seat is the bosom
of God, her voice the harmony of the world. All things
in heaven and earth do her homage, the very least as
feeling her care, and the greatest as not exempted from
her power. Both angels and men, and creatures of what
condition soever, though each in different sort and manner,
yet all with uniform consent, admire her as the mother
of their peace and joy."

LECTURE IV.

THE PRIMARY CONCEPTION OF MORAL SCIENCE.

THE definition of a Moral Agent must form the starting-point of all Ethical Science. Like the definitions of a point, a line, and a surface in Geometry, we must expect that it will touch on what is mysterious and hard to explain. But this mystery will form no adequate hindrance to a true and just conception, capable of preparing the way for a large superstructure of moral truth.

A Moral Agent is a person or individual, endued with the powers of action, feeling or sensation, and spontaneous choice; self-conscious, or capable of reflecting on his own actions, feelings, and volitions; and knowing good and evil, or apprehending a standard of good and right on one side, of wrong and evil on the other, with which his own thoughts, feelings, and actions, and those of others, may be seen to agree or disagree. It seems thus to imply the concurrence of three main elements. The first constitutes a sentient, the second a reflective or self-conscious agent, the third and last, a being conscious of a law of duty which he is bound to obey.

First of all, a Moral Agent is a person or individual being. The negative theory, which turns men and animals into mere bundles of sensations, tied together one knows not how, is fatal to the very existence of Moral Science. But it is fatal to Physical Science also. Until we rise from separate phenomena to the conception of things and persons, by which these are caused, and to which they belong, we stick fast in deep mire where there is no standing, no foothold for the human reason. Let us adopt, for instance, the definition of life which a recent speculator has proposed, that "it is a definite combination of heterogeneous changes, both simultaneous and successive, in correspondence with external coexistences and sequences." Here we have an attempted portraiture of life, where there is no recognition of any living thing or person whatever. We have a series of changes, and nothing more. It is the play of *Hamlet*, where no *Hamlet* is to be found. But our first conception of life is always that there is some one being which lives. No series of changes, whether simultaneous or successive, whether homogeneous or heterogeneous, can possibly give the conception of life, unless they first suggest the perception of some living thing or person, insect, bird, beast, or man, to which they belong.

Again, every living thing suggests and includes the ideas of action, sensation, and spontaneous choice. Whatever is alive acts, and it also feels. But we also ascribe to it some kind of choice or spontaneity. The elements which enter into this choice may vary widely. But even in the lowest forms of life we conceive action to depend in some way on the feeling or sensation of the living thing, and not to be decided directly and simply by external impulses alone.

A living thing, however, may act and feel, and in a certain sense may choose how to act, and still be incapable of reflecting and reasoning upon its own actions. With the power of reflection or self-consciousness we pass from the

animal to the human or rational stage. The very name,
Conscience, from *conscire*, implies a duality, in which the
thinking being is its own object of thought, lives, in some
sort, side by side with itself, and not only has such and
such powers, but is conscious of them, and can reflect upon
them. This power of self-knowledge, in which the soul
can see itself, compare its own feelings, judge of its own
actions and thoughts, and through its own self-consciousness come to recognize the existence of conscience in
others, seems to distinguish man from the lower animals,
and is essential to the conception of a Moral Agent.

The word, I, in contrast to all splendid and pretentious
polysyllables, has thus been truly placed by Prof. Maurice
as a kind of sentinel at the gate of Moral Science. It is
a key, he justly remarks, " to that mystery in words, which
makes them interpreters of the life of individuals, of nations,
of ages; the discoverers of that which we have in common,
the witnesses of that in each man which he cannot impart,
which his fellows may guess at, but which they will never
know."

But a Moral Agent is, further, one who knows good
and evil ; who can not only reflect on his own actions and
feelings, as his own, but compare them with an apprehended ideal of the good and right, and discern, in his
own case, and in that of other moral agents, their agreement or their disagreement. Thus self-consciousness rises
into a conscience of right and wrong, of good and evil.
The comparison will be latent and potential when there
has been no inward experience, or outward observation, of
evil and wrong. It becomes explicit and clear, whenever
evil has been witnessed or experienced, as in the sacred
narrative of the first human transgression,

Knowledge of good, dear bought by knowing ill.

Every sentient, self-conscious being, capable of recognizing an ideal standard of right and wrong, of good and evil, and of being guided in thought, feeling, and action, by motives drawn from the perception of such a standard, is a Moral Agent. He is not only an I, but an I who says to himself, This I ought, and this I ought not to be, to feel, and to do.

The sense of Moral obligation, in every such agent, depends on the union or concurrence of two elements. The first is the power of voluntary choice itself. The second is the capacity of perceiving, in various forms of feeling and action, the moral contrast of good and evil, of duty and transgression, of right and wrong, and of being influenced by motives of this higher kind.

The vexed question of the freedom of the human will enters thus into the very foundations of Moral Science. But it is important to observe the practical limit of the connection between them. We do not need fully to resolve a deep problem, which loses itself in mystery, how far the will is determined by motives, or itself fixes the weight and decides the relative order of the motives themselves. All we need to know is that there is an extreme on either side, which is fatal to moral obligation. Within these limits, our defective knowledge of the nature and actings of the will does not hinder the sense of duty from remaining firm and strong.

Once let us suppose that choice is an illusion, that human acts are decided, like the motion of a planet in its orbit, simply by the concurrence and resulting effect of many external impulses and physical sensations, and then the sense of responsibility, or of a moral character in our thoughts and actions, disappears. Men would then have no more claim to be moral agents than the falling apple or the flashing meteor, than stocks or stones, or the waves of the sea.

On the other hand, suppose the will to act without any motive or reason whatever, by a blind caprice, an impulse without an aim, and responsibility would cease on the other side. Such an agent would be like the fictitious atoms of Epicurus, that turn aside a little from the right line, without any reason why they deviate one way more than another. But he must cease thereby to be a reasonable being. He becomes an embodied chance, a capricious and senseless atom. For surely to act even on a mistaken motive, and from an insufficient reason, is at least one step higher than to act with no motive or reason whatever.

Between these two extremes, of a volition purely capricious on one side, and of mechanical, physical compulsion on the other, there is a wide interval where moral responsibility has its natural home. Man is not so free as to be able to dispense with motives altogether. Yet he is bound by no such chain of fatal necessity as that motives are mere mechanical forces, and can decide his course irrespective of his own inward state, and the character of his whole moral being. How far motives, by their habitual prevalence, form the character, and how far pre-existing character for good or evil varies and affects the force of the motives, are deep and hard problems of the human heart. In these we may be able to see but a little way. But the human conscience, whenever it is not bent on vain self-excuse, and drugged by some fatal opiate, decides at once that these limits do obtain in the actual constitution of human nature. Man is still free enough to be responsible, however grievously, in many cases, he may be "holden with the cords of his sins."

And still he is not free enough to despise with safety the double warnings of experience and of revelation on the power of vicious habits, and the bondage to which they swiftly lead. Those words of the prophet clearly express a solemn and weighty truth,—"Can the Ethiopian change his skin, or the leopard his spots? Then may ye also do good, who are accustomed to do evil."

The power of reasonable and spontaneous choice within these two limits is the ground and basis of moral obligation. The two ideas, like the convex and concave in one and the same curve, are correlative and inseparable. The truth has its inward aspect, towards the agent himself, and his own self-conscious power; and its outward aspect, towards the law of right above him, and the whole moral universe. Every where and in all things Law must reign, and chance is only a shadow. If Man, then, by reason of his higher powers, escapes from the control of a physical necessity, and from laws he cannot help obeying, he must come thereby within the range of a higher law of right and duty, which speaks to him in nobler accents with the voice of a sovereign, and which he knows and feels that he ought to obey.

The close connection of these two ideas, power of reasonable choice, and moral obligation, is doubly confirmed by the cases they include, and by those which lie just beyond their limit. Wherever that power is recognized, however wide the other differences, we own the clear existence of moral duty. Thus the existence of angels is revealed to us in Scripture. Of their special powers, their gifts and modes of intelligence, very little, and almost nothing is known. Still they are clearly set before us as intelligent beings, endued with the powers of reason and choice. Therefore, while ignorant of nearly all beside, we recognize at once that they are moral agents, bound by the great laws of moral duty.

Again, philosophers have pleased themselves with inventing conjectural races for other planets, endowed with reason, but in other respects supposed to differ widely from mankind. But these inhabitants of Venus, these Jovians or Saturnians, are no sooner invested in our thoughts with will, choice, and reason, than we feel that the laws of duty must also apply to them. The same is true of every Eastern tale of magical change of form or supposed transmigration. The magic which changes the shape alone leaves the sense of moral being unaltered. But the moment we suppose reasonable choice to be gone, and blind instinct alone to rule in its stead, the whole moral nature has disappeared.

The same connection reveals itself, no less clearly, when we dwell on those cases which seem to border on moral obligation, without fully attaining it. Three such cases may be specified—children, lunatics, and those domestic or nobler animals which attain some striking resemblance to the virtues and vices of mankind.

The question is often perplexing, at what stage of its life a child first begins to be responsible. So long as the infant merely continues and multiplies its experiments on the outward world, we do not ascribe to it a moral character. As soon as it gives signs of self-reflection, we feel that in that childish bosom a nobler life has begun to be revealed. And whenever this reflection seems to involve a power of comparing its acts and feelings with a law of duty, it becomes plain that the exercise of a moral nature has begun. We place it then at once in the higher category of moral and responsible agents. Those infants only escape from the claims of this law, which, in the words of Scripture, have no "knowledge of good and evil," no sense of a standard of right above and beyond themselves. The case of lunatics seems, at first sight, more perplexing. There is here not only frequent embarrassment, but a strong tendency to mutual divergence between doctors on one side and lawyers and divines on the other. The former are prone rather to extend, the latter to contract, the range of exemption from moral responsibility through the partial failure of reason. The perplexity arises, I think, in no small measure, from confounding pure Ethics with that mixed, composite morality, which is involved in human jurisprudence. The lunatic, in general, does not cease to be capable of strong convictions about moral right and wrong. But, owing to some mental illusion, the connection which may be assumed in other men between certain actions and the answering motives is distorted and deranged. His inward feelings do not lead to their natural and healthy results. His outward acts, when tried by customary rules, do not indicate, with any clearness and accuracy, his inward motives. Thus he does not cease, for a moment, to be inwardly responsible in the sight of God. But the common rules by which human law infers crime and guilt in the heart from the outward actions fail to apply, and if they are enforced, would lead to serious injustice by their application. The method of solution which replaces all forms of punishment by simple detention seems to be rather an idle and clumsy way of cutting the knot, which it would need much care and pains to untie. In avoiding wrong to the individual, it runs the risk of serious danger to society, and of a general relaxation of human law; for all vice and crime is highly unreasonable, and therefore, in one sense, a presumption

of partial madness. Lunatics have been known to attempt
or threaten murder on the ground of their own expected
impunity through mental disease. Surely the true policy,
in cases where criminal acts, by the verdict of a jury, are
connected with strong suspicion or proof of partial de-
rangement, would be to refer the decision on the partial
or entire remission of the legal punishment to a mixed
tribunal of lawyers and eminent physicians, selected
and permanently appointed as a court of special jurisprudence.

Such cases, however complex and difficult in practice,
only bring out the principle itself into clearer relief. So
far as involuntary illusion divorces the outward act from
the motive it would otherwise infer, the action ceases to
wear the moral character which the law, in other cases,
justly assigns to it. But, so far as the mind can choose
and reason, though partly under false impressions, it continues to be morally responsible. The difference is that
more exact care and closer inquiry is needful, to decide
on the moral elements of the inward feelings and intentions, as deduced from the outward acts. An oar does not
cease to be an oar, because, when dipped in water, it
seems to be broken. Allowance needs only to be made
for the diffracting power of the medium in which part of
it is seen. The lunatic continues responsible for his own
motives, feelings, desires and intentions. He is not responsible for his outward acts, so far as they are turned
aside, by involuntary illusion, from the course to which
these inward desires and feelings would lead in a healthier
mind.

Another subject, which tends to obscure the doctrine
of moral responsibility, is the close approach, at least, to
the characteristics of moral vice or virtue, which some

6—2

animals appear to attain. How natural it is to apply
moral epithets of praise or blame, to the dog faithful to
his master even to death, to the vicious, unmanageable
horse, the generous war-steed, the cunning serpent, and
those various domestic favourites, which seem to come
within the shadow of human influence, and assume, in
some measure, the features of a higher nature than
their own !

On the strength of this evident fact an attempt has
been made to found the theory that all moral feelings and
emotions are only animal instincts, slightly transformed.
The view falls in with the doctrine of successive evolution
of species, so popular at this hour with a large number of
physical students, and espoused by them almost with the
zeal of a new religion. The moral sense is said to follow
" firstly, from the enduring and always present nature of
the social instincts, in which respect man agrees with the
lower animals ; and secondly, from his mental faculties
being highly active, and his impressions of past events
extremely vivid, in which respects he differs from the
lower animals. Owing to this condition of mind, man
cannot avoid looking backward, and comparing the impressions of past events and actions. He also continually
looks forward. Hence, after some temporary desire or
passion has mastered his social instincts, he will reflect
and compare the weakened impression of such past impulses with the ever present social instinct ; and feel that
sense of dissatisfaction which all unsatisfied instincts leave
behind them. Consequently, he resolves to act differently
for the future, and this is Conscience. A pointer dog, if
able to reflect on his past conduct, would say to himself,
as indeed we say of him, I ought to have pointed to that
hare, and not have yielded to the passing temptation of
hunting it."

A pointer dog, "if able to reflect on his past conduct," would be a highly intelligent, almost human being. And, if able further to say to itself, "I ought to have resisted that passing temptation, which turned me aside from the law of my duty, and to have pointed at that hare, instead of hunting it," such a dog would plainly be a conscientious being, a moral agent. But the "if" and the "I ought" in this hypothesis are instances of what has been wittily called "the Saltatory Principle," which some have called in to supplement the doctrine of slow development. It leaps over an immense gulf at a single bound. Compared with the Man described just before, who merely seeks to gratify a suppressed and reviving instinct for social pleasures, the dog would rank far higher in the moral scale. The attempt to bridge over the interval between man and the brute is ingeniously made by a double process of change. Man is degraded into a slave of the stronger instinct, and his blind obedience to it is dignified with the name of conscience. The animal is promoted into a self-reflecting, conscientious moral agent; who considers his own ways, and says to himself, like a moralist or divine, "This is a temptation to which I ought not to yield. This, and not that, is what I ought to do."

The only force in an argument doubly fallacious consists in the undoubted fact that the conduct of animals, in some cases, does spontaneously suggest the use of moral epithets. It is natural, almost unavoidable, to apply to them words of praise or blame. How can this be explained, if the power of a reasonable choice and moral responsibility are inseparably linked together?

Now in what cases does the conduct of animals rise into what we feel, at least, a very close resemblance of moral virtue? In every case, I think, it is when some lower instinct, either of indolence or animal pleasure, yields to the higher motive, obedience to a superior will. The faithful dog finds its chief delight in pleasing its master. It listens to his voice. It watches his eye. It follows promptly, and with evident delight, the slightest indication of his will. Endowed with senses and powers of delicate scent or swift motion, superior to his master's, he still takes pleasure in lending them to the service of one in whom he feels instinctively the presence of a nature higher than his own. It becomes to him a second nature, strengthened by a thousand acts, that his master should command and he should obey.

All moral action consists in obedience to a law of duty, which appeals to the highest part of man's nature, even at the sacrifice of lower instincts and momentary pleasures. When united to religious faith, it consists in the recognition of a higher, uncreated Will, supremely good, and in obeying that Will, so far as its lessons are known and understood, at whatever price of self-denial, pain, or suffering.

It is plain, then, that all these instances of devoted attachment, on the part of animals, to which epithets of moral praise are commonly applied, bear the very closest analogy to virtuous actions in moral, intelligent beings. The dog, which looks up fondly to its master, and obeys every sign of his master's wish, follows within the limits of its own power the very same law which constitutes piety and moral goodness in human beings. He practically apprehends and follows his own highest good. His actions are not only naturally good, they border closely on moral goodness. They bear to it the closest analogy and the nearest resemblance. Let us only, by a tacit illusion, add to them the idea of something higher than instinct, of a free and reasonable choice, and they become instances of moral goodness in one of its purest and noblest forms.

How, then, are such acts of animal nature to be distinguished from actions properly of a moral kind? By the want of power in the animal to rise beyond the visible standard, the will of its master, and to compare its actions with a standard of absolute right still higher. A criminal, we may suppose, the owner of a faithful dog, to escape from the police, stirs it up to attack them, and it is killed in defending its master from the hands of justice. We admire and praise its fidelity, to which its life is sacrificed. We impute the blame and condemnation to the vicious owner alone. To obey the human will is the dog's highest law, and it seems to us incapable of climbing higher. When an instinct so noble is perverted and abused through the sin and folly of man, we have simply a proof that man, when he deserts the true standard of his being, is not only made subject to vanity in his own person, but also drags down with him the lower creation in his grievous fall.

But there seems to be a further truth involved in facts of this kind, and which is needed to complete the explanation. There is a singular class of facts in the science of harmony, called the doctrine of forced vibrations. Notes or strings of a particular pitch or length, when their sound is powerful, tend to hinder and quench those vibrations of other strings which are in discord with them, and awaken others which are either in unison, or bear to them the relation of some fundamental chord.

There seems to be a similar law in ceaseless operation in the world of thought and intelligence, when lower natures are brought under the daily and hourly influence of some being of a higher kind. They are attracted by a kind of magnetic influence. Their own instincts are more or less suspended, and replaced by others of a higher sort, the echoes and reflections of that higher nature which dominates over them. They are thus magnetized into the semblance of a higher life than is properly their own. And thus domesticated animals, in proportion as the society of man has its full influence over them, seem to rise into a kind of border land between mere instinct and moral intelligence. They are raised by a foreign power above themselves. A process of elevation is at work, which tends to conceal the interval between instinct and reason, unmoral and moral life, because the lower instinct is guided, controlled, and in a manner subdued and replaced, by a power derived from man's higher and nobler being. The strange marvel, recorded once alone in Scripture, and even there a stumblingblock and jest to the careless and profane, would seem thus like one extreme instance of a general law in ceaseless operation. It may be taken for an outward visible sign of a sacramental privilege of moral elevation, gained by lower creatures through the daily consecration of their best powers to the service of man. When the prophet was perverse and faithless, the ass which had served him faithfully so long, rose for a moment to a share in its master's abused and forfeited privilege. It saw what the man whose eyes had been opened could not see. The dumb ass, speaking with human voice, forbad the madness of the prophet.

The faithful animal, which cleaves to its master with a fond affection, and sacrifices its own instincts in obeying his will, attains thereby the highest type of its own being, and a close resemblance to moral goodness in beings of a higher type than its own. And when this analogy is confirmed and deepened by such daily and hourly intercourse that the higher, intelligent will seems to mould and almost animate the lower, the resemblance is closer still, and seems almost like a direct participation. But these border cases only confirm the truth of the principle, that a power of reason and free choice, and this alone, is joined with the sense of moral obligation. They prove that instinct in its highest and noblest forms is, in the words of Coleridge, like "the shadow of approaching humanity, the sun rising from behind, in the kindling dawn and morning of creation."

But the same principle, the primary and fundamental law or conception of Moral Science, precludes at once, and wholly sets aside three counterfeit theories of conscience, the physiological, the instinctive, and the tyrannical. Let us examine these briefly in succession.

The Physiological Hypothesis in Morals consists mainly in the union of two elements. The first is the process of medical research, by which the consequences of all mental emotions are traced in their effects on muscular and nervous tissues, and on the state of the bodily frame. The second is a vague, ill-defined theory of the perpetual equality of dynamical force, under forms ever varying. All moral emotions, it is thus inferred, are only the results of some strange concentration and transmutation of solar force in the nervous structure of the human frame.

Now it is plain at once that since we ascribe moral responsibility to angels and other possible unknown races, of a physiology wholly different from our own, or bodiless spirits, and deny it to animals, however nearly allied to us in structure, so long as we exclude from our conception the gift of reason, the hypothesis must be an entire delusion. It excludes from the definition of a moral agent what is alone essential, and includes what is accidental and superfluous. Things may actually concur, and that in the whole range of our limited experience, and still we may feel clearly that there is no essential connection between them. Certain changes in the nervous tissues, let us grant for a moment, accompany the moral emotions of love or hatred, sympathy or envy, hope or fear. How can this prove that the physical change is the cause of the emotion, and not its effect? How can it prove that the connection is not wholly arbitrary, and capable of being entirely different for other races, or for men themselves in the life to come? Thus, for instance, we cannot think of a circle, or reason upon it, without some sensible image. There may be many to whom it always suggests the thought, by association, either of a plate in a dinner service, or of the sun in the sky. But if some skilful manufacturer should try to persuade us, that the properties of the circle depend on a knowledge of the earths that are used in making porcelain, or the spectroscopic observer, that they rest on a chemical analysis of the red protuberances of the sun, then, in spite of all their manufacturing skill or scientific attainments, we should justly laugh to scorn so prodigious a folly. And it is and must be a folly no less extreme, when the attempt is made to resolve into some complex medical fact about the waste and change of nervous tissues, those grand fountain truths of moral good and evil, which encompass, guide and sustain the whole universe—those laws of eternal goodness and righteousness, which are the deep foundations of the throne of God.

But the mere instinctive theory of morals is equally set aside by the same test. A man has lost favour with his fellows by some selfish or cruel act, the result of self-

will or animal impulse. He is thus disliked, and his
social instinct is troubled and dissatisfied. To get rid
of this pain, "he resolves to act differently for the
future, and this is conscience!"

Conscience, according to this new and strange definition,
is nothing more than an instinctive effort to escape from
the secret pain of an unsatisfied desire. It would seem
to follow that every one is conscientious, in proportion
to his eager attempt to procure the unbridled and ceaseless indulgence of every lust. The great author of evil,
according to Milton, must have had his conscience in
vigorous exercise, when he set out on his expedition to
deceive and destroy.

> "Gabriel, thou hadst in heaven the esteem of wise,
> And such I held thee; but this question asked
> Puts me in doubt. Lives there who loves his pain?
> Who would not, finding way, break loose from hell,
> Though thither doomed? Thou wouldst thyself, no doubt,
> And boldly venture to whatever place
> Farthest from pain, where thou might'st hope to change
> Torment with ease, and soonest recompense
> Dole with delight, which in this place I sought."

And if a strong social instinct is needful to complete
the definition of conscience, this too is satisfied in the
description of his eager longing for closest "league and
amity" with Adam and Eve and their offspring, which the
arch-fiend has professed just before in his famous soliloquy.
Our great poet hardly could have suspected that a philosophy would arise, which would find all the needful
elements for the genesis and birth of conscience in his
own masterly portraiture of the Prince of darkness, and
the vehement workings of self-tormenting and consummate
evil. Avoidance and flight from evil, and craving for

companionship at whatever cost, are seen there united in
full perfection.

Near akin to this theory of conscience, as generated by
the effort to escape from an unsatisfied instinct, is the
tyrannical theory, which sees in it submission to the will
of the stronger, and a mere result from the habitual dread
of human punishment. On this view it is an artificial
product and creation of the penalties which lawgivers
have imposed. Thus a strong association is produced
between certain lines of conduct, and the dangerous and
painful consequences to which, under the actual constitution of society, they naturally lead.

Now it is doubtless true that by means of human
laws and their penalties we rise most easily to a vivid
perception of moral right and wrong. We are told, on
the highest authority, that "by law is the knowledge of
sin." It seems, however, no less plain that human laws do
not create the conscience of right and wrong, but only
awaken it. Men come very soon to distinguish between
actual laws, and a higher standard of right, by which laws
themselves need to be measured. It is felt that legislation, in some cases, may be unwise and mischievous, and
that punishments, though in agreement with the letter of
human laws, may be unjust. How can water rise above
its source? How can the conscience of man, if it be merely
a product of the fear of punishment, ever pass sentence
on those very laws by which punishment is enjoined?
The authority which such laws carry with them depends
plainly on two causes. Either what they enjoin is seen
to be right in itself, and what they forbid to be wrong; or
else the relation between those who command, and others
to whom the command is given, is felt to involve the duty
of obedience, whenever the command is not in its own

nature morally evil. In both cases alike we are compelled to recognize a source of obligation higher than the
mere will of the lawgiver. In one case it reminds us that
such things were duties, and right to be done, even before
the human command was given. In the other, the higher
law enjoins obedience, within certain limits, to the known
will and command of a lawful superior. But without some
faculty of moral discernment, some standard of right
deeper and higher than human laws, the laws themselves
must be wholly powerless. Nothing would be left of them,
but the power of the stronger to inflict suffering on the
weaker, whenever there is not abject submission to their
will; and the exposure of the weak to be crushed by the
strong, till their turn may come to cast off a hateful yoke,
and become oppressors in their turn.

Once let these theories of morals be condensed into
their simplest form, and stripped of those accessories of
ingenious thought, which disguise their true features, and
they will be spontaneously rejected as wholly incapable of
explaining the real experience and deepest convictions of
the human heart. When a man has committed a frightful
murder, his whole nervous system undergoes a strange and
painful disturbance, and this is conscience! When he has
forfeited the esteem of his fellows by selfishness and vice,
his social instincts are unsatisfied. He resolves to gratify
them in future, and this is conscience! The slave crouches
with fear before a human slave-driver, and shrinks from
the lash he sees uplifted, and ready to fall, and this again
is conscience! Yea, they are conscience in the same sense
that the monkey, the chimpanzee or the gorilla is a reasonable man. There are some strong features of bodily or
anatomical resemblance, but the human heart and mind
are wholly wanting. Such a conscience is no true con-

science, but a poor and wretched substitute where the reality is wholly absent. A murderer may experience strange horrors. The "horrid, horrid dream" of the scene of violence may beset him in his waking hours. He may have the strongest desire, and the firmest resolution, to disguise his crime, that he may still enjoy the pleasures of social intercourse. He may be full of secret terror, lest his course should be detected, and the sentence of the law alight upon him. And all the time conscience may be asleep. He may remain a hardened and cruel ruffian, ready, if only he can reckon on impunity, to repeat the worst of crimes.

True Conscience is a higher and nobler thing. Its ground and root is the conscious possession of a reasonable will, an inward power of choice, dependent on no mere external influence, but on the mind's own conviction of what is fit and right to be done. Its upward growth is towards the light, sometimes dimly seen, as in mist, sometimes as in brighter daylight, of some noble and lofty ideal of human conduct, some bow of heaven, in which the pure light of a perfect love diffracts and varies itself into a thousand forms of loveliness and beauty. It lifts the eye of the soul towards those eternal hills, whence its help for moral conflict and victory must come. The physical elements of man's bodily frame do not and cannot enter into its definition. It belongs to the reasonable mind and will, whether unembodied or disembodied, to angels and to men, to men living as we now live, or unclothed by the stroke of death, or clothed upon with nobler bodies in the resurrection. It deals with voluntary actions in their threefold character, the source from which they flow, the limits within which they move, and the issues to which they tend. But moral tendencies cannot even exist, when moral characters and distinctions, in the will which is the fount of action, are wholly denied. The tree must first be good, that its fruit may be good also. There must be some character of moral goodness in the motives, tempers, and feelings of the heart themselves, before they can have any tendency, in their actings, to produce good even in distant ages, and throughout the whole extent of the moral universe.

The law of gravitation, in the natural world, is wonderful in the consequences it involves, and the results to which it leads. We live, it tells us, surrounded by mysteries without number. All creation is bound by it into one great system of being. Every leaf that withers and falls in the forest, affects, though insensibly, the motion of every planet in that great system. The dew-drop, alighting on the grass, has its speed increased by every gem buried in the Indian waves, and every wave that dashes on the beach of a thousand distant isles. Links of secret influence emanate from our own bodies, from every bird and insect in the skies of summer, and range onward, till they lose themselves in the depths of space. There is nothing solitary in the wide creation. There is no single mote or atom, in earth or air or sea, but is linked fast, by relations science has in part revealed, and which in part are still hidden, to the whole system of created and material things.

Now conscience discloses to us a law of union in the moral world, as wide and far reaching as the law of universal attraction, but of a nobler and higher kind. It is a law, not of physical compulsion, but of moral duty. It pronounces, not what will be done, but what every moral agent ought to be and to do. Revealed to us more dimly by natural conscience, it stands out in still clearer

light in the word of God. But clearly or dimly taught,
the message is the same. The sacred voice may be
repeated, but the vision is one. That law is the great and
simple law of love. It includes love to God, and love to
men and all the creatures of God. It ranges through
every rank and order of sentient beings, as the objects it
includes within its care, though moral, intelligent, reasonable creatures are the only subjects to which it belongs.
It stoops to protect the insect from the lawless cruelty of
the child, and rises to claim the allegiance of angels and
archangels before the throne in heaven. It seems at first,
like the pure sunlight, to be so simple that nothing can
be learned from it, and thus it may be in danger of being
mistaken, by the rash and careless, for an empty truism.
But when it stoops down to earthly things, and passes
through the clouded atmosphere of this lower world, it
discloses an infinite variety of rights, duties, and obligations, which belong to men in their relations to each
other, to the unseen world beyond the grave, and to the
great Author of their being. And when it has ranged
through the wide universe, and stooped down to awaken
high and pure desires in hearts that have been deluded
and darkened by vice and folly, recalling them to the
upward pathway of light once more, it returns to present its gathered wealth of all holy desires, all good
counsels, and all just works, as a freewill offering at the
footstool of that glorious Fountain of goodness, perfect in
all moral beauty and holiness, from whom they proceed,
and to whom they tend as their proper home. For "God
is love, and he that dwelleth in love dwelleth in God, and
God in him. He that loveth not knoweth not God, for
God is love!"

LECTURE V.

THE DIVISIONS OF MORAL SCIENCE.

ALL science, as Lord Bacon truly remarks, has three main subjects, Nature, Man, and God. There are thus three main divisions of human knowledge, Natural Philosophy, Humanity and Theology. Natural Philosophy, again, is simple, because in material things, and mere vegetable and animal life, there is no standard of right and duty, distinct from their actual state. Theology is also simple, because in the great First Cause, what is and must be, what is and what ought to be, through the perfection of the Divine Nature, are one and the same. The true conception of a God includes the highest conceivable perfection. But our knowledge of Man and Moral Agents is twofold. Side by side with the lesson of their actual state, derived from experience, we are compelled to recognize an ideal standard, a law of duty and perfection, which they may or may not attain. And hence there is a twofold Science of Humanity, the Actual and the Ideal. Ethics is the science of Ideal Humanity. It is thus co-extensive with the wide range of experimental or practical human science, and presides over it, as it presides over Physics, being the lawful superior and mistress of both. And it borders on Theology, of which, rightly understood,

D. L.   7 it is neither the rival, the child, nor the slave, but the spouse and ally, subordinate in holy and loving union. For in reality it is only through some awakening of natural conscience that men can rise to the discernment of spiritual truth.

Ethics, again, have science and certain truth, not mere guesswork and probability, for their aim. Such a view is confirmed, not only by the judgment of Locke and my two most eminent predecessors, but by the nature of the subject, and the analogies of geometrical science and physical research. It must be possible, with humble and patient thought, to rise here above the mists and fogs of endless doubt into a higher region of clear sunlight and eternal truth. The definitions are simple, on which the whole superstructure depends. The whole temple of moral truth may be said to rest on these two pillars— a power of reason, will, and spontaneous choice in each moral agent, and a perceived standard of right and wrong, binding on such a free moral agent, as his true ideal of thought, feeling, and action, by its own inherent and supreme authority. That standard, reduced to its simplest form, and summed up in one word, is the great law of universal love, or the first and second great commandments of the Law and the Gospel, bound together in essential, indissoluble, and perfect union.

Such a view of the nature of Moral Science may seem perhaps, at the first glance, to reduce it within the narrow limit of a few barren and almost self-evident truisms. But such an inference would be a fatal misconception. The star we see at midnight may appear, to the careless observer, to be only an insignificant speck of light. But the seeming minuteness results from its distance alone. The sun is a million times larger than the earth on which

we live. Sirius, from modern photometry, has been
inferred to be sixty or a hundred times intrinsically
brighter than the sun. It may thus, for aught we can
tell, be the centre of a material system, vaster and larger
than our own. So also the simplest truths of science, like
the properties of the triangle or the circle, or the law of
gravitation, are the most fertile, when we strive to trace
out the consequences involved in them, and the results to
which they lead. And as soon as we endeavour to map
out the fields of Moral Science, and to form the outlines of
its geography, it will become plain how immense is the
range of thought which has here to be traversed. A rich
and large variety of moral precepts, lessons and doctrines
of high importance, will then be seen to unfold themselves
from its fundamental truths.

Moral Science admits of being classified in three
different ways. The first of these depends on the various
objects or persons whom it includes; the second on the
faculties and powers of the mind, which have to be brought
under the control of moral obligations; and the third on
those moral capacities, which are shown, by the joint
evidence of experience and revelation, to belong to the
whole universe of moral agents.

I. First of all, Moral Science may be viewed with
reference to the objects or persons whom it includes within
its range. It is thus parted at once into three main
divisions, Personal, Social, and Divine. The third and
last of these answers to the first great commandment of
the law. The second, which is like the first, includes the
two others. Theology, based on a supernatural message
from heaven, descends naturally from the love of God, as
the primal duty, to the love of man. But when we
view Morals as a human science, the natural order is a

climax, in which we begin with ourselves, and then travel outward and mount upward. Self-love, the love of our neighbour, or of mankind at large, and the love of God, are thus the three main divisions or kingdoms of Moral Science, as defined by the objects of duty which it includes, and the persons to whom it extends.

Self-love is the first of these three main laws of moral duty. Its just expansion and development open a very wide field of thought. If we are not to love ourselves at all, the command, Thou shalt love thy neighbour as thyself, is robbed of all sense and meaning. It would then constitute a virtual prohibition of every kind of social affection. Personal and social morality are thus inseparably linked by the Divine law. They rest on the same foundation, and must stand and fall together.

This branch of Ethics has been exposed to a double perversion from opposite sides. One class of writers would exalt it beyond its due limits, so as to constitute the whole of Moral Science. Others fall into an opposite extreme, and would exclude it altogether.

All the selfish theories of Ethics come under the first description, or the school of Epicurus, Hobbes, Mandeville, and the lower class of utilitarians, who have not changed their wild olive by grafting it on the more fruitful stock of Christian benevolence. To the opposite pole belong some mystics of the middle ages, the school of Kant, and some few intuitive moralists of modern times. According to the first class of writers, all morality is only a wise expediency, a prudent, foreseeing regard to our own happiness and enjoyment, and a wise calculation of the means of securing it in the fullest measure. According to the other, virtue must be pursued simply for its own sake. Any respect to our own benefit in upright or virtuous conduct degrades it from its proper character of obedience to an absolute law of right, and thus poisons duty at its fountain-head.

The pathway of true wisdom lies between these two opposite extremes. Those benevolent affections, which alone satisfy the wide and large claim of the great law of duty, are more than mere self-love, covered with a thin disguise. The mind, when in a right and healthy state, goes forth directly towards its object. It seeks the good of the loved one for his or her own sake, and does not pause first to make a secret calculation that their benefit will redound in probable or certain gain to ourselves. The benevolent affections, as Dugald Stewart has well observed, "prompt us to particular objects without any reference to our own enjoyment." There is no doubt that actions of outward beneficence may often proceed in their secret source from self-love alone. But then in this case they fail to satisfy the first conditions of social morality.

To the same effect Cicero remarks on the doctrine of Epicurus (*De Fin.* II. 24), "Where can there be a place for friendship, or who can be a friend to any one, whom he does not love 'ipsum propter ipsum,' himself for his own sake? What is it to love, but to wish any one to be enriched with the greatest benefits, even though there should be no return from those benefits to him who desires them? But it benefits me, you may say, to be of that disposition. Nay, perhaps, to *seem* to have it. For you cannot *be* such, unless you *are* such. And how can you be such, unless that love itself has possession of you? And this comes to pass, not by introducing the conception of its usefulness, but it is born of itself, and springs up of its own accord. But you say, I follow

utility. Thy friendship then will last, so long as some
gain shall follow it, and if utility makes a friendship, the
same will unmake and destroy it."

The reasoning of Kant, on the other hand, would exclude
from morality all pursuit of personal happiness. Our duty,
he affirms, is to seek our own perfection, and our neighbour's happiness, but neither our own happiness nor our
neighbour's perfection. This is a strange paradox in a
writer so subtle and profound. It replaces the Divine
command by another, which seems its exact converse—
"Thou shalt love thy neighbour, but not as thyself."
What every one inevitably wills, he says, cannot fall
under the notion of duty, so that it is an intellectual
contradiction to say that a man is obliged to advance
his own happiness with all his might. But surely an
instinctive craving for momentary pleasure differs very
widely from a deliberate, rational pursuit of our own
highest welfare. The first may sometimes be synonymous
with open vice, and oftener still with careless and guilty
folly. But the second, though it may have a further and
wider range, must evidently include the aim at moral
perfection. And thus it must ever form one essential
element of true morality, as approved by the enlightened
conscience, and directly enjoined in the Word of God.

Social Morality, the second main division of Ethics, has
its own difficult problems. What is it to love our neighbour as ourselves? Does it mean that we ought to love
him with exactly the same kind of love? In this case, if
our self-love be excessive, diseased, and impure, we should
have to extend the range of this disease and corruption, so
as to infect the whole range of our social action. If we
love ourselves inordinately and unreasonably, without
candour or equity, the evil would only be aggravated

by exercising an affection of the same kind, even if that were possible, to all around us. Or does the precept mean that we are to love them exactly in the same degree? This is hardly possible in itself. And it is an idea, which seems further excluded by the word, "neighbour." For this naturally implies that nearness enters into, and forms one element in determining, the moral obligation. The true meaning of the command seems rather to be, that the thought of self or not-self is excluded in estimating the relative claims of duty, and that the obligation rests on nearness, neighbourhood, and opportunity alone. We are nearer to ourselves than to others, and have thus fuller opportunities to seek our own good, and to act for it, than for theirs. But beyond this contrast, which cannot be set aside, and is of great practical moment, the rule prescribes that the question, whether the good be theirs or ours, shall not disturb the impartial actings of a wise benevolence, which will thus be found in perfect harmony with a temperate and healthy self-love.

The third and highest branch of Ethics, Divine Morality, or Moral Theology, gives rise to deep questions of another kind. If love consists in a genuine desire for the happiness and well-being of others, or of ourselves, how can it apply to One, of whom not every Christian only, but every intelligent Theist, must believe that He is purely and perfectly blessed? But the answer to this difficulty is not hard to find. Love may assume three different forms or aspects, according to the diverse state and character of the object beloved. It may rest on those who are in want, pain, suffering, and moral degradation. In their case it assumes the form of pity and compassion, of desire for their moral recovery, or their relief from suffering. Again, it may have respect unto those who are upright, sinless and happy, but whose happiness is limited, and their moral excellency still capable of a large increase. In their case love must assume the form of simple benevolence, of desire for the increase of their happiness, and their growth and progress in all things that are good and worthy of praise. But, lastly, love may have for its object the glorious Creator and Preserver of the universe, the Infinitely and Supremely Good, who is blessed for ever. And here it must pass into a higher and nobler form. It becomes a delighted and adoring complacency in the contemplation of His infinite goodness. Divine Love is the exact reverse of selfish murmuring, or of sinful envy. It implies a deep gladness of heart, that He who is perfectly good and holy should be removed far above the reach of pain and evil, and that He should be blessed with perfect and inconceivable blessedness for evermore.

II. Moral Science may be distinguished and arranged, in the second place, by a reference to those faculties or powers of the mind and will, which are seen to coexist in every moral agent. The threefold character of the science meets us here in another form. Goodness, wisdom and power, all infinite, meet in our conception of the Divine Being. Being, knowledge or intelligence, and will, or the *esse, posse* and *velle* of the schoolmen, are equally found in the constitution of every moral agent. So that Moral Science must have a threefold character, when viewed in its reference to the revealed perfections of God, and the constituent elements of every created mind. The distinction is found in the words of the first and great commandment, where the heart, the mind, and the strength, are separately named, and placed alike under the supreme law of perfect love. There is the Morality of good affections and desires, of wise and clear intelligence, and of that active zeal and energy, which carries into effect the decisions of the judgment, and the desires of the heart.

Moral Science, in this aspect, includes, first of all, a pure and lofty ideal of right affection and desire. It does not deal mainly and immediately, like human laws, with the outward conduct alone. Its empire has its foundations laid deep within the heart. It enjoins that the tree shall be good, that the inward feelings and affections of the heart shall be pure, in order that the life may be pure also. It is a mortal enemy to all counterfeit and unreal righteousness, which begins by cleansing the outside, while all within may be full of extortion and excess, defiled with impure lust and selfish passion. Its aim is to cast salt into that hidden fountain of the heart, from whence either sweet or bitter water must unceasingly flow.

This is the first and highest branch of morals, on its subjective side. For here it rises above the mists which settle on the sides of the mountain, or the diffracting influences that flow from the complex conditions of our human and earthly life. In this highest region it is easier than in the rest to trace out clearly the manifold results and corollaries of that great law of love, equally simple and sublime, which binds together the whole moral universe.

But if love has for its first and simplest character a desire for our own good, and the good of others, or delight in the contemplation of the Divine felicity, a second must immediately follow. It must search diligently into the nature of that good which we are bound to pursue, and of those evils from which, both for ourselves and all around us, we are bound to seek deliverance.

Ignorant and unwise affection defeats itself. It hinders

those whom it would help, and harms those whom it
desires, perhaps eagerly and intensely, to succour and to
bless. Human life and happiness are highly complicated
things. There is wheel within wheel in that strange
machinery, on which comfort and distress, ease and pain,
moral progress and advancement, or decline and degradation, are found practically to depend. Mere wishes of
benevolence may too often avail little, if there be complete ignorance or misconception of the true causes and
elements of human well-being. It needs patient, humble,
and persevering toil, self-knowledge, experience of life,
and study of the Word of God, to trace out clearly those
mysterious Nile-sources, that hide themselves from
careless eyes, from whence the wide and ample streams of
human joy and sorrow perpetually flow. And hence one
important division of Moral Science must consist in what
Locke has made the title of a separate work,—"The
Conduct of the Understanding." His remarks, however
weighty, touch only the brink of a wide sea of thought,
and dwell very slightly on those aspects of the subject, in
which its ethical character, as one main branch of morals,
most distinctly appears.

Here the old Socratic or Platonic inquiry—πότερον
διδακτὸν ἡ ἀρετή, whether virtue is something that can be
taught—finds its natural place. It links itself closely with
the deepest problems, not only in natural metaphysics, but
in revealed theology. Into these it would be premature to
enter now. They could not possibly be dealt with in a
few pages, in a manner worthy of their high importance.
It may be enough here to observe that an obligation to
seek the good and promote the welfare of others must
involve the duty of earnest and continued effort to see
clearly wherein that good and welfare really consist.

The homely proverb, that "hell is paved with good intentions" scarcely deserves the wide acceptance it has found. We may say, with deeper truth, and a very solemn meaning, that bad intentions are the real pavement, on which is reared continually the dark superstructure of consummated vice and crime, and of open punishment, whether in this life or the life to come. What may be more truly said, in a figure, to be paved with good intentions is that limbo of vanity, where all things

> Abortive, monstrous, and unkindly mixed,

all perverse, but well-meaning follies, due to careless haste, blind prejudice, or self-satisfied ignorance, wander up and down in darkness as their natural home.

A general desire for happiness is the natural instinct of all men. And some wish for the good of others, however feeble, is so plain a dictate of conscience, that even the selfish and vicious, who do not really feel it, constantly feign a virtue which, as they are well aware, they ought to possess, and the entire want of which must be fatal to their reputation among their fellow-men. But the interval is very wide between the mere instinct, or the feeble, careless, and irresolute desire, and that earnest effort to learn what is good and right, and then to practise and promote it, which is the true sign of a genuine and hearty benevolence.

A large part, then, of our moral duty must consist in the right conduct of the understanding. It must include the diligent, humble effort to learn, both in our own case and that of others, what is the true good which claims our zealous pursuit; what is the nature, and what are the elements of that happiness towards which we ought to aspire, and what are practically the best means by which it can be really attained.

A pretentious and boastful, but blind and ill-judging philanthropy is one of the chief moral dangers of the times in which we live. The grandeur of the object, the seeming nobility of the aim, its wide and comprehensive nature, too often veil the selfish pride, the rash folly, and in some cases the open impiety, which first sets up a mere figment in place of the great reality, and then falls down and worships blindly those wretched theories of human progress and political perfection, which its own fancy has conceived, or its own fingers have made.

True benevolence is humble and modest. It is suspicious of mere phrases. It puts no easy faith in hollow and shadowy counterfeits of that good, so high, noble, and excellent, which it keeps ever in view. It studies carefully the lessons of experience. It listens with reverence to whatever brings the credentials and reasonable marks of a Divine message. It does not despise the helps to human happiness, which spring from wise laws, social freedom, and the progress of men in those arts and sciences, which multiply the conveniences of social life. But it knows and feels that the main sources of peace and comfort must lie deeper, and be sought higher, than all these. They are land-springs that soon dry up and fail. They are plants too feeble to resist the storm, and may soon wither or be swept away in the whirlwinds of human passion. The men whose love to their fellow-men is most real, deep, and earnest, will distrust the cries of the passing hour, the uncertain voices of popular feeling, which vary from year to year, and almost from day to day. They will try to dig deep, and lay their foundation on solid rock, before they claim to become master-builders in so vast a work as the future and lasting regeneration of the human race. Or rather, they will feel that so great and noble an end must lie wholly beyond the range of their own feeble efforts. And while they labour faithfully, to the best of their power, and use whatever light they have attained, for the good of their fellows, they will look up with reverence for the promised working of a higher Power, and place their hopes of success in a goodness and wisdom far beyond their own.

But if high and lofty desire for the good of others be one main division of moral duty, and a second is Moral Wisdom, or growing acquaintance with the true nature of that good we should seek to promote and attain, the third is Moral Energy, or that zeal and earnestness which seeks ever to carry out in practice the inward convictions of the mind and heart.

Energy of will, it ought always to be clearly felt and owned, cannot alone constitute moral virtue. There are other conditions of right feeling, and true knowledge of duty, which must first be satisfied. Where there is neither goodness in the heart, nor wisdom in the understanding, mere activity, however restless and incessant, will only widen the range, intensify the amount, and deepen the shades, of moral guilt. To "do evil with both hands earnestly" can only place men at the widest possible remove from the summit of true perfection. The hero-worship which some, despairing of Christianity, would exalt into a kind of religious faith, is a poor and wretched substitute for Christian morality. Power is not goodness, and energy of will is not moral excellence. And yet, since man was made an active being, in the image of God, on whose ceaseless energy of wisdom and love all things depend, there is a natural fitness and beauty in human energy, even apart from the right or wrong direction it may assume. And when true benevolence is joined with earnest study of the proper means by which its desires may be attained, and with a hearty zeal for its actual attainment, then human virtue, amidst all its weakness and imperfection, becomes a lovely image and resemblance of that goodness which is infinite and divine.

III. Moral Science, however, besides a threefold division from the objects it embraces, and the natural faculties which it involves and requires, of feeling or affection, knowledge, and will, admits a further arrangement or partition of a still deeper kind. This depends on those moral capacities of obedience, transgression, and recovery, which are linked, mysteriously and inseparably, with the very constitution of a universe of moral agents. And here, once more, the whole science naturally resolves itself into three main divisions.

The first of these is Simple or Direct Ethics. Its primary law and formative principle is the love of being, as being. This unfolds itself, as we have seen, into Personal Morality, or Self-love, Social Morality, or the love of our neighbour, Divine Morals, or Piety and the Love of God. Or again, with reference to the human faculties, into Moral Aspiration, Wisdom, and Energy, or the ethics of the heart, the mind, and the strength. This last variety is well summed up in the precept: " Whatsoever thy hand findeth to do, do it with thy might;" and consists in that moral earnestness, which constitutes true heroism, when once it is devoted to the cause of truth and love. But in all these varieties we have first to consider moral duty in itself, or the love of being as being, without reference to the moral contrasts, which experience has revealed.

The second branch is compound, and might also be

styled Diagnostic or Judicial Ethics. It is that branch
of the science which unfolds the law of right feeling and
conduct towards all beings, when viewed as capable of
immense moral diversity and contrast, from Divine perfection, or the highest forms of angelic or human excellence,
to the worst and lowest degrees of folly, vice, malice and
profaneness. Its double law is the love of all good, and
the hatred of all evil. It includes the three kindred
subjects, righteousness, judgment, and justice. First of all
it prescribes a right and just condition of the affections,
in contemplating all the actual or conceivable varieties of
moral character, so as in every case to love and admire the
good, but to condemn, despise, and hate, every form of
moral evil. In the next place it enjoins a sound exercise
of the judgment, so as to discern, not only the broad contrast of good and evil, but also the various degrees of
virtue, moral goodness, and holy love, or of vice, depravity,
lust and malice, and thus to guide the determinations of
the will in all practical questions that may arise. In
the third and last place it includes justice, or the actual,
honest application and development of true convictions
and right judgment, in reference to all those cases of
moral contrast and diversity, which meet us, from time
to time, in the experience of human life, and in the conflicts of a world, where light and darkness, good and evil,
struggle and contend from age to age.

The third main division, which completes and crowns
the whole outline of the science, is Therapeutic or Remedial Ethics. And here we have to begin by admitting a
weighty and solemn truth—the past and present existence
and wide prevalence of moral disease, which needs some
powerful remedy for its effectual cure. Ethics, in this
department, deals with moral beings, neither as upright

and sinless, nor as hopelessly fallen and irreclaimably corrupt, but as those who need recovery, and may be recovered, from decay, weakness, and degradation, to uprightness and moral healthiness once more.

The parent truth, in this vast and large division of the science, is that great fact, which forms the basis of the whole economy of the Christian faith. Man, however far gone from original righteousness, or the standard of a pure and perfect love, is not therefore hopelessly fallen. A way of life, that leads upward, is still open before him. He may yet arise from the dust, loose himself from the bands of his neck, and stand upright, as a moral freeman once more, in the face of heaven. His sickness, however sore and grievous, and incurable by mere human or external remedies, admits of successful treatment by the skill and love of a Divine Physician. And the science of Remedial Ethics, viewed on the side of pure reason, involves these successive elements. First, the great duty of desire and longing for this moral restoration, both for ourselves and others, so far as it is needed, and its possibility has been revealed. Secondly, the duty of learning what are the means by which this great recovery to a new and higher moral life must first begin, and may still be carried on, with all the hindrances to its birth and later progress, and that provision of moral and spiritual agencies, by which these various hindrances may be overcome. Thirdly and lastly, the earnest practical adoption of all the means of recovery and moral restoration, which Divine love and wisdom may have provided for sinful men, and the ceaseless and persevering progress of the soul, from the miry clay of the slough of despond, towards that celestial city which is the dwelling-place of light, purity, and heavenly love.

These three kingdoms of Moral Science, for such they may fitly be called from their largeness and extent, are in other words the Ethics of Paradise, of the Law, and the Gospel. And each of them in turn admits a nine-fold subdivision, from the moral objects with which they deal, and the faculties of the moral being out of which they grow, and on which their existence depends.

Combining all three elements, we may form a comprehensive outline of the geography and whole domain of Ethics, which is, under another phrase, the Science of Ideal Humanity. It will then assume the following form.

A. Simple or Direct Ethics:

Its primal law and basis is Love, or genuine desire for the highest happiness or welfare of all sentient being, as being.

I. Personal Ethics = Pure and unselfish Self-love.

1. Self-love in affection and desire. This implies the aim at our own welfare in the whole range of our being.

a. Bodily welfare or health; (α) as capable of sensation,—pleasure in contrast to pain; (β) as gifted with active powers, or Gymnastics in its proper sense; (γ) as capable of degrees of health and strength,—Dietetics and Hygienics; (δ) as capable of grace and beauty, or Cosmetics and Æsthetics.

b. Welfare in respect of Intellectual Power. "Mens sana in corpore sano."

c. Moral Welfare. The pursuit of moral goodness and spiritual excellence. The heathen maxim in its best sense,

Αἰὲν ἀριστεύειν καὶ ὑπείροχον ἔμμεναι ἄλλων:

or the higher law of the Apostle, "Covet earnestly the best gifts, and yet show I unto you a more excellent way."

2. Self-love, with reference to the powers of the mind, or Moral Wisdom.

    a. Cultivation of sanitary science, wise self-preservation, the converse of the indirect suicide of vice and folly.

    b. Mental Self-knowledge, wise discernment of special gifts leading to a right selection of the pursuits of life, and of work to be done.

    c. Moral Self-knowledge. "Prove your own selves."

3. Self-love in Action, or Practical Culture, under the guidance of moral wisdom, of all natural and acquired gifts of body and mind.

II. Social Ethics — Philanthropy or General Benevolence.

1. Benevolence in affection and desire, applied to all the various relations of human life.

    a. Conjugal or Married Love, in the relation of husband and wife.

    b. Parental and Filial. The right laws of affection in the fourfold relation of father, mother, son, daughter.

    c. Fraternal, or the laws of right affection in brothers and sisters.

    d. Domestic. Relations of master, mistress, and servant.

    e. Local. The duties of neighbourhood.

    f. Friendship. Bonds and laws of special intimacy and affection.

    g. Civic Relations. Magistrate and citizen.

    h. National. Relations of sovereign and subject.

i. Legislative. Varieties of social rank and constitutional privilege.

j. International. The moral laws of right and benevolent feeling with regard to other races, and other civil communities.

2. Benevolence of the Mind, or right study of the means of promoting the welfare of others.

a. The Relations of Sex. *b.* Of Age. *c.* Domestic Economy. *d.* Civil Economy. *e.* Political Economy. *f.* National Economy.

3. Beneficence — Social Morality in practice and outward result, with reference to all the duties and relations of daily life.

III. Divine Ethics = Piety, or the Love of God, including

1. The Religion of the Heart; Adoration, gratitude, obedience.

2. The Religion of the Mind. Divine contemplation, and the use of all means for growth in knowledge of Divine things.

3. The Religion of the Strength, or pious and holy affections, and a true knowledge of God, applied faithfully in the active and outward duties of a religious life.

B. Compound or Judicial Ethics.

Its primal law and formative principle is Righteousness, or to feel and judge of all moral agents, and act towards them, according to their various characters, good or evil, sinless or fallen, penitent or impenitent, proud or humble, advancing or declining in their moral state. And here we have, as before—

I. Personal Ethics, including

a. Self-condemnation and self-hatred, as evil.

b. Self-respect and self-honour, so far as upright, sincere, and faithful.

c. Repentance and humility.

d. True and right judgment on the personal state, whether of moral progress or moral decline.

e. Earnest aspiration after full victory over evil, and a perfect restoration to moral perfection.

II. Social Righteousness, including

a. Love and esteem of the good for their goodness.

b. Hatred and contempt of the morally evil as evil.

c. Moral discernment of the true character of men.

d. Practical righteousness, in praise and blame, reward, censure and punishment.

III. Divine Righteousness.

This includes the whole doctrine of the revealed law of God, with its disclosure of the Divine holiness, its threatenings and promises, in their connection with the Divine attributes, and the application of its truths to the hearts and consciences of men.

C. Remedial Ethics = the Morality of the Gospel, viewed as a Divine provision of mercy for the healing of moral disease. Here Ethical Science rises into a still higher field. It becomes, in the truest sense of the term, Moral Theology, and links itself with all the promises of the Gospel and the hope of the life to come. It is transfigured, and loses its earthly features in a higher light that beams down upon it from heaven.

This outline, however brief and imperfect, may help to give some conception of the width and variety of those

fields of high and sacred thought, which lie open before
the general students of Moral Science. To unfold them
all, as their grandeur and rich variety demand, would far
exceed the work of a whole lifetime. But to open out,
in any degree, their hidden treasures, and to throw clearer
light on any of their hard and difficult problems, is an object
worthy the ambition of every Christian heart. The moral
teacher, who is at all faithful to so high a trust, may have
to encounter misconception from the careless, or ridicule
and obloquy from moral triflers, in an age prone to self-
flattery, and far too impatient of calm and serious thought.
But these difficulties are only like dust in the balance,
and utterly to be despised, when compared with the
privilege of tracing out these pathways of high and holy
thought, which lead the spirit upward to the footstool of
God's throne, there to lose itself in the light which flows
from His presence, who is uncreated, infinite, and perfect
goodness.

This lesson of the true dignity of Moral Science, as
superior to the noblest triumphs of human skill in the
fields of nature, is taught most clearly in the words of the
patriarch, in the oldest book of inspired and sacred poetry.
A modern paraphrase of this voice of early antiquity,
which is full of such deep meaning, may bring this subject
to a fitting close.

Man, we are told by the tempted patriarch, is diligent
in searching out the hidden treasures of the earth. These
are all of them objects of his assiduous and successful
pursuit; the veins of silver, the place of sapphires, and the
dust of gold. "He searcheth out all perfect things, the
stones of darkness, and the shadow of death." He tills
the earth, and reaps its plentiful harvests, so that "out of
it there cometh bread." He turns up its soil, and brings

to light the gems, sparkling like fire, that were buried in
its bosom. There are paths which no fowl knoweth, and
the eye of the vulture cannot see, and which the wild
beasts of prey, roving over the forest and wilderness, have
never trodden. These are the pathways of Man, when he
sinks the shaft of his mine, puts his hand upon the
rocks, and pierces the sides or depths of the mountain,
that he may bring to light all its stores of hidden
treasure. But amidst all his labours, however prosperous,
one thing still eludes his search, and seems to baffle all
his industry, and the pride of his science. "Where shall
wisdom be found? Where is the place of understanding?"
How shall he attain that moral insight, that true ideal
of human action, speech, and thought, whereby he may
guide his steps aright in the weary journey of this mortal
life, in which his days seem often to be "few and evil"?
How may he escape the follies of childhood, and the
snares of youth; and be freed from the misery of a life
wasted without object or aim, cursed with vanity and
vexation of spirit in every moment of its swift progress
to the darkness and mystery of the grave?

Here is a hard problem. The lapidary or the miner,
in the days of the patriarch of the eastern desert, could
not solve it. And it remains wholly unsolved by theories
of evolution, or the researches and discoveries of physical
philosophy to the present hour. We mine deeper than
ever into the bowels of the earth, and bring up fossils,
buried long ages ago, and eloquent of the past, but "the
depth saith, It is not in me." We dredge the ocean with
industry and consummate skill, and from those profound
abysses bring up new materials for the growth of science,
but "the sea saith, It is not in me." We heap together
wealth in its most various forms, and all the costly treasures

of art; but these do not yield that higher gift of which we are in utmost need. "It cannot be gotten for gold, nor can silver be weighed for the price of it." It cannot be bought in exchange for the most precious jewels, for coral or pearl, onyx or sapphire. Nay, even if all the costly things of earth are summed together, and formed into one coronet or diadem of exquisite beauty, they will not buy this inestimable blessing.

"Whence then cometh wisdom?" How shall we gain that knowledge of highest worth, which may guide us through the dangers of life's journey, and bring us to some haven of peace and rest? When Science fails, and all nature, being eagerly questioned, gives up the task of answering in despair, a higher voice makes answer. He who is the Creator of this outer world, with its complex powers and mysterious treasures, is also the God of the spirits of all flesh, the Author and Parent of our moral being. He makes a decree for the rain, and a way for the lightning and the thunder. He fixes the circuits of the winds, and weighs the waters by measure. But this wonderful Geometer is also the Father of lights, the Parent and Guide of the spirits of men. He has not left us to grope blindly among His lower works for that peace and hope, which can never be found in these alone. He does not condemn the children of men to thirst for a wisdom which will never be given, and for light on the wants, duties, and destinies of the soul, which can never be attained. The deeper mines of moral truth are all in His sacred keeping. The precious jewels of truth, wisdom, and love, that may enrich the spirit for ever, are subject to His secret control. Let men only awake to their true dignity, as the creatures of God, dependent on His teaching, and their quest for moral truth and insight shall not be in vain. "When he made a decree for the rain, a way for the lightning and the thunder, then did He see it and declare it, He prepared it, and searched it out. And unto man He said,—Behold the fear of the Lord, that is wisdom, and to depart from evil is understanding."

In this sublime apostrophe of the patriarch, we have a key to the true relation between all physical science, and that higher field of thought which deals with moral right and wrong, sin and duty, the lessons of social Ethics and of religious piety and faith. These lower pursuits, in their own place and order, have a great value. But no abundance in the outward arts of life can ever secure human happiness, while the passions of discontent and pride, envy and malice, are reigning within the hearts of men. To depart from evil alone constitutes true understanding. And this victory over moral evil, whether in the individual or in nations, can never be really and permanently gained, unless moral instincts are confirmed and deepened by the presence of religious faith. The two lessons of the patriarch's message always go together. They have been married by the Supremely Wise, and no human power can effect their divorce and separation. Genuine piety, or the fear of God, must lead the way; and a high social morality, which discerns evil clearly, and then departs from it with a hearty aversion, is the happy sequel that must ever follow.

This lesson of ancient wisdom is receiving hourly new illustrations in the times in which we now live. A vain and misleading philosophy may extol the power and celebrate the triumphs of intellectual genius, and degrade all moral truth into a meagre compendium of worthless and almost unprofitable truisms. But in such comparisons

we have only a proof that its own eyes are dim with age,
so that it cannot see. The grand stars of the moral firmament are settled in the heavens, and shine on for ever.
The wanderer, here on earth, may lose sight of them
amidst the glare of meaner and earthly lights, of passing
and transient meteors, or they may be hidden from his
view by the mists and fogs that thicken around his steps.
But when once he looks upward with patience, in calm
thought, their holy light will dawn upon him once more.
At first it may seem very dim and feeble. But it is the
sign of coming daybreak, the earnest and pledge of
clearer insight and vision that will presently be given.
The higher and nobler the science, the later and the
longest delayed we may expect its full development to be.
"That is not first which is spiritual, but that which is
natural, and afterward that which is spiritual." Even
Physical Science is still only in its childhood, and an
immense progress, with deeper insight into laws of nature
still unknown, seems to be its heritage in coming
generations. But whenever the long-promised moral day-
break of our world shall arrive, all previous discoveries in
the field of physics, however large in themselves, will
seem almost mean and trivial, when compared with the
rich harvests of pure and lofty truth to be reaped in
this higher and nobler field. For Moral Science is nothing
less than the grand ideal of redeemed humanity, of which
the seeds and germs are planted already, but their perfect
growth and expansion can only be when the redemption is
fully come. It deals with that high and pure standard of
human thought, speech, and action, in which heaven stoops
down to the succour of human weakness, and all the
relations of earth are raised and transfigured, and lose
themselves in the light of heaven. The ideal is so bright

and beautiful that our eyes are soon dazzled, when we attempt to unfold its features by reasoning alone.   It can only be seen and known, loved and admired, as it ought to be, when we rise above the diffracted and broken earnests of mere human virtue, and gaze on the true standard of humanity, where all moral perfection is summed up and condensed, without limit or measure, in the person of the Incarnate Son of God.

LECTURE VI.

MORALS IN RELATION TO PHYSICAL SCIENCE.

IN the world of scientific thought, no less than in the sphere of politics, questions of boundary and of jurisdiction are of high importance. Of the former truth our own country has had recent and painful experience. The carelessness or ignorance of negotiators may breed national disputes, even on matters comparatively insignificant, which become a legacy of bitterness and strife to successive generations. And if our country has had recent experience of the evils arising from boundaries ill and ambiguously defined, its earlier history supplies examples, both in its wars with France and Scotland, of the mischief arising from unsettled rights, or claims of jurisdiction and feudal superiority, even on a larger scale. It is a matter, then, of no slight importance, to decide on the true relation between Physical and Moral Science, to know where the boundary lies, and whether there is a just claim, on either side, to superiority and jurisdiction.

In the middle ages, and during the reign of the school-men, there were serious and mischievous encroachments, by theological moralists, on the domain of Physics. Ingenious à priori theories of creation and its laws, such as in their imperfect fancy they ought to be, replaced the

use of diligent and patient inquiry into the facts themselves. The mischief revealed itself in two forms—a
hasty interpretation of Scripture, and a blind reliance
on the authority of Aristotle. And of these the latter
was not the less frequent, while it is less easy to palliate
or explain. When Scheiner announced to his Provincial
his own discovery of spots in the sun, he received this
answer: "I have read Aristotle many times from beginning to end, and can assure you that I have nowhere
found in him anything similar to what you mention.
Go, therefore, my son, tranquillize yourself. Be assured
that what you take for spots in the sun are the faults of
your glasses or your eyes."

These faults of theologians and moralists in former
days seem to have caused a strong reaction in our own.
The turn of Physics has come, to make bold and extensive encroachments on Moral Science. We may
notice two different degrees or stages in the assumptions of superiority which some of its disciples have
latterly made.

The first and most complete may be seen in the
attempt to destroy Morals, properly so called, altogether.
Men may busy themselves so eagerly among laws and
changes of a physical and material kind, that their conscience falls asleep, and they grow insensible to the human
elements of their own being. In this case they end by
denying free-will and responsibility. All changes are
resolved into some mysterious and fatal necessity. Conscience itself becomes an acquired and secondary instinct
of the animal life, or a strange resultant from the combination of material forces, condensed by the nervous
system in some unknown way. Such a theory, it is
plain, puts an end to Moral Science altogether. The

name may possibly be retained for a time, but the substance is gone. What inherits the name of Ethics is merely a branch of physiology, or some transcendental formula of dynamics, which only awaits its solution by some "competent intelligence," some profound and subtle analyst in a future age.

The other form of usurpation or rivalry is more limited and moderate in its hostility. It is willing to allow that Morals have a sphere of their own, and that man is, in some real sense of the word, a spiritual being. But it claims that moral elements shall be excluded wholly from the domain of Physics. It protests against the doctrine of final causes, as a gratuitous disturbance in our search for the genuine laws of nature. It refuses to see, in the frame of nature, in the structure of plants and animals, any real marks of design, and would thus exclude the notion of a Moral Governor and Designer, if not from the whole field of human thought, at least from the range of the material universe.

It becomes, then, highly necessary for the student of Morals, in the presence of such claims and theories as these, to understand clearly, and hold firmly, the true relation between these great kingdoms of human thought. Their entire separation is unnatural and even impossible. It contradicts and reverses that growing tendency to unity, which marks all the recent discoveries of physical philosophers themselves.

The relation, then, of Ethics to Physics may be conveniently viewed under these three heads; (1) Resemblance or Analogy; (2) Difference or Contrast, and (3) Supremacy and Inalienable Jurisdiction.

There is, first of all, between Ethical and Physical Science, a strong resemblance or analogy.

What are the main elements, which enter into all the various and complex researches of Physical Science? There are four main facts or principles, on which, when we examine it closely, the whole superstructure will be seen to depend.

And first, there is a Fundamental Fact of Experience, or the existence of outward objects, which we can see, feel, handle and observe. Thus we gain the conception of Space and a Material World. The materialism, which denies mind altogether, has sometimes, by reaction, given birth to a mystic idealism, which resolves matter into states of thought, and denies the existence of an outward world. Such a theory, if the instincts of common sense did not rebel against it, and set it aside virtually even with its own disciples, would be fatal to the existence of all Physical Science.

A second main element in all Physics is the recognition of fixed and necessary laws or relations among these outward objects, such as the truths of Arithmetic and Geometry. Their distinctive nature is that we not only receive them as true, but we cannot conceive them to be reversed. Their opposite is recognized as a self-contradiction.

A third element, distinct from the last, is the presence of laws which are actual, but not conceived to be necessary, and which are found to link past, present, and future changes together. Their discovery, so as to infer from the present state of the visible world an actual past and an expected future, is the main object of all physical research. These laws do not result from *à priori* reasoning. Their existence has to be determined by careful deduction from observed facts. It is not an inference of pure reason, but depends on actual experience and observation alone.

Lastly, in all physical science there are actual conditions, whether constants or variables, which constitute the materials to which laws have reference, and without which those laws could not even exist. These are almost innumerable, more numerous than the atoms of which the universe is composed. On their mutual relations and incessant changes all the phenomena of Physics depend.

Now Moral Science has the closest resemblance to Physics in these its four main constituent elements. Its fundamental fact is the Conscience, or in other words the existence of Moral Agents, gifted with the power of choice, capable of knowing good and evil, in whom feelings of moral praise or blame spontaneously arise. Its first postulate, answering to that of Physics, is the reality of a moral universe. Next, there are necessary laws and relations, discernible by the conscience, and the opposite of which, when examined, give rise to a feeling of self-contradiction and inconceivability. Such are the truths and first principles of Pure Ethics, the hatefulness of treachery and malice, the beauty and excellence of genuine love.

Still further, in Morals as in Physics, there are laws which are found to be actual, but are not felt to be necessary, so that a different constitution of things may readily be conceived. These are conclusions from actual experience with regard to the faculties of man and his moral capacities, and the special relationships and resulting obligations of human life. Last of all, a completed moral science involves a knowledge of the actual state of the moral universe, at least of that part which is accessible to us, the race of mankind. It includes a wide range of experience, and a full acquaintance with the varieties of human character, and the countless forms of probation, and moral advancement or decay.

In these main features Morals and Physics have the closest resemblance. Both alike include the phenomenal and the real, the actual and the necessary, changing circumstances and invariable laws, facts of experience and deductions of reason. It is on right apprehension of these, in their essential distinctness, and their inseparable union, that the growth and reality of either science depends.

But the relation of Ethics to Physical Science includes also some important features of difference and contrast.

The first contrast, which must strike every candid and thoughtful mind, is in their dignity and importance. Physics, in its narrower sense, deals with lifeless matter. Botany and Zoology rise higher, and deal with living things, plants and animals, of which the highest powers are animal instinct alone. Moral science deals with persons, not with things. And the persons, who form its object, are not merely sentient, but reasonable beings. They are capable of knowing themselves, and each other, and of rising to the knowledge and love of the Father of their spirits, the Creator of the whole universe. Man is higher than mere animals or lifeless matter; and the science which deals with human thoughts and duties, hopes and fears, must be nobler than even the highest departments of philosophy.

There is a further contrast of necessity and freedom. Matter is subject to a law of physical compulsion. It has no choice but to obey. Obedience here is perfect, and deviation impossible. But Moral Beings have a power of choice. The law under which they are placed is one of duty and right, not of fatal necessity. It is one which ought to be kept, but may be broken. The Actual and the Ideal here diverge and part from each other. And as the powers entrusted to such agents are of a higher kind, so in their case there is the possibility of a deeper fall. Experience proves how wide may be the melancholy interval between the law of duty and the actual conduct of mankind.

There is a difference also of colour and tone. For Physics, in a figurative sense of the word, may not unfitly be styled a colourless science. It dwells in a region of dry light. Its truths have only a remote and indirect relation to the feelings of the heart. But Morals are a science to which that name is only sparingly applied, because its truths are more than objects of intellectual perception alone. They are vocal with strong emotion, and awaken deep echoes in the hearts of men. They stir the depths of the spirit with feelings of sympathy and antipathy, of remorse and self-approval, of praise and blame, and open out hidden fountains of pity and grati- tude, of enthusiastic admiration and earnest love.

In the practical aim of the two kinds of knowledge there is also an important difference. Physics increase the power of man over nature, and thus help to secure his comfort in all economy of his outward life. But the deepest wants of the human heart lie beyond its range. Its discoveries, however important in their own sphere, leave these unsatisfied. It cannot tell men why life has been given them, and to what uses it should be applied. It solves none of those doubts and questionings which arise in their conscience, in the pauses of business, or in the prospect of death and the grave. It throws no light on the dark problem of moral evil, on the secret of human guilt, depravity, and sorrow, or on the nature and the symptoms of a disease so melancholy, and the possibility of its cure.

There is another important contrast between Physics and Morals in the conditions on which their progress depends. In Physics these are intellectual only. All that is needed is to bring to the inquiry a clear understanding, and the power of lucid and continuous thought. But moral insight requires moral, no less than intellectual conditions, in those who desire to attain it. There must be singleness of purpose, a real desire to learn the truth, and a willingness to obey that truth, so far as knowledge of it has been attained. The sentence among the sayings of Ali is both simple and profoundly true: "Knowledge calleth out to Practice. If it answer, well. If not, knowledge goeth away." The same principle has the sanction of a far higher authority. "If thine 'eye be single, thy whole body shall be full of light." "Blessed are the pure in heart, for they shall see God." To attain fuller and clearer insight into moral truth, one first requisite is practical obedience to the measure of truth already attained.

But the relation of Morals to Physical Science is not merely one of fundamental harmony and partial contrast. It includes further a lawful claim to supremacy and jurisdiction.

These two main kingdoms of thought, though widely distinct, and marked by some strong features of separation and contrast, are by no means wholly independent. On close inquiry, they will be found to have bonds of close and inseparable union. Whenever ethical truth has to be applied to the actual circumstances of our human, mortal life, Physical Science will be found to have an important bearing on all the details of moral duty. But

Moral Science claims jurisdiction and supremacy over all departments of Physical Study, on the clear and simple ground that these last form one main field of human action. They must therefore abide under the dominion of the great laws of morals, alike in the first opening of physical research, in its later progress, and its final application. Moral ideas are not excluded from the field of Physics, as some in these days have very erroneously conceived. On the contrary, they form one essential and inseparable constituent in all its problems, when once we look below the surface, and examine the deep foundations on which they rest.

To gain such a knowledge of natural laws, that from observation of present phenomena we may be able to trace out past, and predict future changes, is the grand problem of physical research in reference to the outward and material universe. But the lessons implied in this hard problem seem not seldom to be overlooked and forgotten, even by scientific men. Let us suppose the complex and transcendental function to be ascertained, from which future analysts of competent intelligence, whether by integration or infinite series, are to deduce from the present state of our earth the structure of a primitive nebula, countless ages ago, and then to predict with certainty, not only the eclipses and meteoric showers, but the wind and the weather, and perhaps even the flights of locusts and birds of passage, in distant ages to come. Let us lay aside for the present the natural inquiry, whether animal instincts, and still more the human will, may not disturb the meshes of that physical constraint and necessity, in which these theorists thrive, like the Philistines, to bind down the mighty forces of the spirit of man, and make it work and grind in chains in a

9—2

dark prisonhouse of destiny. Still, when this mighty formula is framed, on the solution of which the vast problem is
to depend, it must include the three coordinates of every
atom of matter, or of any physical medium more subtle
than common matter, in the whole created universe.
These are the conditions of the problem, the indeterminates that need to be determined, and on which the solution must depend. The time enters only as one indeterminate in addition to all the rest. Now Physical Science
proposes simply this problem, from the known present to
infer the changes of past time, and predict those of the
distant future. Assuming all the other data to be
ascertained, it would express the state of all the parts
of the outward universe as functions of the time alone.
Thus its utmost triumph is to get rid of one variable out
of a number three times greater than the number of all
the atoms of the material universe—a number amounting
to trillions of trillions, and practically infinite. All these
countless conditions of its own vast problem physical
laws cannot in the least explain. For the laws might be
unaltered, and these elements, on which their application
depends, might be infinitely varied. Let us assume the
existence of a thousand bodies only, and that their
motions, through successive ages, are determined by their
mutual gravitation alone. Still we might multiply a
million into itself a million times, and not exhaust the
conceivable varieties of the first position, by which, in
virtue of the law, every later position would be determined. How, then, can the actual values of these positions be explained? By transferring our thoughts, either
to the remote past or distant future, we do not lessen
their number: it remains unchanged. They can be accounted for in one way alone. From the laws we must

rise to the Lawgiver. We must accept the ideas of creation, and of an Intelligent Cause; a Divine Person, who is capable not only of establishing laws of nature, but of choosing out those elements and conditions for their activity, which satisfy objects of a higher kind, and subserve the purposes of a mighty scheme of universal providence.

It has been affirmed lately, by a skilful and popular experimentalist, that "the scientific mind can find no repose in the mere registration of sequence in nature. The further question intrudes with resistless might—whence comes the sequence? What is it that binds the consequent with the antecedent in nature? The truly scientific intellect can never attain rest until it reaches the forces by which the observed succession is produced. It was thus with Torricelli. It was thus with Newton. It is thus preeminently with the real scientific man of the present day. He knows further that the succession, besides being permanent, is *necessary*. Not until this relation between forces and phenomena has been established, is the law of reason rendered concentric to the law of nature; and not until this is effected does the mind of the scientific philosopher rest in peace."

These remarks are true, so far as they affirm the transition from mere phenomena to causes, forces, or powers, to be the genuine instinct and tendency of a philosophic mind. This is in reality the exact antithesis of Modern Positivism, which places force and power among those hurtful metaphysical abstractions, which mark the immature youth or childhood of science, and affects to limit all sound research to the registration of phenomena alone. But when they affirm that necessity enters into the true scientific conception of every law of nature, they fall into

an error no less glaring and conspicuous than the positive
doctrine which they condemn.   It is hard to explain the
process of thought, by which a view is ascribed to the first
of physical discoverers, and enforced by the authority of
his name, which he has deliberately rejected, and has
even devoted the last pages of his immortal work to its
brief and decisive refutation.   This doctrine of physical
necessity he places in the same rank with the theory of
vortices, and treats it as still more opposed to sound,
philosophical reason.   He writes in his closing Scholium
as follows:—

"Elegantissima haecce Solis, planetarum et cometarum
compages nonnisi consilio et dominio Entis intelligentis et
potentis oriri potuit.   Hic omnia regat, non ut animi
mundi, sed ut universorum dominus.   Hunc cognoscimus
per sapientissimas et optimas rerum structuras, et causas
finales, et admiramur ob perfectiones ; veneramur autem
et colimus ob dominium.   A cæcâ necessitate metaphysicâ
quae utique eadem est semper et ubique, nulla oritur
rerum variatio.   Tota rerum conditarum pro locis et
temporibus diversitas, ab ideis et voluntate Entis necessario
existentis solummodo oriri potuit."

But the falsehood of the view does not rest solely on
the high authority of Newton, to whom an appeal in its
favour has been so strangely and rashly made.   It results
immediately from careful reflection on the nature of known
physical laws themselves.   The only necessity which a
really scientific mind can recognize in them is a hypothetical necessity, or a certain connection between the law,
assumed as real, and acting alone, and motions or positions
that will follow.   Assume such forces to operate, and
that they operate undisturbed and unmingled, and motions
or changes of such and such a kind will assuredly result.

But there is here no answer at all to the question why
these laws, and not others, actually exist, since others are
equally calculable and conceivable. There is no proof, and
hardly a presumption, that these laws, so far as they are
known, may not be hourly modified by other physical
laws, which are still unknown; or intersected and varied,
constantly or periodically, by the action of other laws,
dependent on spiritual agency, of a different and higher
kind. Still further, the existence of the law, when
admitted, furnishes no key to the special elements, almost
infinite in number and complexity, on which its whole
operation depends. These countless indeterminates, amidst
possibilities still more countless, can be accounted for
only by the choice of an Intelligent Creator, who has
selected, out of countless possibilities physically indifferent, those which fulfil the secret aims of His moral
government of an intelligent universe. By this key they
may be perfectly explained, and by this alone.

Moral ideas, then, are not excluded from the field of
Natural Philosophy, but, as Newton felt and taught, are
its highest and crowning portion. The utmost attainment
of mere physical research is to link the details of the
present, by some law of connection, with the past and the
future. But if we would answer the question, why the
innumerable conditions which experience reveals are such
as it reveals, and no other, when our reason clearly
perceives that the possible alternatives, which have no real
existence, are still more innumerable, we must rise beyond
mere Physics into a higher field; and recognize with
reverence the supreme will and choice of the Divine
Creator, " to discourse of whom from the appearances
of things does certainly belong to Natural Philosophy."
The world must have been framed for a higher end than

to give room for the evershifting and aimless motion of lifeless atoms. It was formed, by Divine Wisdom, to be inherited by creatures capable of worship, obedience, and love.

Physical studies, again, in their very outset, need to be guided and animated by a moral purpose.

Why am I to seek a fuller knowledge of the world around me? Is it to be only the satisfaction of a blind impulse, like that of the butterfly that passes idly from flower to flower, or the tiger that seizes fiercely on its prey? Men of science claim instinctively for their pursuits a higher character, and place them above the level of mere selfish trading or luxurious self-indulgence. Truth is the prize at which they aim. They long to pierce below the surface, and to gain a fuller and clearer insight than others around them, or even their own predecessors have attained, into the reality of things. Their ambition is to gain some κτῆμα ἐς ἀεί, a lasting inheritance of truth and knowledge for ages to come.

Such a quest of truth in the field of Physics is right and good in itself. But there are three conditions or moral laws it must obey. First, it should be the love of truth as truth, for its own sake, and not as a mere engine of power to astonish the vulgar, or to secure some mercenary object. They must use all their attainments in the spirit of love, and adopt the well-known prayer of Bacon, that the Father of lights may enrich their fellows with some new benefits through their labours. And it must be a love of truth in its due order and proportion. It is not only an intellectual anomaly, but a moral evil to be condemned and deplored, when truths of secondary importance are sought with eager diligence; while truths far higher, the grand lessons of moral duty, and the mysteries of

religious faith and hope, are passed by with careless indifference, or even rejected with open scorn, and thrust
contemptuously away.

Not only the first steps in physical research, but its
whole later progress, is subject to the laws of moral
obligation. All the treasures it pours at the feet of its
disciples, like mere material wealth, need to submit to a
double rule on which their right use depends. That rule
is one of distribution and consecration. Physical knowledge,
it is plain, ought never to be viewed as a private monopoly,
for the benefit and honour of a few philosophers alone.
And this obligation, too often overlooked or denied in
former ages, is usually recognized in our own day.
But there is another rule of a still higher kind, which
is often disobeyed. The more we learn of the secrets
of nature, the fuller and larger is the tribute of honour
and reverence we are bound to pay to the God of nature,
the Author of that wonderful and mysterious universe,
whose hidden secrets He permits us to explore.

It was said once, in Newton's days, that "an undevout
astronomer is mad." An opposite saying of M. Comte, in
late years, has gained a mournful celebrity, that the
heavens now reveal no glory but that of Copernicus,
Kepler, Newton, Herschel, Laplace, and the other great
discoverers in astronomy. That science, if this were true,
would have become a fallen star. It would have dropped,
like a meteor, from its place in the moral firmament. But
such a hateful degradation of a noble pursuit, however
widely it may spread for a little moment, is unnatural
and monstrous. *Hæ nubeculæ transibunt.* Soon or late
the moral law, neglected for a moment by some physical
students, will resume its just authority, and the words of
the Psalmist become the keynote of all physical research

once more: "In His hand are the deep places of the earth, and the strength of the hills is his also. The sea is His, and He made it, and His hand prepared the dry land. O come! let us worship and fall down, and kneel before the Lord our Maker!" "How excellent, O Lord, is Thy name in all the earth, who hast set Thy glory above the heavens!"

Once more, all physical researches, when successfully completed, need to receive a moral application. This truth is beautifully expressed by Lord Bacon in these well known words:—

"Wherefore, in the opening of our work, we pour out most humble and ardent prayers to God the Father, God the Word, and God the Spirit, that mindful of the cares of the human race and of the pilgrimage of that life, in which we spend days few and evil, they would deign, through our hands, to enrich with new benefits the human family. And this moreover we humbly pray, that human things may not injure the divine, and that from the opening of the gates of sense, and a greater kindling of natural light, there may arise in our minds no unbelief and darkness towards divine mysteries. But that rather, from a pure understanding, purged from phantasies and vanity, and not the less remaining wholly subject to the divine oracles, the things of faith may be given to faith. Finally, that the poison of knowledge, infused by the serpent, whereby the human mind is puffed up and inflated, being put away, we may be wise with sobriety, and cultivate the truth in love."

There are many different ways in which Physics, rightly pursued, may fulfil a high moral purpose, and own the superiority and minister to the progress of ethical truth. They serve to enlarge and ennoble our concep-

tious of the vastness of creation. They reveal, in every
part, the wide dominion and supremacy of law, and thus
convey a lesson of deep significance, when we transfer it
to the higher field of human thought and action. They
exhibit, in a striking picture, in all the celestial motions,
and the unvarying constancy with which the physical laws
of nature are obeyed, the beauty and excellency, among
moral agents, of a perfect and faultless obedience to the
supreme standard of right and truth. They disclose also,
the further and deeper we search out the secrets of nature,
an immense want and void in all mere physical theories
of the universe, which can only be filled up and supplied,
when we pass beyond them, and see in them the outer
porch to a glorious temple of moral and spiritual truth.
And lastly, when we gaze upon the fields of nature with
patient thought, and trace out the structure and manifold
harmonies of the material creation, we may see them
stored with wonderful and various analogies, framed by
the Supreme Architect and Governor, in order to raise our
dull thoughts, through physical emblems and earthly
shadows, to the clearer discernment of the nobler truths
and deeper mysteries of the spiritual world.

The modern theory, which would isolate Physical
Science wholly from moral truth, and form the visible
universe into a gigantic preserve, sacred from all intrusion
of direct spiritual agency, where blind destiny alone is to
rule, undisturbed by any subordination to a moral purpose,
and condemned to roll for ever the stone of Sisyphus,
without ministering to the moral government of responsible creatures—like the old hypothesis of Cartesian
vortices—"is pressed with many difficulties." It contradicts
and reverses that tendency to unity which is one main
feature in the whole course of recent scientific discovery.

It leaves unexplained, and wholly inexplicable, nearly
all the constituent elements of every physical problem,
those constants or conditions, without which no physical
law can exist, and on which its vitality wholly depends.
It leaves the choice of the laws themselves, out of many
others equally conceivable, an enigma of which no solution can be found. It degrades the physical universe
into a wide, vast chaos of unmeaning changes, a machine
with no work to do, and by which no real work is
ever done, a maze without plan, purpose, or object;
where mighty forces are changing their shape every
hour, and still, in every shape alike, are subject to
the curse of utter vanity; where countless suns, and
planets, and systems, and forms of transient, perish-
able life, find their true description from first to last in
the mist out of which they are supposed to have been
born,—

> A thousand wreaths of dangling water smoke,
> That, like a broken purpose, waste in air.

How far nobler and higher is that view of the relation
between Physics and Morals, which genuine science and
true Christian faith equally serve to reveal! "All creatures strive to ascend, and ascend in their striving." All
nature points and looks upward. All outward laws subserve a moral purpose, and are wisely selected to constitute
a worthy theatre for a grand scheme of moral government.
Even when man turns away his eyes from heaven, and
refuses to look upward, he may find, in the wide and vast
ocean of physical change that lies beneath him, the reflections and images of heavenly things. The senses of the
body represent to us the higher moral perceptions and
capacities of the human soul. The starry spaces, and the
unfathomed depths of earth and ocean, represent equally

the vast range of unexplored mysteries in the spiritual
universe. But when we seek to rest in these shadows, and
mistake them for the substance to which they are Divine
way-marks, they disappoint us, and elude our grasp. We
seek a portion in them, but cannot find it. The whole range
of Physical Science must ever remain, to the immortal
spirit of man, a desolate wilderness, a land of darkness,
shadows, and death; until we own in it the work of an
all-wise Creator, the destined theatre for a wide dominion
of perfect goodness. We may then look forward in hope
to a time when order shall come out of seeming confusion,
and light out of darkness; and when all the laws of nature,
and all the perplexing changes of providence, shall be
seen to be the appointed handmaids to one grand, eternal
counsel of Creative Wisdom and Redeeming Love.

LECTURE VII.

MORALS AND POLITICAL ECONOMY.

THE relation of Ethics to Political Economy, even more than to simple Physics, is a subject of deep and growing practical importance in the present day. The want of clear and just ideas on their close connection, with the inseparable dependence of true economical science on the grand lessons and laws of Social Morality, has led already to very serious evils. How these may be resisted and overcome is one of those weighty problems, which claims for its solution the earnest effort of every Christian mind and heart. No remedy can be found for them, unless the basis be laid in sounder and deeper views of the whole question than have usually prevailed.

Political Economy is an ambiguous phrase. The sense in which it has been commonly used diverges sensibly from its proper and natural meaning. For Economy, as Sismondi has well observed, means by its derivation "the law of the house." The compound phrase, then, should naturally denote principles or laws to regulate that larger household, which forms a human state or political society. But the science usually intended by the phrase has a more limited range, and might perhaps be more fitly styled, "Natural Polity." It is that branch of Political Science, which deals with outward nature, and the material objects that surround us, and teaches how these may be best adapted and applied to the social wants of mankind.

The looseness and inexactness of the name has been attended with no slight degree of uncertainty and variety in the definitions of this modern science. Sir J. Stuart says that "its principal object is to secure a certain measure of subsistence for all the inhabitants of a country, to obviate every circumstance which may render it precarious, and to provide every thing necessary for supplying the wants of society." M. Storch says that "it is the science of the natural laws which determine the prosperity of nations, that is to say, their wealth and their civilisation." M. Sismondi defines its object to be "the physical welfare of man, so far as it can be the work of government." M. Say remarks that "it combines the results of our observations on the nature and functions of the different parts of the social body." Mr M'Culloch defines it "as the science of values, or of the laws which regulate the production, accumulation, distribution, and consumption of those articles or products that are necessarily useful or agreeable to man, and possess exchangeable value." But he adds that "its object is to point out those means by which the industry of man may be rendered most productive of wealth, to ascertain the circumstances most favourable to its accumulation, the proportions in which it is divided, and the mode in which it may be most advantageously consumed."

Mr Senior objects to some of these definitions, that they are too ambitious, and include a range which "far exceeds the bounds of a single treatise, or the powers of any single mind. The questions to what extent and under what circumstances the possession of wealth is beneficial or injurious, what distribution of wealth is most desirable, &c., are of great interest and difficulty; but no more form part of Political Economy, in the sense in which we use the term, than navigation forms part of the science of Astronomy." "The subject of legislation," he observes, "is not wealth, but human welfare. On the other hand, Political Economy treats not of happiness, but wealth. Its premises consist of few general propositions, scarcely requiring proof or formal statement, which almost every man, as soon as he hears them, admits as familiar to his thoughts; and his inferences are nearly as general, and if he has reasoned correctly, as certain as his premises. Those which relate to the nature and production of wealth are universally true. But these conclusions, whatever their generality and truth, do not warrant the economist in adding a single syllable of advice. That privilege belongs to the writer or statesman, who has considered all the causes which may promote or impede the general welfare. The business of the Economist is neither to recommend nor to dissuade; but to state general principles, which it is fatal to neglect, but neither advisable nor perhaps practicable to use as the sole guides in the actual conduct of affairs."

Mr Mill agrees mainly with Mr Senior in his definition of the science. It professes, he says, "to teach or investigate the nature of wealth, and the laws of its production and distribution, including directly or remotely the operation of all the causes by which the condition of mankind, or of any human society, in respect to this universal object of human desire, is made prosperous or adverse. It undertakes to set forth as much as is known of the laws and principles according to which those causes

operate." "All know that it is one thing to be rich,
another thing to be enlightened, brave or humane; that
the questions how a nation is made wealthy, and how it is
made free, virtuous, or eminent in literature, the fine arts,
arms or polity, are totally distinct inquiries."

On the strength of these definitions Mr Senior vindicates writers on Political Economy from a charge sometimes brought against them. "It has often," he says,
"been made a matter of grave complaint that they confine
their attention to wealth, and disregard all consideration
of happiness or virtue. It is to be wished that this complaint were better founded. No one blames a writer upon
tactics for confining his attention to military affairs. An
author who, having stated that a given conduct is productive of wealth, should, on that account alone, recommend
it, or assume that it ought to be pursued, would be guilty
of the absurdity of implying that happiness and the
possession of wealth are identical. But his error would
consist, not in confining his attention to wealth, but in
confounding wealth with happiness. Supposing that error
avoided, the more strictly a writer confines his attention
to his own science, the more likely he is to extend its
bounds."

Political Economists in general have by no means
observed the rule Mr Senior lays down for their guidance,
that they are not warranted in offering "a single syllable
of advice." There are few articles of general commerce of
which the production has been more copious and abundant.
Whatever the demand for it, either on the part of statesmen or of the general public, it has usually been far
exceeded by the supply. The consequence, in agreement
with the maxims of their favourite science, has been a
frequent depreciation in the market value of the counsels

they have offered. Separate laws, and whole systems of
finance and legislation, social customs, the conduct of
landlords, manufacturers, merchants, and workmen, have
all in turn been the constant objects of their praise and
censure, from their agreement or disagreement with the
supposed teaching of Political Economy, and on that
ground alone. The claim that other and deeper principles
ought to be kept in view, and that outward wealth is not
the highest aim of personal conduct or national legislation,
has been often ascribed to ignorance or perverseness, and
a culpable neglect of the discoveries of this modern
science. It is clearly essential to settle this internal
dispute among its teachers and disciples, and decide on
its true nature and limits, before we can form a correct
view of its relations to Ethics, and trace the links of connection which bind the two subjects in close and inseparable union.

There are plainly, then, two opposite tendencies at
work among the writers on Political Economy. One class,
of whom Sismondi is one representative, endeavour to
retain the true and proper sense of the phrase, as import-
ing the right guidance and direction of the State, as a
larger household. These enlarge and widen the range of
the science, and make human welfare its true object.
But in the same degree they render it vague as well as
comprehensive, and would make it almost synonymous with
the pursuit of happiness, or the highest good, personal and
social, so as to include wisdom and prudence applied to
the conduct of human life, in all their most varied forms.
Others, like Mr Senior, confine it to the laws of material
wealth alone. Viewed as a science, its proper name would
then seem to be Plutonomy, or the study of the laws by
which wealth is produced and distributed; and as an art,

Chrematistics, or skill in acquiring all those things which are bought and sold in the market, and which money alone can procure. The science, on this more limited view of its nature, gains in precision. But in the same proportion it becomes technical, partial, and limited in its range, and is liable to be deceptive in the highest degree, when we turn from its theories to their practical application. Two alternatives are open to its students. They may understand the science in its narrower sense, and then profess their incompetency to give practical counsel in questions of private conduct and national legislation from its teaching alone. Or they may claim the character of public instructors in all these questions, and widen the range of the science, so as to include mental as well as material riches, and all the moral elements on which human happiness depends. But the most fatal course, and one of the most frequent, is a vague, uneasy oscillation between these extremes. The science is then rigidly confined to the study of material wealth, when its theories are being formed in the closet of its teachers and disciples, and is promoted into the oracle of truth, happiness, and genuine wisdom, when it is sought to apply them for the guidance of men and nations in the actual business of life.

The true and just view of the subject lies between these opposite extremes. Political Economy, in the modern sense of the term, might be more properly called Chrematics, or Natural Polity. It consists in the research and discovery of those laws which regulate the relations between men, and all those outward objects which minister to their life, health, comfort, intellectual progress, and moral welfare. It is therefore part of a greater whole. It deals with men in their relation to the outward world. But the wealth on which it reasons, though an end with

10—2

reference to the processes of production and distribution, is really only a means to a further end, the true good and welfare of men. When divorced from this higher aim, like the manna when hoarded unseasonably, it breeds worms and turns to corruption. The food becomes first husks, and then poison. The gold and silver rust and are cankered, and when the mischief proceeds further, eat the flesh as a consuming fire.

To avoid this great danger, two main aspects of the science must be clearly distinguished, and even contrasted, which too many Political Economists are perpetually confounding together. The first may be called Natural or Physical, the second Moral Chrematics. The first treats of the actual tendencies of production, commerce, and trade, when men apply themselves to the satisfaction of their own wants and desires in the use of outward objects, under the guidance of instinctive self-love or prudential selfishness alone. The second deals with a harder and higher subject, what is the true standard of right and duty in this wide field of human action, and how far the impulses of selfishness, and the calculations of mere prudence and worldly interest, ought to be restrained, guided, ennobled, and sometimes even reversed, by the higher claims of social benevolence and religious faith.

The intimate relation between Moral Truth and genuine Political Economy may be seen in three different aspects of economical science.

The first of these refers to the province of government, and the nature of those elements on which the wisdom of all varieties of human legislation must depend.

Political Economy, we are told, has for its object "not happiness, but wealth." Wise laws, however, must plainly have for their object, not wealth but happiness, or the true welfare of the nation, and the individuals of whom it is composed. The two ideas, it is admitted, are in their own nature distinct and separable. Whenever in practice they diverge and separate, the teaching of the secondary science, which deals only with outward wealth, will have to be modified, and sometimes even reversed, by the just authority of higher truth.

It follows, from the reality of the distinction, that laws may be of four kinds. They may hinder wealth, and diminish happiness, or may be promotive of wealth and of happiness also. Other, again, may encourage the growth of outward riches, and be morally injurious. Others, lastly, may restrain special modes or forms of industrial activity, by which material riches might be increased, but may still, for other and higher reasons, be conducive to the public welfare.

Free trade, when the freedom consists in abolishing laws of the first kind, is an evident gain. It releases industry from shackles by which it had been unwisely confined, which retard its progress, and limit its success, while the direct benefit is outweighed by no attendant evils. But whenever the freedom is opposed to laws of the fourth and last kind, the moral conditions are reversed. Used in this wider sense, free trade must be no gain, but a loss. It becomes a delusive watchword, under which moral opposites are confounded together. It would serve really to erect lawless anarchy of commercial selfishness into the canonized standard of private trade and public legislation among Christian men.

It may tend, perhaps, to clearness of expression to define the object of Political Economy to be the production and increase of material wealth alone. But a science so defined is limited and imperfect by its definition. In the words of Mr Senior, it is not warranted to offer a syllable of advice on questions of private or national duty, till it has borrowed information from other sources than its own. It must be a fatal error to promote conclusions, drawn from such limited premises, and directed to a purely secondary aim, into grand, fundamental laws of social legislation. It is an important boon that commerce should be set free from all selfish, unwise, and needless restrictions. But when, under this plea, a broad indefinite claim is set up, that it should be exempted from restraints and regulations of every kind, the doctrine becomes at once immoral and absurd. Once let the cold, hard, iron selfishness of trade, which disowns the obligations of Divine law, and even the softening instincts of human affection and tenderness, be made supreme in the intercourse of life, and an idol of the worst and meanest kind will have been set up, in the abused name of Economical Science, for universal worship.

But Political Economy is further linked with moral elements in the closest way, because it depends on personal prudence and moral conditions for the success and continuance of that industry which is the only source of private and public wealth.

And first, the moral character and state of the working classes is one of the most vital elements, on which the progress or decline of national industry must ever depend. Let us compare two communities, in one of which the workmen and labourers are sober, industrious, honest, and another in which they are drunken, idle, fraudulent and profligate, and the contrast in their social progress and comfort must be extreme. The words of ancient wisdom are true to the present hour, after all the discoveries of

modern science: "The soul of the sluggard desireth, and
hath nothing." "The drunkard and the glutton shall come
to poverty, and drowsiness shall clothe a man with rags."
The moral and spiritual state of the industrial classes has
a most direct and powerful influence, for good or evil, on the
whole system of trade, and on the progress or decline of
national wealth and greatness. Laziness, intemperance,
feverish discontent, and lawless violence, are equally fatal to
the healthy development of national industry. These evils,
when they abound, take off the chariot-wheels of trade, so
that it drags heavily and laboriously along, and are the
symptoms of some great catastrophe near at hand. And
hence it has been justly observed by Dr Chalmers, in
the preface to his treatise of Political Economy: "Vary
its devices and expedients as it may, it can never secure
its object apart from a virtuous and educated peasantry.
Even for the economic well-being of a people, their moral
and religious education is the first and greatest object of
national policy. While this is neglected, government will
only flounder from one delusive shift and expedient to
another, under the double misfortune of being held
responsible for the prosperity of the land, and yet of
finding this to be an element hopelessly beyond its
control."

But the truth, which applies to the moral condition of
the working classes, belongs equally to the character of
the tradesmen and farmers by whom they are employed.
If these are honest, truthful, liberal and kind, the influence in the promotion of national industry will be
speedily felt. Confidence breeds confidence, kindness in
the master or employer produces, as a general rule,
attachment and fidelity in the workman or the servant.
The wheels of commerce then move on freely, and with-

out friction. But if the employers of labour are close-
fisted, heartless, or even deceitful and dishonest, industry
will be depressed and deadened into dull and lazy
inaction, and the way will be prepared, when knowledge without faith has spread more widely among the
people, for some sudden outburst of revolutionary violence.

When we pass upward, from the middle classes to
the most wealthy, the importance of the moral element
to the economic well-being of society is no less apparent.
If rich men are kind, generous, sympathizing and boun-
tiful, the unequal distribution of the gifts of Providence
ceases to be a perpetual source of heart-burning and
sullen discontent. Society then becomes the counterpart
of that land of promise, where the hills and mountains receive abundantly the rains of heaven, but only to dispense
them in refreshing streams to the well-watered valleys
below.   But let them once become, as a class, miserly
capitalists in one generation, alternating with luxurious,
profligate spendthrifts in the next, and the probable
result, before long, will be an amount of sullen and morose
discontent, accumulating from year to year, before which
the foundations of the social system may at last give way,
and wealth and industry be buried in the common ruin.

But besides the indirect dependence of national wealth
on social morality, through the higher or lower standard
of industry and prudence which the community and its
various classes of workers have attained, there is a further
connection of a still more direct and intimate nature.

Moral Science, from its very definition, extends its
claim to the whole range of human action, speech and
thought. It does not rest content with a partial service,
the church or the closet alone. It follows men into the
street, the market, the warehouse, and the field, and

claims to guide and control their actions in all the various relations of commerce, industry and social life.

The words of the Apostle, "None of us liveth to himself," if viewed as the assertion of a universal fact, would be wholly untrue. But interpreted as a moral precept, they proclaim a law of universal obligation. They apply to the pursuits of trade and commerce, as well as to every other field of human activity. Purely selfish bargaining is in no case lawful for Christian men. To buy in the cheapest market, and sell in the dearest, may be a maxim of wide range in commercial transactions. But there are certain moral limitations it is bound to obey. When these are neglected or denied, it becomes immoral and mischievous. It would canonize the hideous principle that, in the affairs of trade, they were at liberty to put to sleep every higher instinct of humanity, and to be guided by the promptings of pure and absolute selfishness alone. The maxim, "caveat emptor", may embody the results of a large experience. But its full and perfect development must require a world of devils. Its traders would be men whom the fear of discovery alone deters from the grossest frauds, and who have the balances of deceit perpetually in their hands.

The reasonings of political economists often rest on a secret assumption, that men, in all relations of worldly business, are actually guided, and may lawfully be guided, by self-interest alone. Now, even as a statement of facts, the simplification is excessive and untrue. But when accepted as the ideal basis of a science, it becomes an outrage on the simplest lessons of true morality. On such a foundation of universal selfishness a perfect industrial state can never possibly be reared. For the purely selfish in aim can never be far-sighted. The nearer

present, the seeming immediate gain, will eclipse from
their view the loss which is sure to attend, soon or late, on
dishonesty, violence, and oppression. But shortsighted
selfishness is fatal and ruinous in trade and commerce,
no less than in the higher fields of politics and religious
faith. Its grapes are grapes of gall, and their clusters are
bitter. For credit, that is, faith between man and man,
is the life and soul of commerce. But when selfishness
reigns, and sits enthroned on the altar of perverted
science, the atmosphere of the whole world of commerce
becomes mephitic and stifling. Frauds will multiply and
increase without limit, and credit will grow sickly, and
soon expire.

But we have not yet exhausted the lines of thought,
which prove the close and vital union between Morals
and Political Economy. It may be traced further and
deeper still. The truths to which we are led by
further search will prove the imperfect and provisional
character of many conclusions, which modern writers
on Political Economy are accustomed to invest with a
character to which they have no just claim, not as the
results of an imperfect hypothesis and a rude approximation, but as absolute and undoubted truths of a perfect
science.

I have reasoned hitherto on the assumption that wealth
can be defined, wholly apart from every moral element,
and that moral truths are needful only for its right use
and-application. But the admission, made for the sake of
argument, has no real foundation in truth. True Wealth,
by the very origin of the name, is not wholly distinct
from "welfare," but involves the same idea, embodied
and transformed. It consists really in the outward means
of welfare, when possessed and employed by those who

have the wisdom to use them aright. The word "goods"
has a like derivation, and points to the same lesson.
Things are not goods by virtue of a process of manufacture
alone, but because they are applied, or may be applied,
to promote the real good of those who own them.
The right application of the products of industry is the
secret condition, too often overlooked, on which their
character as wealth really depends.

The idea of value lies at the foundation of Political
Economy, just as the conception of space is the basis of
geometry. And yet the definition of value has been one
chief perplexity of writers on the science. One eminent
writer confounds it with cost, and has thus involved
his whole treatise in hopeless perplexity and confusion.
Many identify it with market price. Another, in a separate treatise on the subject, denies it any fixed meaning,
and looks upon it as a mere term of relation, in which one
article rises and another falls, but no absolute measure is
possible. Mr. Mill boldly affirms that nothing remains for
any future writer to clear up, and that "the theory of the
subject is complete." It may be affirmed, with more
truth, that its first elements are hardly laid, because the
main principle on which a true understanding of it
depends is overlooked or forgotten.

The source of these perplexities is not hard to discover.
It arises from a persistent effort to separate the *body* of
wealth, its outward and familiar form, price in the market,
or a sum of money, by which anything may be purchased,
from its *soul*, without which it ceases to be wealth,
and becomes a worthless corpse, a glut of unused, or an
excess of abused commodities. That *soul* of wealth, without
which things are things only, and not goods in the proper
sense, is their real application to some end, which is bene-

ficial to the owners.   When this condition is not fulfilled, wealth ceases to be wealth, having nothing to do with human welfare, but becomes either waste or poison.

The whole of economical science may be said to depend on two or three fundamental equations, which are the moving forces in the whole system of trade. Cost, increased by a first profit, is the market value. Market value, increased by a second or third profit, is the worth, or value in use.   But cost may be either real or imaginary.   There is the same contrast of true and imaginary worth.   The mechanism of trade depends on the cost and worth, as defined by the mere fancy, often the erring fancy, of the producer and consumer.   But the benefits of trade depend on a comparison of the real cost and the real worth, and of these alone.   The great and all-important contrast between a cost and a worth which are real, and one which rests on erring and mistaken impressions only, is the principle on the recognition of which it depends whether Political Economy shall be a moral or an immoral science.

Mr Mill, for instance, lays down the principle that "Political Economy has nothing to do with the comparative estimate of uses in the judgment of a philosopher or moralist.   The use of a thing, in Political Economy, means its capacity to satisfy a desire or serve a purpose." Here the fundamental defect comes clearly into view. The object of Political Economy, as thus defined, is to multiply the production of things desired, however vicious, hurtful, and even ruinous, the indulgence of those desires may be.   If men are swine, its object is to provide more husks and refuse for the troughs in which they feed. If they degenerate into devils in malice and hatred, it is to multiply the desired engines of mutual destruction.

But a science thus defined, and violently severed from all consideration of right and wrong, of the true welfare of man, or hurtful delusions that work his greatest harm, can be no science of human action. It may amass materials, from painful and humbling experience, to teach what fools, misers, and profligates are likely to do. But it renounces the attempt at such an estimate of the wise and just objects of human pursuit, and of the right use of the ample materials for happiness the God of nature has spread around us, as can alone form the basis of a genuine science, and fit mankind to exercise wisely their sacred trust of ownership over this lower world.

Etymology is often a guide to truth, when it is overlooked by those who are busied in framing some artificial theory. The term now in question is an instance of this kind. Value has a double relation to weight and health. It denotes, first, what anything avails in the sober estimate of sound reason, when it weighs men, actions, and things in an even scale, and rates the last according to their real worth, or power to promote man's solid and lasting welfare. And it implies, further, a quality in outward objects, akin to health in the human body, which fits them for the discharge of some useful and healthy function in the complex economy of human life. And no Political Economy can advance human happiness, or escape from the risk of nursing mischievous delusions, which does not accept the teaching of a nobler science than its own, and draw a wide contrast between substance, which has weight, and shadow mistaken for substance; between objects which satisfy the desires of health, and those which minister chiefly to the restless cravings of indolence, miserly greed, destructive profligacy, and all the varieties of moral disease.

The vast importance of the truths here advanced, and neglected or disowned by many writers on economical science, has received, and is receiving at this hour, a striking illustration from the course of modern history.

Since the days of Adam Smith, the founder or reviver of Political Economy in its modern form, there have been two successive stages in the history of its progress and effects. The first stage seems nearly completed. The second, its converse, has only just begun.

In the first stage, which owes its development to many distinguished writers, there has been much acute and sagacious, and also not a little fallacious reasoning, on the tendencies of trade, and the laws of the production and distribution of wealth, so far as determined by motives of pure commercial self-interest alone. The science, on this view, is one neither of mere practical observation, and inferences, *à posteriori*, from the observed facts of trade and agriculture, nor yet of moral duties, and what course men, in the commerce of life, *ought* to pursue. It is a hypothetical science of the tendencies of trade, assuming self-interest, which has doubtless a very wide range, to be the only motive in ceaseless operation. Such a study of the tendencies of commercial self-interest, whether sinking into hard, cold, shortsighted selfishness, or rising into that moral prudence and discretion which is one of the main Christian virtues, may be highly useful, if honestly pursued, and kept within its own proper bounds. But in this case, speaking generally, a double mistake was made. To render the inquiry definite, like those of geometry, moral elements were thrust out of sight, and the question whether things had real value, or were only conceived to be valuable through error and ignorance, was ruled to be entirely beyond the range of the new science.

And still it was forgotten that this exclusion thrust it
down to a position almost servile. It became a theory
of the tendencies of commercial selfishness alone, and was
guilty of plain usurpation, when it affected to lay down
imperative rules for private conduct or national legislation.
And next, the inquiry into tendencies themselves was
warped and distorted by this confusion of thought. There
was a constant disposition to idealize that self-interest,
which was accepted for the supreme law of trade, to
purge it from the scum of those grosser forms of selfishness, with which it is always largely combined in actual
experience; and to leave out of sight those two mighty
sources of unknown disturbance, the selfishness of the rich
and covetous, when capital accumulates, and tho rival
selfishness of discontented multitudes, when the contrasts
of society widen into a chasm, bridged over by no instincts
of humanity, and by no common hope of a nobler life to
come.

That selfish school of Political Economy, which dates
from Adam Smith, and is really a Hypothetical Science of
the tendencies and laws of commercial and productive self-
interest, seemed to prosper greatly in its first stage. Trade
was gradually set free from many hurtful restraints, some of
them possibly useful in former days, but grown antiquated
and worthless, and therefore mischievous, and others, even
in their origin, due to some form of blind selfishness or
jealousy alone. The new discoveries of the steam engine,
the steamboat and the railroad, and the opening out of
the vast hidden treasures of force in our coal measures,
concurred in the mighty change. There was an immense
increase of productive power. Labour was partly displaced, but still more stimulated and quickened, by a vast
variety of mechanical inventions and discoveries. It was

an era of growing capital. Our national wealth and resources were greatly increased. But side by side with this gain was the dark shadow of a great and growing evil. Along with the growth of wealth there was a growing inequality in its distribution. Acquired wealth, under an accepted rule and law of pure selfishness, and when capital is worshipped as the chief good of a nation, has increasing power to beat down the price of labour, and secure the main share of its fruits; until a rival power, still more dangerous, the brute force of myriads and millions, banded by common discontent, and ready to look upon all the wealthier classes as cruel and worthless oppressors, arises to struggle for the mastery, and to transfer the sceptre of trade to other hands.

That second stage in the history and development of a selfish commercial philosophy has now set in. It would have visited us long ago, if the defects of the new science had not been counteracted by a large amount of Christian charity and kindness, softening the hard rigour of the economists by lessons of a deeper and holier kind. The factory laws, and other kindred efforts, proved that spurious lessons of a maimed, imperfect science had not wholly paralyzed the national conscience, and destroyed the instincts of humanity. But, in spite of many things which have delayed its advent, the later stage has arrived, and a reaction, long seen to be inevitable by thoughtful minds, has begun. A new name, the proletariat, has been invented for the working classes, and represents the widespread impression among them, that they have been used by the selfishness of wealth as mere machines for the production of riches, and hardly been regarded as fellow-men and fellow-Christians. By the spread of a cheap literature, and the means of rapid locomotion, their opportunities for combining together have been greatly increased. The separation of remote towns and provinces has been replaced by one of another kind, the sharp contrast of classes, differing in social level. Trades' unions, national and international societies of working men, have been formed on a wide scale. Strikes, concerted by their leaders, and carried out with a military discipline, and under the terror of punishment little short of death, have become of yearly and almost hourly occurrence. Communism in theory, or a total denial of the right of property, has spread widely, and fascinates tens of thousands with the hope of an entire social revolution. The selfishness of capital, in the ascendant for two generations, and almost consecrated into the chief of virtues by modern system-builders, is now encountered and confronted by a force still more terrible, the organised discontent and self-will of the most numerous classes, on whose willing labour the whole system of trade and commerce hourly depends. From the operation of these new forces our great metropolis has had a narrow escape from the double danger of midnight darkness and winter starvation. In one word, Political Economy, in the hands of many of its chief writers, has committed the fatal mistake of affecting to be independent of all moral truths, and still to constitute a double guide for personal conduct and for national legislation. "The greatest happiness of the greatest number" has been its professed aim, and "the greatest discontent of the greatest number" would almost seem, from the present signs of the times, to have been the result actually achieved.

What, then, is the remedy for this social crisis, which threatens to replace one great evil by another still more perilous, and perplexes both monarchs and republics, at the present hour, with the fear of disastrous change? The

efforts of many hearts and minds, the unfolding of many
high truths, the culture of many Christian virtues, are all
required for this hard task.   But one main duty is plain.
We must "moralize" Economical Science.   We must
relegate the science which has usually borne that name
to its true, but subordinate place, as a science of tendencies,
not of duties; an hypothetical, not an actual science, because it deals with the working of one class of motives
only, and those neither the highest nor the best, those
of self-interest and money-making alone.   Side by side
with Natural Chrematics, which has usurped the higher
title of Political Economy, we must create and develop a
higher science of Moral Chrematics, or the laws of social
duty, by which man is bound both to God and his fellow-
men in the right use, social adaptation, and religious consecration, of all outward and visible things.   It is not
universal free trade, least of all its freedom from moral restraints, but universal uprightness, integrity, and brotherly
kindness, in trade, labour, commerce, and all social relations,
which is the true and effectual remedy for these threatening
evils.   The whole system of trade, the manifold treasures
which human skill and industry derive from their parent
earth, when once they break loose from the great law of
love, may soon lose themselves in outer darkness.   But when
they learn to submit reverently to this higher law, they
revolve harmoniously in their own orbit, and are bathed
in a light and beauty which shines on them from above.
And the first lessons and definitions of a Political Economy,
thus reclaimed to its true dignity, and placed on firm and
moral foundations, may be found in four sentences of the
Divine law, which form a climax of heavenly wisdom:
"Six days shalt thou labour, and do all thy work." "A
man's life consisteth not in the abundance of the things

he possesseth." "If ye have not been faithful in the unrighteous mammon, who will commit to your trust the true riches?" "Charge them that are rich in this world, that they be not highminded, nor trust in the uncertainty of riches, but in the living God, who giveth richly all things to enjoy: that they be rich in good works, ready to give, glad to distribute, laying up in store a good foundation for time to come, that they may attain eternal life."

LECTURE VIII.

MORALS AND POLITICAL SCIENCE.

THE intimate connection between Ethical and Political Science has been generally recognized from the time of Aristotle down to the present day. But it is not very easy to attain a clear view of the exact nature of the fundamental relation which exists between them. The path of truth and wisdom seems to lie between opposite bye-ways of shortsighted, prudential selfishness, and of mere utopian theories, and it is only too easy to wander from it on either side.

In every field of human thought, which aims at the guidance of practice, truths and facts, science and experience, *à priori* and *à posteriori* elements, are two factors which need to be combined, and seen in their mutual harmony. This is eminently true in Political Science. It cannot receive a safe and full development, unless we recognize the authority of great ethical truths, or at least the guiding and controlling power of deep moral instincts, side by side with the cultivation of practical statesmanship, and of those lessons of a wise expediency, by which the laws and customs of every nation are adjusted to the varying wants and altered circumstances of society from age to age.

There are thus two opposite dangers to be avoided, in tracing out, practically, the relation between public legislation and the principles of moral science. Nations and their rulers are liable, on the one side, to be wrecked on the Scylla of some impracticable theory, mistaken for a moral law of binding and eternal obligation. Or else, in shunning this danger, they may be sucked into the Charybdis of an expediency, devoid of all social principle or religious faith, in which nations float blindly at the mercy of the winds and the waves. Principles, laid down without warrant as fundamental laws of political duty, may encroach on the just and proper range of social expediency. The firmness and stedfastness of moral truth, in its own nature, is then transferred to social customs, national laws, and political constitutions, and a diseased fancy clothes them with that immutability, which is really a Divine prerogative. Out of this error there naturally grows up a superstitious and blind conservatism, which forgets the true saying of Bacon, that Time is the great innovator, worships the dead forms of the past, and overlooks the fact that national life implies growth and change, and that altered conditions impose new duties on each successive age. The other evil, often caused by recoil from the first, is perhaps wider and deeper still. It is when mere expediency encroaches on higher ground, where fixed principles and laws of social and religious duty should reign supreme. All national sense of moral right and wrong, the sacredness of treaties and covenants, the axioms of public duty and religious faith, are then flung aside, and the place left vacant by their removal is filled up by a blind subservience to the momentary impulses of popular self-will. The true standard of excellence is forsaken and reversed,

which was laid down by a heathen poet for the guidance
of the upright statesman :—

> Virtus, repulsae nescia sordidae, in-
> contaminatis fulget honoribus;
> Nec sumit aut ponit secures
> Arbitrio popularis aurae.

Such a diseased liberalism, which neglects every higher
and deeper law of national duty, and flatters and obeys
the momentary impulses of public opinion, that fluctuate
from hour to hour, is inconsistent with all political stabi-
lity. It thrives in an atmosphere of excessive and ceaseless
change, and builds on the loose sand, which the last tide-
wave of the ocean may have heaped on the shore. To
shun these opposite errors on the right hand and the left
is the hardest and highest triumph of true political wisdom.

Moral Science, when rightly pursued and clearly attained, reveals those fixed laws of duty towards God and
men, which are binding at all times and in all places, not
only on individuals, but on communities and nations.
They are the first elements and dominant truths in a vast
scheme of moral government, which is in ceaseless operation. They are the stars of the moral firmament. They
live, in the words of Sophocles, "not only yesterday and
to-day, but evermore, and no one knows any hour when
they first were born." Whenever these are transgressed,
however strong may be the temptation, and however
plausible the excuses by which men or nations try to conceal their shame, the penalty is sure, and the stars, in
their eternal courses, fight against the transgressors.

But laws and customs, however firm their moral basis,
need to be adapted to the wants of successive ages, and of
the various tribes and races of the human family. The
general duty requires to be embodied in special details,

for practical use in the affairs of life. And these details
of social law and usage are mutable in their own nature.
They may and ought to be "changed according to the
diversities of countries, times and manners." And true
wisdom, both in laws civil and ecclesiastical, consists
mainly in the avoidance of "two extremes, too much
stiffness in refusing, and too much easiness in admitting"
the variations by which they are fully adapted to the
actual state and wants of human society.

Now there is a moral superstition, often very mischievous in its results, which confounds the secondary
and derivative laws with those primary lessons and
principles of good and evil, of right and wrong, on which
they are secretly founded. The error, in political thought,
bears a close resemblance to the doctrine of transubstantiation in theology. The outward sign and visible clothing
of moral truth is confused with the truth itself, till the
form is blindly worshipped, and the substance obscured
and lost. The natural result is some form of political
idolatry. But the nature of the idol may vary from time
to time. Sometimes it is an antiquated and worn-out
usage, sometimes a particular flag, or family, or some worthless pretender to a throne, long ago forfeited by human
guilt and folly, when the just sentence has been sealed by
Divine Providence through successive generations.

To see clearly, then, the true relation between Ethics
and Politics, the first essential is a firm hold on the contrast between Pure and Applied Morality. The great
truths, which appeal directly to the heart and spirit and
conscience of man, have to be distinguished from their
application, in detail, to all the varying forms and conditions of social life.

The laws of truth, love, righteousness, and grace are

of absolute and universal authority. They belong alike
to all moral agents—to men, to angels, and to unknown
races, distinct from both, if such there be; and to men in
every age of the world, of every race and tribe, and under
all the varieties of political constitution or social change.
But their application, in social jurisprudence and outward
law, admits of large varieties. It depends partly on
experience of what men have been and are, and of their
actual state in moral capability, progress, and attainment,
and not simply on what they ought to be. Laws, that
would be admirably suited to a state of high moral
feeling and advanced intelligence, may be wholly un-
suitable among a race of savages, and in a state of social
barbarism and abounding passion. They may then even
become mischievous, and only aggravate the evils they
attempt to restrain or cure.

> Quid vanæ sine moribus
> Leges proficiunt?

This first contrast lies thus at the basis of all wise and
wholesome legislation. Pure Morals are fixed, absolute,
invariable. There can be no curvature whatever in a
straight line. But Applied Morals, in their own nature,
and by virtue of their definition, are largely variable. For
they include all those social conditions, as elements in
their wise adjustment, which themselves vary widely,
from country to country, and from age to age.

But there is a further contrast, more liable to be overlooked, which is also highly important, and even vital to a
just and comprehensive view of the whole subject. Positive Law or Applied Morals has two different aspects, one
human, and the other divine. And these are distinct in
their aim, and involve important differences in their
practical development.

Tho object of outward laws, in their human aspect, is merely the repression of vice and crime, so far as they tend to injure or destroy the life, comfort, and social welfare of men. Its leading and defining character, then, is to be restrictive of evil.

The Divine aspect of Law goes further. It includes, indeed, this first and more immediate object, the repression of open crime. But it has a wider and deeper range, and includes, as one main end, the discovery of evil, with a view to its more perfect abatement and cure. It enters "that the offence may abound." It is not simply a power and force to restrain evil It is detective also. It does not confine its aim to the security of life and property for the moment, but reaches after the higher object of moral renovation.

Human laws themselves, when guided by true wisdom, as soon as the first end is secured, should pass on to the higher. The first endeavour must be the repression of outward vice and crime, in those forms which strike directly at the peace and comfort, and even the existence of society. The second and higher is the awakening of conscience from its slumber, and the creation and culture of a higher moral standard. In this way laws themselves may become one powerful means of moral education.

Positive Laws, when divinely revealed, may deal more largely with the higher and nobler object. Their seeming failure, when viewed only as expedients to hinder the growth of open crime, may be really the fulfilment of a higher object of God's moral government. The discoveries of human evil, which through successive ages they have not overcome, but rather have placed in a clear and full relief on the page of history, may prove the best preparation for more effectual displays of the Divine goodness,

and of redeeming love. But such laws, when only of
human origin, must be content with a more limited aim.
They cannot, indeed, without serious evil, entirely set
aside the higher object. But it needs to be cautiously
and temperately pursued. It is a half truth, though it
is only a half truth, that you cannot make men moral by
acts of parliament. Human laws should be in advance,
but can only with safety be a little in advance, of public
morality. Else, in attempting too much, there will be
serious risk, almost the certainty, of entire failure. Instead of producing habits of virtue, they will then breed
a plentiful crop of mischievous and odious hypocrisy.

Legislation, then, to be practically perfect, requires a
real accommodation of human laws to the actual moral
attainments of society, while still avoiding with care any
sanction of immorality. Like the law of Moses, but on
a still more extensive scale, it must suffer some things,
without inflicting penalties, because of moral blindness
or hardness among the multitudes for whose good it provides. And hence the true principle by which it should
be guided is neither moral despotism, nor moral indif-
ferentism, extremes which tend to generate each other;
but Toleration, or the public recognition of a contrast
between what the law condemns and punishes, and what
the lawgiver fully approves. It is a watchword, which
bigotry may dislike, and charge with moral weakness, and
which may be resented as an insult by the pride of lawless
self-will; but no other principle, in a world like ours, can
satisfy the imperative claims of high-toned morality and
true political wisdom.

A third main element, essential to a just view of the
intimate connection between Morals and Political Science,
is a clear apprehension of those Formative Principles, on

which the right and wise establishment of every system
of positive law must depend.

Political Law deals with men under three distinct, but
closely related characters, as Men, as Children, and as
Brethren. Hence in all social law there will be found to
co-exist three main and vital elements,—Humanity, Piety,
and Brotherhood. Or, in other words, to bring the truth
into closer relation with a favourite modern watchword,
with which it agrees in part, and partly disagrees, its
three principles are Liberty, Inequality, and Fraternity.
Neglect of any one of these is mischievous. Its deliberate
and entire reversal, whenever seriously attempted in the
social constitution, must be fatal and ruinous.

The first of these essential principles of wise legislation
is that of Humanity or Liberty. Men, in order to be the
fit subjects of social law, must be free moral agents. The
freedom thus affirmed is no contradiction of that unhappy
bondage to habits of sin, which Scripture and experience
alike reveal as a mournful and widespread disease. On
the contrary, it is the condition without which moral
health and moral sickness are both impossible. Bondage
of such a kind is the disease of agents, morally free, and
is possible to these alone.

Laws, then, being designed for men as free moral
agents, must deal with them according to their true
character. If they are treated as mere things, chattels
of a master, or mere tools for the manufacture of goods,
whether this be done in the name of political absolutism,
commercial selfishness, or a fatalistic and material philosophy, morality is quenched, the hearth of human affection
is left cold and desolate, and social life must expire and
die away.

The evil, to which this great principle is opposed, may

assume at least three different forms. In philosophy it
reveals itself in that cold and barren fatalism, which would
resolve the heart, mind, and conscience of man into a
transcendental product of solar force; and pretends to
believe that our feelings of right and wrong are bound
hand and foot in the toils of some vast dynamical theorem,
which awaits the birth of a competent intelligence in one
of its own countless variables, for its own complete integration. In politics, the same evil appears in the two different
forms of mere absolutism, when all rights of subjects are
displaced by the caprice of a supreme despot; or of caste
absolutism, when a claim to life-long service is perverted
into a denial of all the rights of humanity, and instead
of servants, more honourable than mere hirelings, who
honour their masters, and receive from them what is just
and equal, we have selfish oppression on one side, and on
the other a race of degraded helots and slaves. The same
evil reappears even under the outward show of extreme
liberty, when men and children are treated by their fellows
as mere tools and instruments of production, and all their
higher characters are lost sight of and forgotten. A
third form of the same evil is found in hasty over-legislation, when human lawgivers attempt a task beyond
their power, and in the pursuit of some political object,
or in the mistaken assertion of their own authority, bind
down the social life of the nation with burdens hard to
be borne, which experience proves to be intolerable, and
which, when long continued, lead to discontent and social
revolution.

This first principle, then, of Humanity or Liberty,
prescribes a threefold law for the guidance of all social
thought and action, and of all wise legislation. First, in
doctrine, the clear assertion and firm maintenance of

human responsibility, in contrast to the immoral voices of
a material philosophy, and even to those subtle physiological excuses for crime, which forget that all wrong
doing, when traced deep enough, must be real insanity
and madness in the sight of perfect wisdom. Next, in
the national constitution, the same principle points to
power limited by law, or the settled order of constitutional
government, in contrast to the despotism either of lawless
multitudes, or of some solitary tyrant. And lastly, in
practical politics, the same truth points to the duty of
large toleration and forbearance. It will lead statesmen
to remember the limitations of their own power, and to
avoid the serious risk of over-legislation. They will feel
it not only lawful and expedient, but even one primary
obligation of their high office, to leave wide scope for
human freedom, without which life becomes mechanism,
and society degenerates into a herd of slaves.

The second formative principle, on which the moral
character of human legislation depends, and by which it
ought to be controlled, is Piety, in the primitive and classic
meaning of the word, which includes reverence to human
superiors, and especially to parents, as well as towards
God and the unseen world. It is the principle, in other
words, of Inequality or Subordination.

Men, by the very constitution of their twofold nature,
are born unequal. The opposite statement, however
widely current in modern times, is either a strange
misnomer, or a prodigious fable. Each child of man is
first a child, and only much later becomes a parent. A
contrast, wide and deep, between experience and in-
experience, authority and subjection, manly strength and
infant weakness, is inwrought into the constitution of
human nature, and reveals itself anew in every successive

generation. There is no strict equality even among the hosts of heaven. There are angels that excel in strength, the rulers of celestial hierarchies, thrones, dominions, principalities and powers, dimly and mysteriously revealed. Far less can such equality be found among men. It has no place, still lower in the scale of being, among the animal creation and the vegetable world. We must stoop lower still, to the first elements out of which lifeless objects are composed, and there alone, if anywhere in creation, equality must be found. The atoms of chemistry are unequal, from hydrogen to gold. Comets and asteroids, satellites, planets, and suns, the hyssop and the cedar-tree, the insect and the elephant, reveal the law of inequality in the natural world. And it extends still further, and mounts higher, in the contrast between the newborn infant, the strength of manhood, and the wisdom of age; between the drunkard and the savage, and saints, and prophets and apostles, the lights of the Church in every age. It is thus one all-pervading law of the natural, the intellectual, and the moral universe.

> Order is heaven's first law, and, this confessed,
> Some are, some must be, greater than the rest.

Strict and absolute equality would unmake the universe, and resolve all its wonderful beauty and endless variety into a chaos of warring atoms and a sea of nebulous mist once more.

This law of order, which underlies the whole world of political life, and binds it to the great doctrines of ethical science, assumes the double form of social and religious piety. It involves, in its manifold and weighty lessons, the subjection and obedience of children to their parents, the reverence of the young to their elders, the subordination, in loving union, of woman to man, and the dominion exercised over the floating, variable, and inconstant wishes of a people by fixed and abiding laws of national life. Its higher form is seen in the dependence of the whole community on the will and word of the Supreme Creator. And the two great evils by which the principle is disowned, and political science is disjoined and severed from moral truth, are social insubordination and national irreligion. The first of these evils is sometimes a penalty, which follows upon the second. When religious faith declines, and its sanctions lose their power, there follows, naturally and inevitably, a relaxation of those bonds which form the cohesion of society, and bind it together. The warning description of the prophet is then fulfilled. The child behaves itself proudly against the ancient, and the base against the honourable.

The third moral principle, which is inwrought into the whole texture of human society, and prescribes a law to the form and course of wise national legislation, is that of Brotherhood or Fraternity.

Men are born children, but they grow up to be brethren. The brotherhood of a common nature, of common wants, rights, and duties, of capacities for moral progress, and dim yearnings after some higher happiness still unattained, exists side by side with all the inequalities of age, sex, talent, wealth, social position, intellectual gifts, and moral attainments.

This grand truth of man's universal brotherhood limits and guards the other maxim of inequality and subordination, and hinders it from lapsing into a serious error. The two principles, like polar forces in the natural world, balance, and in balancing strengthen each other. The peasant, the workman, the pauper, the newborn

infant, is a brother or sister to the wisest philosopher,
the most gifted poet, the most absolute sovereign; and to
those who are higher than mere philosophers, poets, and
kings, to those prophets and apostles, who in moral
dignity and honour are highest and noblest among men,
who stand in the presence of the Lord of the earth, and
convey His messages with authority to their fellow-men.
And this brotherhood has its rights, which cannot be
violated without guilt and danger, and must form one
main guiding law in the whole course of wise legislation.

The evils in political life, which contradict this great
law of social brotherhood, are many and various. First in
order is the selfish pride of rulers and governors, when
they look upon their office as a means for personal
aggrandisement, whether in the grosser form of wealth and
opulence, or the more subtle shape of ambition · and
historic fame; instead of seeing in it a sacred trust, to be
used for the benefit of their fellow-men. This evil reveals
itself outwardly in the form of caste legislation, or the
tendency to confine the main benefits and privileges of
the social system to a favoured minority alone. The
second, near akin to the first, consists in the pride and
exclusiveness of social distinctions. The lesson of order
and gradation is thus exaggerated, till it hides from view
the common dignity of our human nature, and the further
claim of affinity and brotherhood. A third evil is the degradation of woman. The recoil is easy, from the lessons or
customs of a high-flown chivalry, which treats woman, in
terms, with a fond and blind idolatry, and sets aside the
truth of her subordination, so clearly revealed, to a refined,
but debasing sensuality; and then, as the moral darkness increases, to a coarse, ungenerous and heartless abuse of men's
superior power, till the object of idolatrous enthusiasm

to the knights of romance, or a sentimental philosophy, is turned once more, as in savage tribes, into a victim and a slave. A fourth evil, akin to the last, is the oppression of childhood. Some painful forms of this evil were too frequent among ourselves, till they were checked by wise and Christian legislation. Others, it is to be feared, survive still to the present day. When idle and drunken parents indulge their own vices through the hard earnings of their young and almost infant children, a blight must have passed over some of the sweetest and holiest instincts of our nature. The aggravated guilt is too likely to be followed, in later years, by the opposite and not less hateful evil of childish lawlessness and disobedience, till the springs of family life and love are poisoned and destroyed.

The last and crowning denial of human brotherhood is that of direct slavery. Only it should be well observed that the definition of slavery, which brings it under this just sentence, is not a legal obligation, on the part of one man to another, of lifelong service. It is the treatment of man by his fellowman as a mere thing, and not a person, a tool for producing wealth, and not as a moral agent, sharing the same nature with himself, and forming a true part of the wide and sacred brotherhood of mankind.

These great principles, on which the connection between Ethics proper and Political Science seems really to depend, involve a large variety of weighty practical lessons. We may apply them, in succession, to the duties of subjects, of magistrates, and legislators; and, rising still higher, of those who attempt to frame or remould that constitution in any state or kingdom, which may decide and determine the whole course of future legislation for ages to come.

The first duty, then, of subjects, which flows directly

from the first of these truths, is to be freemen indeed.
They are to be subject, not to lawless caprice, under
whatever titles of honour or sacred names it may be
disguised, but to law and just authority alone. This is
their birthright, and they cannot without guilt and shame
barter it away. This truth is the living root of all constitutional government, in contrast to political or ecclesiastical slavery, the mere despotism of Pope or Emperor,
of tyrant or priest. No man, whatever his rank, spiritual
or political, has the right to claim absolute, unlimited
obedience from his fellow-men. Those religious orders,
which lay down such a rule for their members, may gain
an effective organization, so powerful as to make them
dangerous to their enemies. But they purchase it by
sacrificing Christianity itself, and stifling the voice of
natural conscience. He who consents to be the slave of
a superior or a priest ceases thereby to be a freeman of
Christ. And the evil is nearly the same in abject submission to political tyranny. By such a blind subser-
viency the cause of order gains nothing. It rather incurs
a serious loss. Doctrines like those of the *Leviathan*, with
the corresponding practice of political servility, form the
natural prelude to those fierce and bloody revolutions, in
which all the foundations of social order are overthrown
and swept away.

But if the first duty of Christian subjects is to be
freemen, who bear in mind the dignity of human nature,
not destroyed, though obscured, by human sin and guilt,
and which constitutes the very basis of human society—
their next is to be men of order, or law-honouring, and
law-abiding freemen. They are bound to render to lawful
government, and all the authorities placed over them, no
reluctant and enforced submission, but a willing and

cheerful obedience. The outward acts of submission
are due to Cæsar, and may be enforced by Cæsar's law.
But the free and cheerful spirit in which their obedience
should be rendered lies beyond the range of Cæsar's
power to enforce and secure. It is a debt which is due to
that higher Power, by whom kings reign, and princes
decree justice. Only they who obey human laws in this
temper fulfil the nobler and more sacred duty which they
owe to their Maker, and "render unto God the things
which are God's."

But these two principles of order and liberty, contrasted yet harmonious, do not exhaust the moral elements which enter into the wide range of the political
duty of every citizen in his public life. From the truth
of human fraternity or brotherhood a third main duty
must follow. They ought to be men of kindness. Their
moral obligation, as members of society, cannot be satisfied by obedience to the mere letter of human laws, however undeviating and complete that obedience may be.
There are other and deeper laws of brotherhood, which
find no place in human statute-books, and would flee
away, like the delicate colours of the rainbow, if hard-
headed lawyers strove to draught them in legal phraseology, and embody them in some supplement to a
human code. But though unwritten, they are of real
and binding obligation. In the Divine law two or
three cases are written down as specimens of the rest.
"Thou shalt not see thy brother's ox or his sheep go
astray, and hide thyself from them; thou shalt in any
case bring them again to thy brother. Thou shalt not see
thy brother's ass or his ox fall down by the way, and hide
thyself from them; thou shalt surely help him to lift
them up again." But this law of brotherly kindness is

12—2

too wide in its range, and too pervasive in its fragrance, to
be fully expressed in any code of written obligations.
Whenever such attempts are made, that fragrance exhales
and begins to pass away.   It finds its development in a
thousand instincts of high-souled chivalry, and in countless amenities and courtesies of social life.   And whenever
it is ennobled and purified by the higher lessons of Christian faith, it raises human intercourse from the mere
mechanism of law, or the drudgery of mere workers in a
vast hive of industry, into a lively pledge and earnest of
all the sacred fellowship which Christianity assures to the
faithful in a happier and holier life to come.

These same principles, which involve the chief laws
of moral duty binding on subjects in their political and
social life, apply no less to magistrates and lawgivers
themselves.   They ought so to legislate, that these truths
may be embodied in the whole course and tenour of their
legislation.   And this will lead them to avoid three main
evils, which it is the task of true political wisdom to resist
and put away.

The first of these is over-legislation, with its natural
and inevitable tendency to legal tyranny.   To meddle
with social intercourse at every point is not the task of
wise human legislation.   Such a prerogative belongs to
Divine enactments and the deeper laws of moral duty
alone.   But in the laws of men a wide scope must and
ought to be given to human freedom.   The true limits
may be hard to define.   Mr. Mill's treatise on *Liberty*,
while it contains much that is true and important, lays
down the principle too broadly on the other side.   It
assumes that personal convictions, if sincere, absolve from
all right of social restraint, not only on the opinions
themselves, but on the social acts to which they lead.

And it justifies this view by an appeal to many instances of social persecution, which, even when most mischievous, have been honest and sincere. But it is plain that the rights of individuals on one side, and of society on the other, depend on the real truth, and not on false opinions which either may entertain. The problem is too hard and vast to be solved by general aphorisms, investing either individual conscience, or human society as a whole, with a factitious supremacy, to which truth and liberty are sacrificed on either side. So much, however, seems to be practically clear that, in an age like our own, over-legislation must be more than usually dangerous, and that many evils should be wisely tolerated, so far as direct legislation is concerned, lest attempted remedies should be worse than the disease. But whenever special forms of selfishness or vice are proved to work extensive social mischief, and the public mind is prepared for some decisive action, it is dangerous, on the other side, in obedience to any abstract theory of personal rights, to neglect the just use of authority for the restraint of evil. It is a most unwise antithesis when it has been said that to "England sober" we should prefer "England free," as if the spread of national drunkenness were not, in its own nature, adverse and fatal to the only freedom which deserves the name.

The second evil, against which these principles ought to be a moral safeguard, is that of blind, selfish, and democratic levelling.

Human equality, unless the phrase be so limited as to become wholly unmeaning, is a great and evident falsehood. Legislation, whenever it is based on such a principle, must be a building of sand. Whenever it deals with men as mere units, and leaves out of sight the deep con-

trusts and immense varieties of human life, it tends rapidly
to political chaos and confusion. For our very conception
of chaos is that of a state in which countless atoms

> Swarm populous, unnumbered as the sands
> Of Barca or Cyrene's desert shore,

but fight only under their party colours, and have no law
of mutual cohesion, no gradation of life and dignity, but
decide their quarrels, ever renewed, by shifting numbers
alone. Wherever such a policy is pursued, the instinct of
order, violently repressed during the chase after an impossible ideal, is sure to break out in some new and
unexpected form. Plebiscites of mere floating political
atoms, in which every law of social and moral order is
cast aside, and number alone is supreme, swiftly breed
despotic rule as the natural and almost necessary antidote
for a worse evil. Plato's genealogy of the forms of government is then fulfilled. The nation, which drinks deep of
licence under the name of liberty, falls speedily under the
yoke of some skilful and prosperous tyrant.

A third and last evil on the part of rulers, from which
these great moral principles of humanity, piety, and fraternity should be a constant safeguard, is the more subtle,
but hardly less dangerous fault, of class legislation. This
fights plainly against the great law of human brotherhood.
When the interest and welfare of large classes of men are
systematically set aside, or even carelessly overlooked and
forgotten, because legislators are selfish, and abuse the
power vested in their hands, there is sure, soon or
late, to be a dangerous recoil. Their sin is great in
abusing a sacred trust, and it will be sure to find them
out. They are bound, as legislators, to consult impartially
for the general good, and the omission of any class from

their study for the common welfare is a serious wrong.
It is true that they are bound to consult for all, not as
mere abstract units, or apart from all the distinctions of
sex, age, knowledge, character, on which the constitution
of society depends; but for all alike in their true place,
and according to that weight which they may justly claim
in the political organism, and in God's wide plan of universal providence. All men are not equal, far from it.
But all are equally brethren. The rights of brotherhood
belong to all, from the least to the greatest, and cannot in
any one case be safely or lawfully set aside. All are free
agents, and ought therefore to be treated as moral beings,
and in no case as animal machines alone. All are immortal, to whom the present life is probation for another
life soon to follow; and are to be treated with honour, as
called, by Divine invitation, to partake in the Christian
hope of that better life to come.

The same principles apply to the still higher duty of
those who aspire to frame national constitutions, or to
determine the fundamental laws and guiding maxims on
which the whole course and tone of national legislation
is to depend. When great moral truths are forgotten, and
politics degenerate into a mere strife of party, or a series
of spasmodic efforts to combine discordant elements into
momentary union, and thus to secure at any price the
majorities on which power and influence depend, political
life must suffer a rapid and sure decline. But I forbear to
enter on a subject so wide, which suggests to thoughtful
observers grave and anxious reflections on the future of
our own country. One thing is sure, as the pillars of
heaven and earth. It is not the abundance of private
wealth, nor the largeness of the national revenue, which
can secure the lasting happiness and welfare of an empire

like our own. Our national safety depends on deeper
causes, and the true talisman of our lasting prosperity and
greatness is of a higher kind. It consists in the supremacy
of justice, mercy, and faith in the public counsels of the
land; and in the mingled and harmonious culture of the
great laws of freedom, order, and brotherhood, sustained
and quickened by faith in men's immortality, among the
dwellers in countless homes of domestic purity, peace, and
love.

LECTURE IX.

MORALS AND REVEALED RELIGION.

THE relation between Moral Philosophy and the Christian Faith, a subject highly important at all times, has acquired new interest in the present day. It has a most intimate connection with nearly all those great philosophical and religious questions, which, in an age of peculiar intellectual activity, occupy the thoughts, and divide the judgment of educated men. Very opposite views have been zealously advocated in former days, and are still maintained. There are Christians of earnest faith, who conceive that all study of Ethics, as a purely human science, whether based on moral intuitions, or on calculations of far-seeing prudence, is set aside and rendered superfluous by the fact of a Divine revelation. All moral speculations, depending on experience and natural reason alone, seem to them nothing better than feeble tapers lighted at noonday.

The exact converse of this view is held by disciples of the idealist school of sceptical philosophy. The clearness and certainty of Ethics, as a science of pure reason, seems to them so complete and self-sufficing as to dispense with all need for supernatural revelation. A religious creed, designed for a moral purpose, and still dependent inseparably on historical records, and needing external confirmation from alleged miracles and prophecies, must therefore, on their principles, be only a useless incumbrance of an ethical system otherwise complete, by which its scientific character is disguised and obscured. It must be little better, in their eyes, than an improbable fiction, an unmeaning superfluity.

Such a view of Moral Science is the basis of Tindal's once famous work, *Christianity as old as Creation.* It has been unfolded, in his own peculiar style, by Immanuel Kant in his essay on *Religion within the bound of Pure Reason.* It has been more lately expounded, in a popular style, with zeal and eloquence, by Theodore Parker, in his *Discourses on Absolute Religion.* It is warmly espoused in a recent work on *Intuitive Morals,* and has plainly found, at the present hour, a wide acceptance among persons of general culture and intelligence, who retain a vague and loose profession of Christian faith. They look upon Christianity as simply the republication of a code of moral duty which had been taught mankind by the light of reason alone. To this extent they will freely allow that it may have, in a practical sense, some real worth and value. But as soon as it attempts to travel beyond this limit, and to set up any claim of a higher kind, to proclaim mysterious doctrines, or remove the veil from the unseen world, they deny its authority altogether. It then lies open, in their opinion, to the serious charge that it encumbers a pure and lofty science with Jewish superstitions and prejudices, histories of doubtful and uncertain truth, a multitude of worthless ceremonies, and dogmas morally useless and hopelessly obscure.

This view of Tindal and other kindred writers was prominently recalled to notice a few years ago, in the sixth of the *Essays and Reviews,* which discussed at some

length "*The Tendencies of Religious Thought in England,
1688—1750.*" A real effort to throw light on the difficulties of the subject would have been a most valuable gift
to thoughtful and perplexed inquirers into the nature and
claims of Christianity. But of such an effort there is no
shadow of a trace. The aim seems rather to be, in a
series of hasty criticisms and rapid historical sketches, to
render the mists which easily gather around a difficult
subject still more dense and impenetrable, and the darkness deeper than before. The only conclusion drawn,
when a dozen theories have been discredited and set aside,
is that no Christian in our days, it is highly probable, has
any clear perception on what ground his faith ought really
to rest. The historical kaleidoscope is lightly shaken, and
a dozen diverging opinions are made to pass before the
eye in swift succession, but the youthful reader receives
not the slightest help to guide or assist his own judgment.
Such a purely literary and curious treatment of the
gravest questions of moral duty and religious faith is one
of the most worthless and mischievous of occupations.
Moral indecision and religious uncertainty are weeds
which grow rapidly enough of their own accord, and have
no need of any artificial culture, by such negative and purposeless criticisms, to secure an ample and luxurious development in superficial minds. My own aim will be the
exact reverse, to unfold on this subject some clear and
definite principles, which may serve as waymarks to earnest
minds, impatient of mere literary trifling in grave moral
questions, who long to feel beneath them a firm foundation of solid truth, on which their faith and conscience, in
harmony with enlightened reason, may safely rest.

There are three mistaken views of the relation between
Moral Science and Divine Revelation, which must first of

all be set aside, before any approach can be made to a just solution of the great problem we are now to consider.

The first of these is the opinion, not unusual with a large number of devout Christians, that Revelation excludes Ethics as a Science, and renders all reasoning on questions of morals needless and presumptuous. The saying of Omar, in the doubtful tradition of Abulpharagius, has found its exact counterpart in some modern reasonings of Christian men. "If these writings of the Greeks agree with the book of God, they are useless, and need not be preserved. If they disagree, they are pernicious, and ought to be destroyed." But such a view, though its advocates may intend, in advocating it, to do honour to the Bible, is one which the Scriptures themselves set aside and condemn. They give no warrant whatever for that blind, superstitious faith, which, in order to establish its own supremacy, and reign without a rival, begins by stifling the voice of natural conscience, and seeks to condemn it to utter silence.

The very first page of Scripture contains a clear proclamation of the moral gifts and faculties of mankind. For man, we are there told, was created at first "in the image of God." Whatever else the words imply, they evidently include the affirmation of those moral capacities, and of that spiritual nature, by which man resembles his Divine Creator, the Holy One who is a Spirit, and is thus widely parted from the beasts of the field. The same truth reappears in another form in the severe expostulation by the prophet: "Woe to them that call evil good, and good evil; that put darkness for light, and light for darkness; that put bitter for sweet, and sweet for bitter." And still later, in the New Testament, our Lord himself, the supreme authority with every Christian,

makes an appeal to his adversaries on this very ground—
"Yea, and why even of your own selves judge ye not that
which is right?" The presence of a moral faculty in man,
which can judge, and ought to judge, even with respect to
the character of a heaven-sent messenger, and the moral
features of a message claiming to be Divine, is thus affirmed
from the opening to the close of the Christian revelation.

Again, the Scriptures teach that there is a standard
of right and wrong, not wholly inaccessible to mankind,
and morally binding on them, even apart from messages
supernaturally revealed. The Gentiles, as St Paul plainly
teaches, were "a law unto themselves," although they had
no law, in the sense of a Divine code, like that of Moses,
externally revealed. And, a thousand years before, the
same truth had been proclaimed by the Psalmist in his
simple and sublime description of the testimony of the
heavens,—"Their line is gone out into all the world, and
their words unto the ends of the earth." The doctrine
which denies the moral nature of man is a vain and
fruitless attempt to silence these heavenly voices. Their
calm and solemn accents never cease, though they may
fall too often on dull and heedless ears.

The Scriptures teach us also, with equal clearness, that
morals are a progressive science. For although, as in
physical science, the truths themselves are permanent, and
do not change, their range is vast and boundless, and there
is growth in the knowledge and apprehension of them by
individual minds. All the terms which we use habitually,
to describe the most real knowledge of sensible objects,
are transferred everywhere in the word of God to this
higher field. It speaks with high praise of those who
make constant advance in a pursuit so high and excellent,
and thus "by reason of use have their senses exercised

to discern good and evil." And a similar analogy, from
outward light, and the faculty of vision, is used in the
Sermon on the Mount to describe the effect of moral
singleness of aim in giving clearness to the understanding,
and firmness and consistency to the moral judgment. "If
thine eye be single, thy whole body shall be full of light."
The communication of fresh gifts and higher privileges
is described, by the same Divine authority, as mysteriously
linked with the right use and improvement of those
already received. "To him that hath shall be given, and
he shall have more abundance; but from him that hath
not shall be taken away even that he hath."

The principle is also clearly recognized, that moral
truths, apprehended by a moral faculty, are one main and
essential part of the evidence of a Divine revelation. By
this means alone can its reception be fully distinguished
from mere credulity and blind superstition. There is an
abundant appeal, it is true, to evidence of a lower and
more sensible kind. But even here the presence of a
moral element is implied. The miracles of Christ were
themselves works of mercy, and parables of Divine grace;
and the prophecies, to which appeal is made, are described
with emphasis as the words of holy men, who spake under
the impulse of the Holy Spirit of God. But in other
cases this moral element in the testimony stands alone,
and appears in fuller relief. "Which of you convinceth
me of sin? and if I say the truth, why do ye not believe
me?" And the Apostle, treading in the steps of his
Divine Master, describes the main object of his own
preaching in those impressive words,—"By manifestation
of the truth commending ourselves to every man's conscience in the sight of God."

Christian Faith, then, by the testimony of the Scrip-

tures themselves, does not exclude all moral science, or
supersede natural conscience, but recognizes its reality,
and the duties which flow from it, in the plainest terms.
But an opposite error, still more dangerous, must equally
be cleared away, before any just view of the whole subject
can be attained. For Moral Science, whether under the
earlier title of a "Christianity as old as creation," or the
modern name of "Absolute Religion," has been held to exclude all need for supernatural revelation, such as Christianity plainly claims to be, and to make it superfluous and
unmeaning. By the help of this maxim men have been
invited to rise "from the transient shows of time to the permanent substance of religion, from a worship of creeds and
empty belief to a worship in Spirit and in Life;" and the
claim is made, by this process, to have "removed the rubbish
of human inventions from the fair temple of Divine truth."

But the error of this opinion, that the perfection of
Moral Science, or of the absolute religion of reason, makes
any further and positive revelation superfluous, is shown
by a single thoughtful glance at the actual state of mankind. Nowhere in heathen or even in Christian lands are
there any signs of such abundance of moral light, of so
high and advanced a stage of moral attainment, as plainly
to show that any gift of supernatural revelation would be
a needless superfluity. The only reasonable objection to
the claims of Christianity must be of an opposite kind.
It may be urged, with some plausibility, that the moral
state of Christendom is so little raised above the level of
heathen countries, as to discredit the notion that the
gospel is a Divine message, and to countenance the view
that it is only one transient and imperfect phase of a
purely human development. But clearly the natural conclusion from such a premise can never be that all reve-

lation is superfluous. It must rather be that the light
of Christianity itself is too limited, partial, and obscure;
and that, even after eighteen centuries during which
its influence and teaching have widely prevailed, some
fuller and clearer message from heaven is still to be
earnestly desired, in order to scatter the still remaining
darkness. Now this is the exact reverse of the conclusion which Tindal and his successors have drawn, from
the alleged clearness and certainty of ethical truth, to
set aside the claim of the gospel to be a Divine message.

This dream of sceptical philosophy is disproved, not
only by a direct appeal to the lessons of a long and painful experience, but by a just perception of the higher
necessity and importance of moral truth, when compared
with the discoveries of physical science. An increase of
man's knowledge of the outward laws of nature is desirable,
both as a healthy exercise of human intelligence, and for
the practical results, promotive of social ease and comfort,
to which it leads. Still the knowledge which men require,
to provide for the animal necessities of life, is of an elementary and familiar kind, and all beyond seems almost
to belong to the class of social luxuries. But uprightness,
honesty, and truth, social kindness and good will, the restraint of selfish and angry passions, the culture, if not of
high and heroic excellence, at least of temperance, prudence, and sobriety, and the domestic virtues, are almost
essential to the peace and welfare of society, besides their
connection, which reason shows to be probable, and Christianity proclaims on Divine authority, with the nobler
hopes and wider prospects of life beyond the grave. It
may be wise and kind in the great Author of our being,
when man has once attained such knowledge of nature
as enables him to provide for the wants of his animal life,

to lay the world before him for ceaseless research, and leave him to discover its laws and harmonics by his own unaided efforts. But if selfishness and passion have clouded the eye of the soul, and make it hard for him to discern higher truths, far more vital to his present and future welfare, the same wisdom must surely point to an opposite course. We may well infer from the Divine goodness, that help for the discovery of moral and spiritual truth will be given to those who sojourn in a land of twilight and shadow, so to assist their feeble efforts to escape from the darkness, and to guide their feet into the way of peace.

This presumption, drawn from the actual wants of mankind, and the urgent need for a practical attainment of moral insight, is confirmed when we reflect on the deep and mysterious nature of these truths, which it is so needful for them to know and understand. Man is higher and nobler than lifeless matter. Human conscience, will, and intelligence, are harder to explore than the facts of physiology, and the laws and instincts of mere animal life. Man, even as he now is, amidst all his follies and vices, is a more difficult study than the depths of ocean or the stars of the sky. But Man, as he ought to be, the knowledge of his high capacities of moral growth and attainment, his duties and dangers, the means and helps of his progress, the noble and perfect standard he should strive to attain, is a subject harder and nobler still. Now this is the great subject of Moral Science. The simple nature of its first elements cannot remove the vast complexity, the unsearchable mystery, which must belong to its full development. It rises from earth, and climbs towards the highest heaven. It passes beyond the bounds of space and time, and reaches into eternity. It strives

to reach the mountain-tops of creation, and there still to
gaze upward on the unsearchable mysteries of eternal
and uncreated love. Some thoughtful minds, when they
look on the past and present state of the world, may
have doubts and misgivings, that haunt them like dark
spectres, whether any direct light from heaven has ever
dawned on mankind, or can be reasonably hoped for in
time to come. But surely to reject the idea of supernatural revelation on the ground of the clearness of moral
and spiritual truth, and the perfect ease of its attainment,
so as to render all such help superfluous, is the worst
madness of human pride, a climax of unreasoning folly.
The grandeur, difficulty, and loftiness of moral truth, no
less than the greatness of the moral wants of mankind,
form a strong and almost irresistible presumption, that
those who are walking in mist and darkness may reasonably hope for some help to clearer vision from a God of
infinite wisdom and perfect love.

The same view is confirmed by all the analogies which
human parents and teachers supply in every field of
human thought. Men are never left to raise themselves
out of ignorance by their own unaided efforts. Life begins
with a course of education, in which the child passively
drinks in the lessons which are set before it by a knowledge higher than its own, and profits by all the stores
of truth accumulated by former generations. But moral
truths, which involve the duty and the destiny of man,
the ends for which the present life is given, and the prospects of another life after death, are subjects in which the
best and wisest of mankind, in proportion to their wisdom
and loftiness of thought, feel most keenly their own ignorance
and weakness. Their highest attainment is the spirit of
a little child, which feels how ignorant it is, and longs to

be taught and guided by a wisdom far beyond its own. Such an instinct, in thoughtful minds, who feel how steep is the ascent of the mountain-side, and still look upward, is the pledge of its own fulfilment. All human teachers, and the instructions given to children by their own parents, are multiplied proofs, to reflecting men, that our race have not been abandoned, like orphans, to their own self-taught progress in moral wisdom and insight by their Father in heaven.

These reasons, to disprove the strange and wild paradox that revelation is rendered superfluous by the clearness and self-evidence of Moral Science, are further confirmed by the great fact that Christianity, on the very face of it, is a remedial system. It is no message to creatures in a state of moral health, who need no physician. It implies and assumes, on every page, the existence of a dangerous moral disease. It is feet to the lame, and recovery of sight to the blind. It starts from the assumption that men's faculties of moral discernment, though not destroyed, are grievously impaired, and that restoration to health is needful, as well as the provision of external light, before healthy vision can ensue. This view, so plainly taught in the divine message, is confirmed on the largest scale by the past history of the world. The claim, then, that men can dispense with all supernatural revelation, and may safely rely upon their own unaided reason in the whole field of moral inquiry, is like a suggestion that the inmates of a blind asylum may easily build an observatory, provide it with transit instruments and telescopes, with spectroscopes and heliometers, and discover all the magnificent truths of modern astronomical science, without the help of any teacher, oculist, or physician, by their own spontaneous efforts alone.

13—2

A third view of the connection between Moral Philosophy and Christian Faith is that which enforces a policy of mutual isolation. Though more usual in its application to Physics, it is often extended to this higher field of thought. Each subject, it holds, must be studied separately, and treated in entire independence of the other. We are to have "no hankering after seeming reconciliations." The geologist, "if loyal to science, will marshal his facts, as if there were no book of Genesis," and the interpreter of Scripture "will explain its meaning, as if there were no science of geology." Attempts to unfold the harmony of revelation and science, even by divines of eminence, have been called "restless, feverish, and sad," and condemned severely, not simply for errors and faults in the execution, but as if the effort, in its own nature, were a criminal and mischievous folly, instead of being an intellectual necessity with every thoughtful and reverent mind.

Such an entire separation, however, in the case of morals still more than of physics, is unnatural and impossible. It could be attained only at the price of two fearful and immense evils, that religion should become immoral, and moral philosophy irreligious and profane. The remark has sometimes been made, that the different source of the two subjects is enough to warrant their entire separation. Human philosophy or science, it is said, depends on experience and induction, but religious faith on Divine authority alone. They ought therefore to be kept entirely apart, and neither of them to be suffered to interfere in the least with the free and full development of the other.

Such expedients, however, to avert all risk of conflict between revealed religion and human science and philosophy, must be wholly unavailing. However good the

intention of their advocates, they fight against the fixed
laws of human thought, and must utterly fail. We cannot
believe contradictions, whatever the sources from which
they are derived, or however diverse the evidence or
authority on which each rival doctrine is supposed to rest.
One of three results must certainly follow. We must re-
nounce the alleged authority of the Divine message, or
deny the certainty of the supposed science, or set aside
the alleged contradiction, and maintain, on reasonable
grounds, that it is illusive and untrue. But we cannot
seat our theology in one lobe of the brain, and a philosophy which flatly opposes its teaching in the other.
When seeming contrasts arise, we may defer the attempt to reconcile them, believing the materials for a full
solution to be insufficient, and may be content to wait for
a day of fuller light. But the unavoidable result must be
either dimness and uncertainty in our faith in the Scriptures, or some large reserve of doubt and incredulity in
accepting conclusions propounded to us in the name of
ethical philosophy or natural science.

The whole drift of thought, in modern times, is opposed
to the view, in politics or in science, which would find
safety, whether for creeds or for countries, in a kind
of Japanese isolation. Every where, through all the
various fields of human thought, the essential unity of
all truth is becoming more and more apparent. The
principle is too deeply true to be overlooked and contradicted without loss and danger, whether by Christian believers or by men of science. The latter are bound to receive the evidence of well-attested facts, even if drawn from
those fountains of sacred truth which they are sometimes
tempted to overlook or despise. The former are bound to
serve God with a reasonable faith, and never, in reading

those Scriptures which they believe firmly to be the word
of God, to neglect the light which must be thrown on
their real meaning from all successful and honest study
of the works of nature, and from the predicted growth of
natural science in these latter days.

Moral Science then, if it be truly a science, must be
in full harmony with all genuine revelation. A Divine
message, on the other hand, if genuine, must be in
harmony with the lessons of true morality. And such
is really the relation in which they stand to each other.
They are not rivals, but friends. Christianity reinforces
lower and plainer truths of morality, and unveils the
higher, which are less attainable, and hardly accessible
to men's unaided reason. Ethical Science recognizes
the moral excellence and purity of the Christian revelation. Whenever their harmony seems obscured, it
either serves directly to remove false constructions of a
message, so plainly worthy of a Divine origin, in all
its main features, or else it teaches the wisdom and
duty of distrusting our first impressions, when they
would impute, to some particular doctrine or narrative,
inwrought into a code so pure and lofty, moral inconsis-
tency and contradiction. The objections in most cases,
as in the noted example of Abraham's sacrifice, are due
only to the rashness and hastiness of superficial thought,
which a juster and deeper view of the genuine conclusions
and teaching of Moral Science would be sufficient to
expose and condemn, and to reveal the perfect harmony
of the sacred narrative with the noblest and most comprehensive maxims of true morality.

These false theories once removed, the way is open
for a brief survey of the true connection between genuine
Ethics and Christian Theology. Christianity confirms and

enforces the main principles of Moral Science. That
Science, in its turn, is a needful handmaid, which ministers
in various ways to a right reception of Christian faith.
Christianity promotes ethical culture, and supplies the
largest helps for progress towards the true standard of
moral excellence; while Moral Philosophy, in its systematic study, contributes, in many different ways, to the
growth and full perfection of Christian Theology.

Christianity, first of all, confirms and enforces the
great principles of Ethical Science, because it affirms so
clearly the moral element in the constitution of human
nature. The first utterance of Scripture, when man is
brought on the theatre of sacred history, is to proclaim
that he was created in " the image of God." The words
are full of the deepest significance. They express the
wide interval, which some anatomists strive to bridge
over by fixing their eyes on bodily resemblances alone,
between all the lower animals, and a being endowed with
reason and free will, capable, as a spirit, of communion
with the Father of spirits, and of knowing, loving, and
serving the Supreme Creator. This keynote, struck so
early, resounds through every later page of the Bible. It
appears once more in the New Testament, where the main
object of the Gospel is said to be the restoration of the lost
or defaced image of God to the souls of men. It is this
full recognition of man's moral nature, this tone of lofty
thought, in which he is viewed as a creature standing
apart and alone, made in God's image, lord of this lower
world, but subject to a Divine law, and placed under the
moral government of the righteous and holy Governor of
the universe, which makes the Bible, even where its special
doctrines, and the force and drift of its separate messages,
are hardly received, or scarcely known, so mighty an instru-

ment, in all ages, for the moral awakening and elevation of mankind. In the light of true morality, its exclusion, in a Christian land, from the outline and course of early education because of the strifes and divisions of Christians themselves, would be at once a folly and a crime. No sadder exhibition could be made of the power of human perverseness to dishonour and cast aside the most precious gifts of Divine love.

Again, the Scriptures reinforce the fundamental truths of Ethical Science, when they insist so strongly, in every part, on the essential contrast between moral good and moral evil. Human probation, in all its forms and varieties, is made to depend on this great and fundamental truth. The commands of the law, the warning voices of the prophets, appeal to it continually. Man is gifted with the knowledge of "good and evil." He is responsible to God for this knowledge, and is bound to use it in choosing good and refusing evil. Life and death are set before him, and he is commanded to choose life, that he and his children may live. A solemn woe is denounced on those, more guilty than the robbers of some earthly inheritance, who seek to remove the moral landmarks, which are the common inheritance of all mankind. A severe invective is pronounced against those who have no knowledge to do good, but are wise to do evil. Our Lord himself appeals to conscience as the eye of the soul, and proclaims the result of its blindness through passion and vice to be the darkening of the whole intellectual being. St Paul teaches that the light of nature, shining in the outward works of God, leaves men without excuse, when they yield themselves to the seductions of sensual vice, and forget or deny the Creator, who has stamped the signs of His own wisdom and greatness on all the works of His hands. Each in-

spired Apostle, in turn, makes his appeal to this moral
faculty in the mind of man. "To him that knoweth to do
good, and doeth it not, to him it is sin." St Peter exhorts
the first disciples to maintain "a good conscience, that
those may be ashamed who falsely accuse their upright
conversation." St John lays down the high standard at
which the Christian ought to aim: "If our heart condemn
us not, then have we confidence before God." And St
Paul sums up the whole outline of moral duty in that
comprehensive appeal: "Whatsoever things are true,
whatsoever things are honest, whatsoever things are just,
whatsoever things are pure, whatsoever things are lovely,
whatsoever things are of good report; if there be any
virtue, and if there be any praise, think on these things."

But further, the Bible confirms and establishes the
foundations of Moral Science, because it teaches plainly
that the standard of right and wrong is no arbitrary thing,
which comes into being through positive appointment, or
some changeable act of the Divine will, but a law which is
true before its own revelation, and on this account has
been revealed. It does not fear to refer the acts of the
Almighty to this standard, and thus teaches that Eternal
Goodness is a deeper and holier attribute than even Almighty Power or Omniscient Wisdom. Its voices by the
earliest patriarchs are these: "Shall not the Judge of all the
earth do right?" "Shall he that hateth right govern, and
wilt thou condemn the Most Just?" It sets before us the
Supreme Creator making this appeal to His own creatures:
"Are not my ways equal? are not your ways unequal?"
It crowns the messages of the law with that most glorious
of all moral aphorisms with regard to the stainless perfection of the Divine goodness: "He is the Rock, His work
is perfect, all His ways are judgment; a God of truth and

without iniquity, just and right is He." And in its later messages it sets before us, as the highest object of Christian desire, to make trial, in our own conduct and course of life, what is "the good, and perfect, and acceptable will of God."

Another way, in which the Scriptures confirm the reality, and enforce the authority of Moral Science, is by laying it down for a fixed law of Christian duty to make progress continually in spiritual discernment, and in the apprehension of spiritual truth. No countenance is there given to the crude fancy that Ethics, viewed on their practical side, are a barren and unprogressive subject of thought. We rise into a purer atmosphere, where the mephitic choke-damp of such depressing theories finds no place, but is swept away by the fresh wind of some holier influence, and the human conscience breathes freely once more. The voices it utters are full of reality and of hope. They encourage, while they stimulate, the willing learner to climb higher and higher up the hill-side of truth. "To him that hath shall be given, and he shall have more abundance." "The path of the just is as the shining light, which shineth more and more unto the perfect day." The soul, we are taught, has senses resembling those of the body, only more wonderful and mysterious. And these, like their outward counterparts, grow keener and finer in their perception, when rightly employed, so that Christians, "by reason of use", may attain a fuller and clearer knowledge, both of good and evil. Such a growth of knowledge, in the case of unreal shadows, is plainly impossible. The reality of Moral Science is plainly implied, when such various degrees of moral discernment lie open to the attainment of the sincere and humble Christian.

But the New Testament supplies a still deeper con-

firmation of the same truth by the description which
it gives of the main drift and aim of its own message.
What is the great end, to which miracles and prophecies,
the ordinances of the Christian church, and all the
secondary features of the revelation contained in the
Scriptures, are subservient? What is the standard of
hope and desire, which its disciples are taught ever to
keep in view? It is not blind submission to the decrees
of almighty power, or the dull, unreasoning apathy of the
fatalist, but the full, intelligent harmony of the created
will with the felt and known perfection of the Divine
goodness. Its highest message is not couched in the
sentence that "God is Power," but that "God is Light"
and that "God is Love." It teaches us to see a moral
goodness, perfect and without stain, seated on the
throne of the universe. Towards this high and perfect
standard it represents it as the privilege and duty of the
Christian continually to aspire. And thus it leads us to
rise above the domain of natural sequence and mere
physical law, in which the ebb and flow of material changes
is subject to rules of quantity and direction alone; till we
reach a higher region, where the intelligent will, gazing
on a perfect standard of Divine wisdom and love, approaches nearer and nearer to the glorious object on
which its gaze is fixed unceasingly, shines more and more
with some real though faint reflection of its Divine
beauty and glory, and sees light in the light of heaven.
The character of the Christian revelation is wholly mis-
conceived, it is true, when it is taken merely for the
republication of a code of morals, in which no remedies
are provided for the moral disease of mankind, and no
powerful helps are given, and no mighty attractions of
Divine grace are revealed, to replace the barren acknow-

ledgment of a law perpetually transgressed by the peace of forgiveness, and conscious progress towards the recovery of the lost image of God. But still it is certain that the aim and purpose of the gospel is the moral elevation and spiritual recovery of those to whom its message is given. And no surer pledge could be given to us of the unspeakable dignity and importance of Moral Truth, when contrasted with mere physical progress, than a just view of that wonderful economy of Divine grace which the gospel reveals. Its final aim, as clearly announced by prophets and apostles, is to plant the laws of duty once more in the hearts of men, so as to provide an effectual remedy for the moral disease which has spread so wide, and lasted so long; and in due season to establish a kingdom of purity and love, of righteousness, peace, and joy, which may form an image and reflection on earth of the moral beauty and perfection of a higher and brighter world.

LECTURE X.

MORALS AND REVEALED RELIGION.

THE reality and excellence of Moral Truth, viewed as a science and object of human thought and study, is confirmed, and not contradicted or impaired, by Christianity. But the relation of the two subjects is mutual, as well as intimate, and Morality has an important office to fulfil in connection with the right reception of any message which claims to be Divine.

How may we discern between a true and a pretended revelation? The credentials of such a message must answer to the perfections of its Author. They are Divine power, far-seeing wisdom, and supreme goodness. All these attributes, though perhaps in various measure, may be expected to leave their impress on every oral utterance or sacred writing, which really comes from God. The moral evidence cannot usually stand alone. In that case the reception of a heavenly gift would be made to depend on the perfect and healthy working of a faculty, grievously imperfect and diseased, which creates, by its disease, the need for this Divine remedy. But though moral evidence alone is not enough, because of the state of those to whom the message is given, it is one main element in the credentials of any true revelation. Its presence is essential, in order that the acceptance of the message, as

really divine, may be an act of genuine faith, and not of
blind credulity. The unholy and impure must be quite
unable to pass a true moral judgment, in detail, on every
part of a record which claims to be Divine.   Still, if
it be otherwise well attested, they may be perfectly able to
judge whether its general tone is worthy of a message
from the God of heaven; or whether, from its low tone,
and confused moral teaching, it is wholly unworthy to
be received in the high character of a genuine revelation of His will.

Ethical Science, again, prepares the way for Christian
Faith, because it acts as a powerful detective to disclose
the moral wants of mankind. All spurious moral teaching
lowers and debases the standard of right and wrong, so as
to quiet the uneasy conscience, and bring down the rule of
duty to the level of the actual state and conduct of men.
But true morality teaches a widely different lesson. It
refuses to lower its standard, in order to relieve its subjects
from the painful consciousness of wrong-doing. It brings
out into clear relief the wide and deep contrast between the
laws of right, and the actual state and history of the world.
And thus it reveals on the side of science, and seals by the
voice of natural conscience, that lesson of the wide and
universal spread of moral evil among men, which forms
so main a feature of Scriptural Theology. It re-echoes, in
tones of power, those heavenly voices, which announce
to mankind the presence of sore disease, and their need
of some effectual and Divine remedy.

Again, Moral Science, when pure and genuine, includes
and recognizes those deep instincts of creature dependence
and conscious weakness, which, in a race like our own,
render a Divine revelation the natural object of hope
and earnest desire. The full soul loathes the honeycomb.

It is possible for those who have been reared amidst the
light of Christian teaching, and who are still averse to
the high and pure morality of the gospel, to turn away
with a cold indifference from whatever appeals to them
in the name of God, and claims to be Divine. The state
of mind which proclaims all knowledge of the Creator
impossible to be attained, and then proceeds, without one
pang of regret or sigh of bitter lamentation, to frame its
own theories of a universe consigned to eternal and hopeless darkness, is one which finds unhappy illustrations in
our own day. But the moral instinct, when really awake
and in vigorous exercise, and moral science, when its voice
is truly heard, teaches a widely different lesson. Its voice
is that of the ancient patriarch in his hour of sorrow,
"O that I knew where I might find Him! that I might
come even to His seat." Even in heathen lands it will
prompt a secret yearning of the spirits of men, to "feel
after the Lord, if haply they may find him." It imprints
on every thoughtful mind a deep conviction that contentment with entire religious ignorance and uncertainty, far
from being the sign and test of advancing science, is the
sure mark of a deep and ineffable moral degradation.
There are only two states of mind, which, in the light
of sound ethical teaching, can be safe or right in a creature
like man, gifted with such high powers, and still conscious
of their past abuse—to know and love God who has been
actually revealed, or to seek with earnest longing of desire
after the God who is still unknown.

Right and sound moral teaching, when a divine message has been outwardly received, will aid in the work
of setting aside false interpretations, to which it must
always be exposed, and which tend to obscure or pervert
its meaning, and thus to defeat the object for which it

was given. The best and noblest gifts of God are liable to serious abuse, when entrusted to the keeping of sinful men. The Scriptures may be wrested, as an Apostle has warned us, by men of perverse mind to their own destruction. And even where the abuse is not so extreme, genuine faith and piety may be mingled with no small amount of superstitious ignorance or blind credulity. Under the plea of reverence for the word of God, the faults of good men may be mistaken for virtues, holy words may be wrested from their context, and violently forced into the mould of imperfect human systems, or supplemented with human guesses and fancies, till their true meaning is obscured or wholly forgotten. Here a genuine knowledge of ethical truth may prove an important safeguard against serious dangers. It will teach men that records of human error and sin, even when they are found in a Divine message, do not suffer a moral transformation, and become examples of moral excellence; and that special duties, depending wholly on some special command of God, are no laws for universal guidance. Actions, which would be highly criminal, when their motive is the mere caprice of self-will, or the excitement of passion or revenge, may sometimes be proofs of heroic faith or earnest love, when done in obedience to the express command of God, to fulfil some great end of His moral government. And outward and ceremonial precepts, in which the principles of moral duty are mingled with details, and applied to variable and transient circumstances, may be set aside by the Lawgiver who appointed them, and still His wisdom may be perfect alike in their earlier institution and in their later abrogation.

Again, Moral Science, rightly understood, is the spouse and ally of Christian Faith, because it reveals and enforces the supreme importance of that knowledge of Divine truth, and of the character and perfections of the Creator, which it is one main purpose of the gospel to impart to mankind.

The doctrine, lately taught by some eminent writers, that nothing can be known of God and His moral nature, because He is an infinite Being, is directly opposed to the whole scope and aim of the Christian revelation.   Its effect, whenever consistently held, must be to destroy all Theology and all Ethical Science at one common blow. In the hasty recoil from speculative theories of religion, the rivals and substitutes of Christian faith, it would plunge the world and the whole church into a gulf of hopeless darkness.   But the view is not more opposed to the teaching of Scripture than to the voice of conscience and sound reason.   All truth is so closely linked together, that a fatal necessity of entire ignorance in any one field of thought must extend its influence, like a mist of gloom and obscurity, to all the rest.   If we know nothing at all on any subject of which our knowledge is not exhaustive or complete, no person or thing in the wide universe can ever be really known.

Moral Science, when its truths are clearly and firmly held, teaches plainly the opposite lesson.   It thus becomes the natural ally and handmaid of Christian faith.   We do not know ourselves perfectly, either in body or soul ; and in this life, perhaps even in the next, we can never fathom all the mysteries of our own being.   Yet we know that we have an inward power of choice, and are bound to use it aright.   A light shines down upon us, which bids us seek continually a perfection not yet attained. We do not know perfectly our nearest relative or dearest friend.   The social ideas, on which all human fellowship is based, are mysterious and obscure. Yet we know and are sure that kindness and love to all, but especially to neighbours and friends, are our bounden duty and high privilege. Our ignorance of the secret heart of others, and of many hidden laws on which their health and comfort depend, cannot set aside the great maxim of the Apostle, " To him that knoweth to do good, and doeth it not, to him it is sin."

The same principle must apply when we travel upward in thought to a higher sphere. The greatness of the Creator is unsearchable. The Infinite Being transcends, and must transcend, the full comprehension of every finite understanding. The voice of the ancient patriarch is no recent discovery of an improved philosophy in modern times : " Canst thou by searching find out God ? canst thou find out the Almighty to perfection ?" But when a fatal necessity of entire and absolute nescience is inferred from the mystery, which hangs around the horizon in every field of human thought, and is then applied to religious truth alone, the reason, conscience, and heart of man protest against a conclusion no less illogical and baseless than debasing and repulsive in its moral aspect.

There are many dark lines in the solar spectrum. It shares this feature, though in more abundant measure from its superior brightness, with flames of earthly origin and inferior brilliance. Yet the spectrum is light, and not darkness. These lines, though dark themselves, could never have been discovered by those who were wholly blind. And the same principle clearly applies to a higher subject. The very power to perceive and know the mysteriousness of the Divine nature is a proof that some partial knowledge is attainable. Minds which can speculate on the persistency of force in all nature amid cycles

of perpetual change, on the secret undulations of light, and
the mass and velocity of stars almost infinitely remote, have
certainly powers by which they can know, and ought to
know, their Almighty Creator, and thus to echo the voice
of the Psalmist : " Be sure that the Lord, He is God ; it
is He that hath made us, and not we ourselves." They
may feel, and ought to feel, the certain truth of that
moral axiom of the Apostle : " The invisible things of
Him, from the creation of the world, are clearly seen,
being understood by the things that are made, even His
eternal Power and Godhead." And from this great fact,
as its fountain, another truth must naturally flow, that
contented ignorance of that God, in whose hand our breath
is, must be always and in all circumstances a grievous and
inexcusable folly. It is a threefold offence, against the
true dignity of man as a responsible creature, against the
bonds by which all human society is held together, and
against the authority, love, and kindness, of our Father
in heaven.

Christian Theology, in many different ways, confirms
and deepens the claim of moral truth on the minds and
consciences of men. It republishes the great facts of
man's moral nature, and of his responsibility to his Maker
and Preserver, and proclaims them anew with Divine
authority. By the voice of that law of holy love which
it clearly reveals, it awakens the conscience from its frequent slumber, and brings to light once more the secret characters once engraven there by the finger of God, but since
obscured, as in some palimpsest, by worldly habits and
selfish passions. It rescues men from that palsy of hopeless despair, which is liable to seize on them, when once
aroused from the stupor of moral indifference, and
when they see how far above their actual state is the

14—2

standard they ought to have fulfilled, of which the obligation can never cease, and feel how unable they are
to attain it by their own feeble efforts. By new and
higher motives, drawn from the revealed facts of the
gospel, it calls their moral faculties once more into
vigorous exercise, animates them with new grounds of
hope, and stirs the heart with a noble ambition to seek
for glory, honour, and immortality in the paths of humility,
obedience, faith, and Christian love. It provides tests, by
which to discover moral progress or decline, and sacred
landing-places in the ascent of the soul from lower to
higher states in the knowledge and discernment of spiritual truth, and its practical application to the guidance
of the life and the culture of the heart. The beatitudes,
for instance, are like a ladder of moral ascent and progress, of which the foot rests upon the earth in the
confession of human weakness, but the top reaches to
heaven, where the soul attains to a full resemblance of
the Divine perfection. And besides its other characters,
which make it the most powerful instrument of ethical
progress, it is one great excellency of the Christian revelation, that it provides, in every part of its inspired and
holy messages, such large and ample materials for the
illustration and practical enforcement of almost every
variety of moral truth.

But the converse is equally true, and seems to claim
a fuller development, so as to remove the suspicion which
some Christians have entertained, that Moral Philosophy
in its systematic study is a dangerous rival and adversary
of Christian faith. Such a view, however it may be pal-
liated by the unbelieving tone of some ethical speculations,
is highly unreasonable. Its acceptance, by any number
of religious men, would be a dangerous stumbling-block

in the way of simple minds. For indeed Moral Philosophy, when true and genuine, must be the spouse and ally of Christian faith, and minister in various ways to its progress and full perfection.

First of all, sound ethical teaching confirms and ratifies the grand outlines of revealed morality. It discerns in them great, fundamental, unalterable truths, applicable to mankind in every age, and in all the varying circumstances of human history, and worthy to be enforced anew by direct messages from heaven, supernaturally revealed.

It has been remarked, in a recent defence of utilitarian ethics, that the morality of consequences, to be true and sound, must include not only Epicurean, but many Stoic as well as Christian elements. Such a statement serves only to disguise the real truth. Three main elements really enter into all moral questions, and ethical systems are distinguished and contrasted by the way in which they deal with them. The first is a law or rule of right and wrong, going before; the second, the moral faculty or capacity of moral feeling and judgment, by which that law is apprehended; and the third is the discernment and anticipation of results that will practically follow from morally right or wrong conduct. The transcendental and ideal philosophy of modern times relies on the first alone, and attempts to soar out of the region of common sense and practical expediency into one of absolute, inflexible reason. The old Stoic morality of nature, and its modern counterpart, the ethics of conscience and the moral sense, dwells exclusively on the second element, or the harmony of human action with the voice of personal conscience, as a faculty properly and rightly supreme. The morality of consequences, whether in its older selfish and Epicurean form, or modified by a tacit adoption of the law of universal philanthropy, dwells on results alone. But Christian Morality includes all three elements alike, and assigns to each its due place. It exhibits, first of all, a law of essential right, which it is the duty of man to learn and apprehend for his own guidance. It recognizes, next, a faculty of moral discernment, a conscience, the eye of the soul, which needs to be kept single and pure, and neither warped by pride nor selfishness, that the whole body may be full of light. It dwells further on the truth, that the consequences of actions, soon or late, must answer to their moral character ; so that, by an inverse process, their good or evil results will serve in most cases to illustrate and confirm that ethical contrast on which they secretly depend. Thus the genuine teaching of Moral Science, and the voice of Christianity, will be found, the more closely they are examined, completely to agree.

The Bible needs to adopt no foreign element, whether Stoic or Epicurean, to complete its own ethical teaching. It contains within itself whatever is true and sound in either system, as well as in modern transcendentalism, but combines their divergent and imperfect theories in a higher unity of balanced and perfect truth. On the other hand, while it includes the elements necessary to a complete and harmonious system, it does not attempt to exhibit them in a systematic form. And thus the genuine progress of Moral Science must fulfil, towards the ethical precepts of revealed religion, a double office. It will reveal more and more the truth and consistency of those principles which underlie the whole range of Bible morality, in its high appeal to laws which are "settled in heaven," its direct challenge to the human conscience, and its constant reference to practical consequences, in life or death

in blessings and curses, that follow on well or illdoing.
But it will also develop those principles in other directions,
which do not lie within the special aim of the Christian
message. For as the Scripture records sunrise and sunset,
but does not anticipate the discoveries of Astronomical
Science, so its enforcement of great moral truths, and
of their sure consequences both in this life and the life
to come, leaves still a wide and ample range for the
reasonings and conclusions of Ethical Science, when it
traces out more fully the first principles themselves, and
applies them in fuller detail to all the countless varieties
of human character, and the vast and ever multiplying
diversities in the complex economy of human life.

Moral Science, when its first lessons are clearly apprehended, performs another service to Christian truth.
It establishes, on grounds which are unassailable, the
mournful contrast between the true ideal standard of right
conduct and the actual state of mankind. And thus it
bears witness to that great fact, which is also the fundamental doctrine of the Gospel, that the state of men
is one of sin, guilt, and unholiness, of wide departure
from the true and inflexible standard of the good and
right, and therefore calls for the intervention of some
Divine remedy. Every form of spurious morality strives
to lower the standard, in order to get rid of this mystery
of evil, so solemn and mournful, and to reduce its own
requirements nearly to the level of the habitual practice of mankind. The lowest varieties dispense with the
law of duty altogether, and make prudential selfishness
the only rule of human conduct, subject to no other
penalty than the natural results of a defective calculation. In this way, however, not only the harmony of
Morals and Christian Faith is at an end, and replaced by

direct opposition, but Ethics, as a science, having definite
objects and laws of its own, is wholly destroyed. It becomes a mere branch of arithmetic. Its problems retain
in this case no moral feature whatever. They merely
propose for solution certain equations of a very high
order, involving countless coefficients, in which not only
the quantity sought, but nearly all the coefficients by
which its value is to be determined, are equally unknown.

This harmony, however, between genuine Ethics and
the truths of Christianity, is not confined to the mere
discovery of widespread moral disease, which proves the
desirableness of some supernatural provision for its cure,
and opens the way for the disclosure of a remedial system
of grace and a Divine Physician. It extends further, to
the Incarnation, one great central doctrine of the Christian
faith.

There is much in the statement of the Gospel, that
" the Word was made flesh," and that the Supreme Creator
has been manifested in human flesh, to stagger the faith
even of devout men, and to awaken the active opposition
and incredulous disbelief of mankind, when we view it
on the side of experience or natural probabilities alone.
The question of Solomon—" Will God in very deed dwell
with men ?" presents itself here to the reflecting mind in
a startling and almost oppressive form. It can be no
matter for surprise that multitudes, not wholly incredulous, shrink from a doctrine which involves so deep a
mystery, and feel an utter disproportion between the
littleness of man and the place of our planet in the universe, and the alleged union of the Divine nature with
our own in one historical Person, who has lived and
died, like a man, among his brethren of mankind.

But here the teaching of Moral Science comes to the

aid of Christian Faith, and throws an immense weight
into the same scale, when loaded so heavily with doubts
and objections on the opposite side. For it teaches clearly
two main truths, which go far to confirm the doctrine, so
startling at first sight, and still so clearly announced in
the Scriptures. First, it assures us of the doctrine, the
secret foundation of all genuine Ethics, that the great
First Cause, the Creator and Preserver of the universe,
is a Being possessed of all moral perfection, a God of
spotless holiness and perfect love. And then it assures
us, further, that infinite condescension must be one
integral and inseparable element in our conception of
all-perfect goodness. It is true that the forms of this
condescension, and the special features it may assume,
or the moral limits that regulate its exercise when it
encounters sin and evil in its objects, are too high and
hard a problem to be solved beforehand by the guesses
of human wisdom alone. Such knowledge is too wonderful for our powers of discovery. But when revealed in
another way, the truth may be seen at once to harmonize
with the deepest and purest lessons of Ethical Science.
For goodness does not and cannot consist in selfish pride,
or in haughty isolation. True dignity does not depend on
empty state and outward show, but on moral excellence
alone. Genuine love delights in stooping to want and
sorrow. Supreme perfection can belong only to a Being
supremely gracious, and in its modes of disclosing its
Divine preeminence may be expected to surpass the dim
anticipations of our narrow minds. It is morally worthy
of the Most High to " have respect unto the lowly;" and
the starry heavens, while they reveal the glory of the
Maker, only add new emphasis to the moral beauty of
the truth, of which the Incarnation is the highest proof

and illustration, that the Lord of all worlds is mindful, with most tender love, of all the creatures of his hand.

The "unknown God" whom the Athenians ignorantly worshipped, was no other than the Father of spirits, who has revealed himself under the gospel in the person of Jesus Christ. But "the unknowable God," which some schools of modern thought offer for our acceptance under that name, is widely different. A Being, of whom nothing whatever can be known, who abides apart, like the gods of Epicurus, in solitary isolation and inaccessible mystery, never to be broken by one gleam of heavenly light, is something worse than a mere negation and intellectual void. If the great mystery of Christian faith overwhelms and dazzles us by the bright vision it presents of an infinite condescension, surpassing our largest efforts of thought to conceive its greatness, this negative theology, which pretends to replace it, is incredible for an opposite reason. It offers to us a moral paradox of the most prodigious kind. A Being of unlimited power, who still is unable or unwilling to have communion with any finite intelligence, who shrouds himself in a mystery never to be broken by one gleam of light, and leaves the world to run in one vast cycle of wearisome and perpetual change, abiding in the selfishness of an eternal isolation, can be no object of honour and esteem, much less of loving awe and holy adoration. It is a spectral vision of darkness, the moral incubus and nightmare of a deserted and desolate universe. Physical Science disclaims the doctrine as an idle, inconceivable figment. But Moral Science goes further, and proclaims this apotheosis of perfect and eternal selfishness to be hideous and impossible.

There is, in reality, no main element of Christianity, which does not find some direct support and confirmation

of its truth in the lessons of genuine Ethical Science.
For this discovers, in the light of a long and mournful
experience, the moral feebleness and impotence of man,
the wide extent of corrupt desire and wayward and
perverse action. And thus it shows the suitableness to
the wants of human nature of that great promise of the
Divine Sanctifier, the Lord and Giver of spiritual life,
which constitutes one main part of the Christian message.
It rescues the doctrine from those intellectual subtleties,
by which it has been overlaid and disguised in the many
controversies of the church, and presents it, in all its
Divine simplicity, as a truth in full and deep harmony
with the known wants of the human race, confirmed
by the history of the world in every age. It cannot of
itself resolve the hard problem, how a Being of perfect
goodness and infinite condescension may be expected to
deal with a race so morally helpless, and even perverse,
as mankind in general are proved, by long experience,
to be. But it points our thoughts in that exact direction, where the sunrise dawns upon us in the gospel,
revealing the fact of a Divine Comforter and Sanctifier,
provided by the goodness of a heavenly Father for the
urgent moral wants and necessities of mankind. It confirms, by the voice of natural conscience, gaining fresh
light in proportion as it meditates more closely on the
laws of duty, the revealed warnings of a judgment to
come. It discloses further the complete harmony between
the deepest instincts of our moral being, when once
thoroughly awakened and aroused, with its dim longing
after a moral perfection seen in the far distance and not
attained, and the great and glorious hope, revealed in
the gospel, and assured to those who receive its message
aright, of a perfect and sinless life beyond the grave. As

in water face answers to face, so do the natural instincts of the human heart respond to this voice of Divine revelation, and echo not only its warnings of future judgment, but its hope of a higher life and purer moral excellence, to be attained hereafter by all who are true and upright in heart.

Once more, Moral Science vindicates the Bible from a large class of objections, and helps to remove a fertile source of objections to its authority, while it points out, in the fact of a series of progressive revelations, a wise correspondence with the actual wants of the human race.

Wise expediency is not the sole duty of man. It is only one aspect, and neither the highest nor the noblest, of Moral Truth. But it is an aspect inseparable from the rest, and it claims the fullest prominence in the case of legislation, whether human or divine. For the main object of positive laws is to supply the want which arises from the shortsightedness of men in general, and their vice, perverseness, or moral weakness, by the higher wisdom and foresight of the lawgiver, and his freedom from the disturbing influence of mere self-interest and passion. When moral laws have to be applied to the varying circumstances of mankind from age to age, variable elements must enter into their wise application. It is thus a natural and certain corollary from the first principles of moral truth, that a revelation, to be wise, must be moulded, in part, by the actual state of those to whom it is addressed; and that, while the principles on which it is based must be firm and unchangeable as the pillars of heaven, successive modifications in the outward form of the message, far from obscuring and contradicting, only tend to confirm and establish its Divine origin.

There is no reason, then, why firm believers in Christianity should look with a jealous and unfriendly eye on the earnest cultivation of Ethical Science, and still less why the students of that science should turn aside in sceptical doubt, and with secret repugnance, from the messages of Holy Scripture. The distinction between Moral Philosophy and Christian Theology is important, and needs ever to be kept in view. But the elements of union between them are more important and vital than the partial contrasts. In the nineteenth Psalm, long ago, we have a Divine prophecy of their perfect reunion. All the voices of nature, whether of the stars in the firmament, or of natural conscience in the human heart, whenever their sound goes forth to the whole world, tend to resolve themselves into a still nobler utterance, and to lose themselves in a clearer and brighter light, the written word of God. For this proceeds originally from the same source, but, when rightly welcomed, approaches nearer and nearer in its progress to the full and perfect daylight of the better life to come.

LECTURE XI.

ON ETERNAL AND IMMUTABLE MORALITY.

FROM the spiritual geography of Moral Science, or its
relation to the various branches of knowledge which compose the great cycle of human thought, I proceed now to
consider separately some of those main elements on which
its truth and authority depend. It includes three different
aspects, the source and ground, when parted from each
other, of conflicting ethical systems, and on the union of
which, in their due order and proportion, Moral Philosophy
must be founded, if these debates are to be reconciled in
a deeper harmony. The first and highest is the objective
aspect of Morals, which recognizes an eternal law of right
and wrong, prior to the perceptions of the individual conscience, and independent of its errors; a lofty and inflexible
rule of righteousness, uncreated and everlasting, based on
the essential relations of moral agents to each other and
to their Creator, an ideal standard of perfect goodness
in all its forms, whose seat is the bosom of God, and
her voice the harmony of the world. The second is
the subjective aspect, which recognizes conscience as an
inward faculty of the soul, naturally claiming precedence
and supremacy over all the rest. It is this great fact,
which makes man "a law unto himself," bears witness to the

claims of duty, and awakens inward approval and disapproval
on the contemplation of virtuous or vicious actions in ourselves and others. The third aspect of Morals is that which
unfolds the connection between right and wrong conduct,
good or evil actions, and the wide-spreading consequences
that must naturally ensue. It is the great fact which
forms the basis of utilitarian theories of Ethical Philosophy. However defective and dangerous, when laborious
calculations of pain and pleasure are used to set aside the
law of God without, and the direct voice and authority
of conscience within, it is an element of moral reasoning
which can never be overlooked without serious peril on the
other side. A practical code, tested by experience, and
suited for the real conduct of life, would then be likely
to be displaced by some high-sounding and pretentious,
but thin, abstract, and barren theory.

Eternal and Immutable Morality is the title of a
well-known work of Dr Cudworth, a contemporary of Dr
Knightbridge, and one of the chief lights of Cambridge
two centuries ago. The objective certainty of moral truth
is there maintained with much ability and learning. But
the long delay of the publication, which took place forty
years after the author's death, when a new school of thought
had set in, and still more its scholastic style, have con-
spired to rob it of its due influence. It needs pains
and effort to separate its solid ore of thought from the
learned dust and sand in which it is almost buried. Dr
Whewell has remarked that "though always mentioned
as one of our standard works on Morals, it produces little
impression on most of those who view it as an ethical
work." One reason he assigns is that its principles are
not made to bear manifestly on moral questions, and are
too abstract and general in their form. But I conceive

that the chief cause for the want of any wide influence
is the scholastic mould into which many of the thoughts
are cast. Such a passage as the following, though a really
important and vital truth lies hid beneath its surface,
is not likely to secure a wide school of disciples in the
present day.

"It is a thing we shall easily demonstrate that moral
good and evil, just and unjust, honest and dishonest, if
they be not mere words without any significance, cannot
possibly be arbitrary things, made by will without nature;
because it is universally true that things are what they
are, not by will, but by nature. As for example, things
are white by whiteness, and black by blackness, triangular
by triangularity, and round by rotundity, like by likeness,
and equal by equality. Neither can Omnipotence itself,
to speak with reverence, by mere will make a thing white
or black without whiteness or blackness, or by mere will
make a body triangular without having the nature and
properties of a triangle in it; nor circular without the
nature of a circle, that is, a circumference equidistant
everywhere from the centre. The reason is because all
these things imply a manifest contradiction, that things
should be what they are not."

To place the subject, if possible, in a clearer and more
convincing light, it may be well to consider, first, in what
sense moral truth must be owned to be contingent, and
neither immutable nor eternal ; and next, in what sense
these high titles of honour may be fitly applied to it, and
express a view of its nature, essential to its vital influence
and practical power over the human heart.

Now here it is needful, first of all, to distinguish three
main divisions of Ethical Science, the morals of desire or
affection, of knowledge or intelligence, and of outward

action. The first of these is the subject of Pure, the third of Applied Ethics; while the second, which deals with the right conduct of the understanding in all moral subjects, holds a kind of middle place, and serves to form the transition from pure moral truth to its outward applications.

Even Pure Ethics, or the morals of internal affection and desire, involve plainly some contingent elements. They assume the existence of moral agents, with their power of choice, and mental attributes of will and desire. No laws can be in actual force, where there are no persons to whom they apply. The absolute and perfect goodness of God, the secret fountain on which all the streams of moral duty depend, and from which they flow, is so distinct in kind, and so mysterious, as scarcely to be included in the general conception of its nature. For this requires a superior, whether some person, or only a law, to which obedience is due. Now all created being is and must be contingent. Hence Morals, so far as they assume the existence of moral agents, bound by ethical laws, must be contingent also.

Morality assumes the existence, not of the moral agent alone, but also of other beings, towards whom he lies under various obligations. In all social ethics the objects of duty, as well as the agent himself, have only a contingent and not a necessary being. And thus the eternity and immutability of all moral truth of a social kind must be doubly limited, from the mutable, dependent nature of the subjects in whom it inheres, and of the objects to whom it belongs.

In the morality of the intellect other elements of contingency appear. For this class of moral duties depends on the existence of powers and capacities in the human mind, by which the good and desirable may be

B. L.   15

known, and on the actual limitations in our faculties,
which involve the need for slow and gradual progress
in the acquisition of truth of every kind. It includes
further all the special conditions in the means available
for the increase of knowledge, which may vary widely,
according to diversities in natural gifts, or in the states
of society. All these elements may introduce some corresponding diversity into the actual laws and limits of
moral obligation. Truths, fixed in themselves, may thus
be elastic and contingent in their application to real life.
How much every one is bound to learn and know, even
in moral questions, will depend in part on his own natural
powers of thought, and in part on the variable means of
progress and improvement which he may have enjoyed.
The lesson, taught by an Apostle, clearly affirms this great
principle of Ethical Science, which links human duty with
the opportunities of knowledge previously given: "To
him that knoweth to do good, and doeth it not, to him it
is sin."

In Applied Ethics the element of contingency enters
in still larger measure. Here diversities arise from all
the varieties of actual power in every moral agent. The
larger his own gifts, the fuller will be his responsibility.
All the differences which exist in the capacity of sentient
beings for pleasure and pain, all diverse experiences of
good and evil in our fellow-creatures, multiply the possible variations in the practical rule of right or wrong
action. The great law of love mounts upward, from the
lower animals to men, from subjects to rulers, from men
to angels, from creatures to God. It includes the whole
range of sentient being. But in every stage of ascent,
short of the highest, it must include many contingent
and visible elements, depending on the actual gifts of

our fellow-creatures, and the present constitution of the world in which we live.

No universe, whether natural or moral, can subsist on geometrical or necessary truths alone. Some positive law seems essential to the nature of all created being. Such are plainly the laws of attraction and cohesion in the outward and material world. In the higher field of moral activity, there need also to be positive laws of Divine appointment, which are not incapable, in their own nature, of reversal or change. Actions may be linked with certain results in a manner which all experience confirms, but which we are unable to trace to any abstract or fatal necessity. These laws may be of two kinds. Some of them may refer to the human body, and to the construction of the material world. Others are mental, and refer to the laws and associations of human thought. The murderer, who plunges a dagger into the heart of his victim, commits a hateful crime. But the essence of that crime consists in the malice and hatred, which knows that life is precious, and intends to destroy it. That this outward act should imply deep malice depends on those laws of human life which experience has revealed, and on the murderer's knowledge of the preciousness of life, and of the means by which it can be irreparably destroyed.

Morality, then, cannot be eternal and immutable, so far as it must depend, practically, on a large variety of contingent and variable elements. The positive laws which the Creator has appointed, and which enter so largely into the whole economy of human life, must have a great influence on the application of ethical rules and maxims, however deep and firm their foundations may be.

Still, when every needful concession has been made, there is a sense, deeply important, in which we may claim for moral truth, in the words of Cudworth, that it is eternal and immutable. Even in geometry, the most fixed and certain of human sciences, we must begin by assuming the existence of an outward and spatial world known to us by experience. When this assumption has been made, the relations of geometrical science necessarily follow. They are discerned as necessary, and not contingent, by the general consent of thoughtful and educated minds. Even those philosophical heretics, who strive to resolve them into arbitrary inductions of a partial experience, capable of reversal, will usually be found, in the course of their reasonings, to bear unconscious testimony to the truth they seek to disprove.

The nature of Moral Science is, in this respect, precisely the same. To prove the existence of a moral world, or of beings possessed of will and the power of choice, we must refer back to our own consciousness, and to the experience of others gradually acquired in the course of life. But when this first step has been taken, the power of choice and the sense of moral responsibility are found to be inseparable. In strict agreement with the moral faculties, as soon as their existence is recognized, thoughtful minds are compelled secretly to own that there is some standard of duty or transgression, of right and wrong, binding in its own nature on every moral agent. That standard, embodied in its simplest expression, is threefold, in reference to the threefold faculties of the reasonable mind. It is love in the desires and affections, truth in the understanding, and energy in the will. And the passions or evils which are the contrasts of these, are self-condemned; in the affections, selfishness and malice; in the understanding, ignorance, error, and delusion; and idleness and violence in the field of outward action.

This great truth, however simple in its own nature, is capable of a large and various development. It extends to an immense variety of objects through the whole range of the universe of being. It includes the Creator and all His creatures, angels and unseen spirits, as well as the human race. It comprehends all the various and complicated relations of human life; and even tho lower creatures, so far as they are capable of pain and pleasure, cannot be exempted from the circle of its just authority. It is modified by all tho immense variety of sensible, intellectual, and moral capacity for pain and pleasure, good and evil, in those who are the objects of right or wrong action from their fellows. It is further extended and varied by innumerable diversities in the conditions of moral influence, and by the differences and contrasts of spiritual condition, which experience reveals in the members of the human family, and of which dim revelations are given us, extending beyond our own limited experience to higher or more distant worlds.

The doctrine that Morals are eternal and immutable may be viewed in contrast to two main errors or falsehoods, which have widely prevailed.

And first, the truths of morality are not to be looked upon as if they were "by will, and not by nature," or arbitrary results from some appointment of the Supreme Creator. This doctrine has been held not only by philosophers but divines, who have strangely supposed that they honoured the Almighty Power of God by advancing a doctrine which makes the Divine goodness a fiction without meaning. The view has been maintained in two different forms. The first of these assigns moral distinctions in the law of right and wrong to a direct, positive appointment of God. He might have enjoined hatred instead of love, selfishness instead of kindness, falsehood and treachery instead of truth, and on the principle of these writers the obligation would equally have followed. It would have been a duty to follow in the wake of the sovereign command; so that, in their hypothetical world, to call evil good and good evil, to put darkness for light and light for darkness, instead of incurring a solemn curse and woe, would have secured and deserved a blessing.

But the same principle has been adopted and maintained, indirectly and circuitously, by some who strongly denounce it in its bare and naked form. They refer all right and wrong, for their immediate source, to certain emotions of approval or disapproval, which rise spontaneously in the human heart. But they refer this constitution itself to the category of positive ordinances of the Supreme Creator. In this way the dependence of Morals on will, and not nature, the doctrine which Cudworth condemns, after being rejected in its simpler and more naked aspect, reappears under a thin disguise.

This great oversight has a signal illustration in the ethical lectures of Dr Brown. He condemns strongly the view of some theologians, who would resolve right and wrong into the one idea of obedience or disobedience to the commands of God. If this view were just, he argues with truth, "what excellence beyond mere power could we discover in that Divine Being whom we adore as the supreme goodness? If the virtue depend exclusively on obedience to the command, He must have been equally adorable, though nature had exhibited only appearances of unceasing malevolence in its Author, and every command He had given to His creatures had been only to add new voluntary miseries to the physical miseries which already surrounded them." But in other passages he looks upon the moral feelings themselves as nothing more than an arbitrary and reversible constitution of the human heart by the Divine Creator, and writes as follows:

"Our minds have been so constituted as to have these emotions, and our inquiry leads us to the provident goodness of Him by whom we were made. God, the author of all our enjoyments, has willed us to be moral beings, for He could not will us to be happy in the noblest sense of the term without rendering us capable of practising and admiring virtue." "Virtue is a felt relation to certain emotions, NOTHING MORE. We speak always of what our mind is formed to admire or hate, not of what it might have been formed to estimate differently. The supposed immutability has regard only to the existing constitution of things under that Divine Being, who has formed our social nature what it is; and who, in thus forming it, may be considered as marking His own approbation of that virtue which we love. Such is the moderate sense of the immutability of virtue for which alone we can contend."

This indirect denial of the essential character of moral distinctions seems to me now, as it did forty years ago, no less mischievous than when the same principle is advanced in its open form. "That which defines cannot, from its very nature, become a property; and thus we cannot justly speak of the Divine Will as good, so long as we regard it as constituting of itself the final standard of right and wrong. But it is plain that we are brought equally to such a conclusion, whether we view it as directly propounding itself for such a standard, or as implanting feelings arbitrarily, to which it afterward refers. The path leads by a longer circuit, but the issue is the same.

Indeed, when searched narrowly, the difference is only that a sense of deception, painful to entertain for a moment, aggravates the evil of the former view. The contrast is the same as between the sway of an arbitrary sovereign, who should claim obedience on the sole ground of his power; and one who should claim further the praise of his subjects for governing with the sanction of a senate of his own appointing, blindly and tamely subservient to his will. Yet surely this would be a faithful emblem of the Divine government, could we conceive the moral emotions to be of mere arbitrary appointment, and liable to be reversed at will, so that what we now condemn as evil we might in such a case have been brought to praise as good. From such a view the mind recoils even more than from the former, and takes refuge in the expostulation of the Psalmist: 'Shall the throne of iniquity have fellowship with thee, which frameth mischief by a law?'"

Again, Morals are eternal and immutable in this further sense, that they do not depend for their truth and certainty on the caprice, the ignorance, or the moral diseases, of those who are subject to their authority.

Pleasures are of many kinds. They may either be pure and healthy, or vicious and diseased. And hence, if moral duty depends on a mere summation of pleasures, and an attempted calculation of their total amount, irrespective of any higher standard, it must be as mutable as those pleasures themselves, which form its component elements. No chain can be stronger than its weakest link. In the view of pure utilitarianism, when the doctrine abides in its native simplicity, and is neither infected nor improved by an attempt to ally it with Stoic or Christian elements, moral right must be as mutable as the capricious likings and dislikings of the most fretful, the

most childish, or the most vicious among those who are
included in the wide universe of moral agents. It may be
inferred logically, from the principle thus laid down, that
it is as much one part of moral duty to gratify the lusts of
the impure, or the malice of the devilish, as to please the
pure and the benevolent, and win the approval of the best
and wisest of mankind.

Still further, moral truth is eternal and immutable,
because it depends very partially, and in only a limited
sense, on those variable elements, which enter into all the
experience of human life, and diversify the great laws of
duty in their outward application. Truths, however fixed
and sure in themselves, contract a seeming variableness
when they are wedded to those facts, derived from experience and testimony alone, which do vary continually.
The principle extends to every department of applied
science. The truths of pure arithmetic are fixed and
irreversible, but the data of statistical science are dependent on the accuracy of human observation and memory,
or the veracity of human testimony. And the same
principle must clearly apply to the higher subject of
ethics. There is and must be large room for the exercise
of a wise expediency, based on actual experience, when
the general doctrines of moral science are brought to bear,
in detail, on the actual wants and business of life. The
courses of the stars in the sky are fixed and stedfast in
their own nature. But when their light shines on the
troubled ocean, or even on the calm and peaceful lake
that sleeps amidst the hills, the image fluctuates and
trembles with every breath of wind that creates a passing
ripple or wavelet on the face of the waters.

The treatise of Cudworth, however encumbered with
scholastic forms of thought, which detract in some measure

from its value, contains some important truths, vital to the integrity of moral science, and no less seasonable at the present hour than when the learned writer first gave them utterance.

And first he maintains earnestly, and with real force of reasoning, that moral distinctions are no creation or appointment of arbitrary power, but are founded essentially on the nature of responsible agents, and of all created being. Descartes had laid down the opposite principle, that the Divine Omnipotence implied the dependence of all things, the truths of geometry, and the distinctions of right and wrong, on some fiat of almighty power, and that "no good or evil can be conceived, of which any idea was in the Divine intellect, before the will of God determined to make it such as it is." On this view Cudworth observes as follows:

"If the natures and essences of all things depend upon a will of God that is essentially arbitrary, there can be no such thing as science or demonstration; nor can the truth of any mathematical or metaphysical proposition be known otherwise than by some revelation of the will of God concerning it, and a certain fanatic faith and persuasion thereupon, that God would have such a thing to be true or false for such a time, or so long. And so nothing would be true or false naturally, but only positively, all truth and science being arbitrarious things. Neither would there be any moral certainty in the knowledge of God himself, since it must wholly depend on the mutability of a will in Him essentially indifferent and undetermined."

"As for the argument that, unless the essences of things, and all truths and falsehoods, depend on the arbitrary will of God, there would be something independent of God, if it be well considered it will prove a mere bug-bear. For no other genuine consequence is deducible from this assertion, but that there is an eternal and immutable wisdom in the mind of God, and thence participated by created beings, independent of the will of God. Now the wisdom of God is as much God as the will of God; and whether of these two is best conceived to depend on the other, will be determined from their nature. For wisdom hath in itself the nature of a rule and measure, as a most determinate and inflexible thing; but will being, as considered in itself, indefinite and indeterminate, has the nature of a thing regulable and measurable. Wherefore it is the perfection of will, as such, to be guided by wisdom and truth. But to make wisdom, knowledge, and truth to be arbitrarily determined by will, and regulated by such a plumbean and flexible rule, is quite to destroy the nature of it. Now all the knowledge and wisdom that is in creatures, whether angels or men, is nothing else but a participation of that one eternal, immutable, uncreated wisdom of God, or like so many reflections of one face made in several glasses, whereof some are clearer, some more obscure, some standing nearer, others farther off."

"Moreover, it was the opinion of the wisest of the philosophers that there is in the scale of being a nature of goodness, superior to wisdom, which therefore measures and determines the wisdom of God, as His wisdom measures and determines His will. Wherefore, though some make a contracted idea of God, consisting of nothing else but will and power, yet His nature is better expressed by others in the mystical representation of an infinite circle, whose inmost centre is simple goodness, the rays and area, all-comprehending and immutable wisdom, the exterior periphery or circumference, omnipotent will or

activity, by which everything without God is brought forth
into existence. Wherefore the will and power of God
have no command inwardly on the wisdom and knowledge
of God, or on the moral disposition of His nature, which is
essential goodness ; but the sphere of its activity is without
God, where it hath absolute command on the existences
of things; and is always free, though not always indifferent, since it is its highest perfection to be determined
by infinite wisdom and infinite goodness."

His remarks on the hypothesis of some writers,
agreeing nearly with that of Protagoras, that nothing
can be known as absolutely true, but only on the assumption that our faculties are rightly made, have a
striking application to some later speculations, which
deny that any knowledge is attainable of "things in
themselves."

"If we cannot be certain of the truth of any thing,
but only *ex hypothesi*, that our faculties are rightly
made, of which none can have any certain assurance but
only He that made them, then all created minds whatsoever must be condemned to eternal doubt. Neither
ought they ever to assent to any thing as certainly true,
since all their truth and knowledge is but relative to
their faculties, arbitrarily made, that may possibly be
false, and their clearest apprehensions nothing but perpetual delusions. Wherefore, according to this doctrine,
we have no absolute certainty of the first principles of
all our knowledge, as that equals added to equals produce
equals, or that every number is either odd or even. We
cannot be sure of any mathematical or metaphysical
truth, or of the existence of God or of ourselves."

"For whereas some would prove the truth of their
faculties from hence, because there is a God whose nature

is such that He cannot deceive, this is nothing but a circle, and makes no progress. For all the certainty they have of the existence of God and of His nature depends upon the arbitrary make of their faculties; which, for aught they know, may be false. Nay, according to this doctrine, no man can certainly know that there is any absolute truth in the world at all. And this is very strange to assert, that God cannot make a creature which shall be able certainly to know either the existence of God, or of himself, or whether there be any absolute truth or no."

"The ultimate resolution of theoretical truth, and the only criterion of it, is in the clearness of the apprehensions themselves, and not in any supposed blind and unaccountable make of faculties. So that the certainty of clear apprehensions is not to be derived from the contingent truth of faculties, but the goodness of faculties to be tried by the clearness and distinctness of apprehension. For to suppose that faculties may be so made, as to create apprehensions of things that are not, is much like that opinion of some, that all the new celestial phenomena, as of the Jovian planets, and the mountains in the moon, are no real things; but that the clear, diaphanous crystal of the telescopes may be so cut, ground, and polished, as to make all those clearly to appear to sense, when there is no such thing."

"It is a fond imagination to suppose that it is derogatory to the glory of God, to bestow or impart any such gift upon His creatures as knowledge is, which hath an intrinsic evidence in itself... It cannot be denied that men are often deceived, and think they clearly comprehend what they do not. But it does not follow, that they can never be certain that they do clearly comprehend anything; which is just as if we should argue, because in our dreams we think we have clear sensations, we cannot therefore ever be sure, when we are awake, that we see things as they really are."

This doctrine of Cudworth, when rightly explained, and freed from exaggerations which disguise its true sense, that moral truths, or the contrasts of good and evil, of right and wrong, of duty and transgression, are fixed, eternal, and immutable in their own nature, and no mere product of animal instinct or prudential arithmetic, no arbitrary creation of an absolute will, lies at the foundation of all Ethical Science. Whenever it is set aside, Moral Philosophy expires, and nothing but a lifeless corpse or shadowy phantom is left in its stead. Wherever the attempt is made, and gains a wide acceptance, to replace it by truths of a lower kind, drawn from the discoveries of physiology, or the calculations of worldly prudence, the fountains of thought are poisoned, and a moral palsy must quickly seize on all the springs of national and social life. The warning of Him, who is the true Light of the world, applies to every variety of moral speculation, which impinges on the firm, granite-like foundations that underlie the superficial varieties of ethical teaching :—"If the light that is in thee be darkness, how great is the darkness!"

It is a great evil to neglect the monitions of conscience, to silence its calm and secret whispers through the power of vice and selfish passion, and to give the reins, in practice, to the lowest instincts of the human heart. But the evil is far greater, and still more deeply to be deplored, when selfishness is turned into an ethical theory; or when uncertain guesses, in physiology, on the resemblances between man and other animals, are made the excuse for denying conscience altogether, and replacing

it by the instinctive craving of men or beasts not to be
shut out from the company of their fellows, or by the
fear of slaves who dread the lash, and shrink from the
penalties of human law through dislike of suffering alone.
The logical defect in all such theories is no less striking
than the moral degradation to which they inevitably lead.
Their advocates need to pass over in silence the very
point on which the whole science of morals really depends.
The human animal has acquired, in some way or other, a
liking for society. But how can the mere indulgence of
a social instinct awaken any sense of moral approval?
There are many cases in which a refusal to indulge it, and
an abstinence from social intercourse in forms diseased or
excessive, may be one test and sign of real virtue.

> For Wisdom's self
> Oft seeks to sweet retired solitude,
> Where, with her best nurse' Contemplation,
> She plumes her feathers, and lets grow her wings,
> That in the various bustle of resort
> Were all too ruffled, and too much impaired.

Again, the stage may easily be reached of dreading
the punishments of social law, and striving to escape
from them either by obedience or by concealment. But
how is this instinctive dread, too often the parent of
fraud, falsehood, and cunning, to rise into the dignity of
heroic virtue? Only when, in the voices of human law,
the soul catches dim echoes of some far-off music from a
higher sphere. And, supposing that a perfect calculation
of the results of every action, both pleasant and painful,
could be made, how can this sum in arithmetic be raised
from its own to a higher level, and be made to infer a
moral conclusion, a lesson of right and wrong? Why
ought we to prefer the integral to its own differential, the

collective series to its first and nearest term? How am I
to know that it is right, and a moral duty, to trust my
calculation, and stifle the instinctive desire for a present
and immediate enjoyment, when the rightness and excellence of pleasure is the basis and postulate of the whole
calculation? We cannot rise, without the gift of reason,
from mere animal instinct to intelligent prudence, and
foresight of the distant future. And without the gift of
conscience, or some power of reason to discern a law of
good and right binding on the soul by its own authority,
we can never mount from the lower level of mere prudence to the sense of duty and moral obligation. The
great truths which form the objects of Moral Philosophy
are no mere gas-lights of earth. They are stars which
shine down upon us from the upper firmament. Their
light may too often be clouded and obscured by the mists
of earth, and lost for a time from our view. But let the
mists be dispersed, and they shine out once more, pure
and bright as in the first infancy of the world. And
when we follow their sacred guidance, they lead our
thoughts upward from this land of strife and shadow
where we have often to walk in darkness, to a region of
light, purity, and peace, the ante-chamber of His palace
who sits enthroned in the beauty of holiness without
stain, and goodness without measure, above the water-
floods for evermore.

LECTURE XII.

THE NATURE AND OFFICE OF CONSCIENCE.

THE doctrine of Conscience forms the subjective element of Moral Science. It holds a middle place between that aspect of the truth, which dwells on moral laws or principles as fixed in their own nature, immutable and eternal, and that doctrine of consequences, which traces out the connection between the moral character of actions, and results which either may be reasonably expected to follow, or do really follow. The first, when separated from the others, tends to a dreamy, unpractical idealism, the second to a self-satisfied, capricious individualism, the third to a cold, selfish, calculating, mechanical expediency. It is only when the relation of the three principles to each other is apprehended in its real harmony and proportion, that ethical speculation can be freed from the risk of serious evils.

Some of the main questions which may be started respecting the place of conscience in a moral theory are these. First, what is its nature and true meaning? Next, what are the extent and proper limits of its authority? Thirdly; is it capable or incapable of right education? Lastly, if capable of it, on what must its sound and healthy training depend, and what is the external standard which it requires for its guidance?

There are four doctrines, distinguishable from each other, which have been held respecting the nature of conscience. The first views it as an instinct of the animal nature, developed and transformed; the second, as a separate sense or faculty, analogous to the senses of the body, a special and arbitrary endowment of the human mind; the third, as a power of prudential calculation, linking itself, by association of ideas, with strong emotions of hope and fear; the fourth, as the reason itself, exercised on truths of a special kind, or the moral relations between intelligent agents. On this view the distinction is not so much in the faculty itself, as in the character of those truths with which the mind is occupied, whenever we speak of the working of conscience, and the moral emotions of the heart.

The first view of conscience may be dismissed in few words. It has been thus expounded in a recent work. "Man cannot avoid looking backward, and comparing the impressions of past events and actions. He also looks continually forward. Hence, after some temporary desire or passion has mastered his social instincts, he will reflect and compare the now weakened impression of such past impulses with the ever present social instinct, and he will then feel that sense of dissatisfaction which all unsatisfied instincts leave behind them. Consequently he resolves to act differently for the future, and this is conscience. Any instinct which is permanently stronger or more enduring than another gives rise to a feeling, which we express by saying that it ought to be obeyed."

It is strange how such an explanation of conscience or moral emotion can have found acceptance with any thoughtful mind. It assumes the existence in man of those powers of meditation on the remote past and distant future, which distinguish him from mere animals, and constitute him a reasonable being, susceptible of moral laws; and it then proceeds to account for moral emotions, apart from any higher truth, or any relation to these specially human faculties, by the effect of animal instinct alone. Does then every strong impulse, often yielded to, create the sense of a moral obligation? Is it not the voice at once of a frequent experience, and of the deepest philosophy, which is expressed in the words of the Apostle, "The good that I would I do not, and the evil I would not, that I do"? The yielding to a social instinct, which has been violently thwarted, is an impulse of the animal life, but no act of duty; and, standing alone, has no moral character whatever. It needs, in the phrase of Professor Grote, to be "moralized," by the inquiry,—"Is it right or wrong for me to satisfy this instinct? Is it one which ought to be followed, or resisted and controlled?" Only after such a decision does the act assume a really moral character. Feelings of malevolence, in our actual world, are often very strong and very enduring. The Indian will mark his victim for death, and pursue him for years with undeviating aim and unrelenting malice. Does this warrant the conclusion that the instinct is very strong, and therefore ought to be obeyed? Strength and Force, in the old Greek legend, were the servants of Zeus, by whom Prometheus was bound, but the heathen poet never dreamt of exalting them into the parents of all virtue. He looked on them, rather, as the most fitting impersonations of blind, servile obedience to arbitrary and despotic power. It is neither the strength of an instinct, nor its frequent recurrence, which the human mind, unless demoralized by vice or false philosophy, will dignify with a righteous character, and pronounce that it

16—2

"ought to be obeyed." That strain is of a higher mood. That voice speaks of a higher element in man's being than animal instinct, or the craving for society alone. It is a response and echo, within the soul, to a voice that speaks to it from above. It bears witness to the great truth that man is not merely a magnificent specimen of zoology, but a being only a little lower than the angels, created at first in the image of the invisible and eternal God.

The opinion, which looks upon the conscience as a moral sense, resembling those of the body, or a distinct and peculiar faculty of the mind, deserves a fuller notice. This is the view of Lord Shaftesbury in his *Inquiry concerning Virtue,* and in the *Characteristics,* as well as of Dr Hutcheson, and in substance it seems to be shared by Butler also. "The mind," says Lord S., "observes not only things, but actions and affections. The mind which is thus spectator and auditor of other minds cannot be without its eye and ear, so as to discern proportion, distinguish sound, and scan each sentiment or thought which comes before it." "The true spring of Virtue," observes Hutcheson, "is some determination of our nature to study the good of others, or some instinct which influences us to the love of others, as the moral sense determines our approval." The phrase is based on a true analogy. But, as employed by the writers who introduced it and made it widely current, the truth it implied was mingled with a serious defect. A concrete, positive, and arbitrary character was thus assigned to all our moral emotions and decisions, as if they depended on our being created, through an act of Divine sovereignty, with a sense or faculty of this peculiar kind.

Dr Brown condemns in words the theory of the "Moral

Sense," but adopts substantially the very same view. He writes as follows :

"The great error of Dr Hutcheson and others, who treat of the susceptibility of moral emotion under the name of the moral sense, appears to me to consist in their belief of certain moral qualities in actions, which excite in us what they consider as ideas of those qualities, in the same manner as external things give us, not merely pain or pleasure, but notions or ideas of hardness, form, and colour. It is on this account the great champion of this doctrine professes to regard the moral principle as a sense; from its agreement with what he conceives to be the accurate definition of a sense—'a determination of the mind to receive any idea from the presence of an object, which occurs to us independent of our will.' What he terms an idea, in this case, is nothing more than an emotion, considered in its relation to the action which has excited it. A certain action is considered by us, a certain emotion arises. There is no idea but of the agent himself, and of the circumstances in which he was placed, and the physical changes produced by him, and our ideas of these we owe to other sources. To the moral principle, the only principle of which Hutcheson could mean to speak as a moral sense, we owe the emotion itself, and nothing but the emotion."

Here, as in several other instances, Dr Brown, while professing to detect and remove an error, retains it, and makes it greater than before. "Susceptibility of moral emotion," when compared with "the moral sense," is a more cumbrous and circuitous, and certainly not a more distinct or intelligible phrase. We might call the power of eyesight "a susceptibility of physical emotion from visible objects," but in so doing we should neither improve our style, nor add to the clearness of our conception. The doctrine of a moral sense has its strong and its weak side. Its strength consists in the doctrine that there are moral truths or relations without us, in moral agents and their conduct, which have a certain analogy to the relations of outward objects to each other, perceived by the senses; that these relations are equally true with the other, and that we have a sense or faculty whereby they are perceived. Its weakness consists in the notion that the conscience is a special organ or faculty, like the eye or ear of the body, constructed or implanted for this especial purpose, as the eye for noting form and colour, and the ear for sounds, and in seeming to press this partial analogy so far as to overlook an important contrast. For certainly our perception of rightness or wrongness in actions, and of virtuous or vicious character, is not exactly of the same kind as our sensation that honey is sweet, that fire burns, and ice is cold.

Now Dr Brown seems to oppose or abandon that aspect of Hutcheson's and Shaftesbury's view, which forms its strength, and adopts and amplifies its weakness. The term, sense, may suggest the notion either of truths or facts without us, which we are able to perceive, or of some present, transient sensation and feeling alone. Dr Brown rests his ethical theory on the latter view of the subject. We have certain emotions, however they may arise. We have strong feelings of liking for some actions, and disapproval of others. So far we can go, but no further. Vice, virtue, merit, demerit, obligation, duty, eternal truth, Divine law, are all pronounced to be one and the same fact variously disguised, a susceptibility of the emotions of moral approbation and disapprobation. By this view the subject is said to be freed from much superfluous argument. But the simplicity is of the same kind, as if we strove to replace all the reasonings and conclusions of geometry, and the wide range of geographical and astronomical discovery, by reducing them all to floating, transient impressions of daylight and colour produced in individual minds. We must first see, before we can observe and discover. We must have a sensation of sound through the ear, before we can arrive at a science of acoustics, or drink in the rich and complex varieties of human speech and musical harmony. There could be no moral science if we were not capable of seeing in our actions, or those of others, those moral features which awaken feelings of shame and indignation, or else of approval, sympathy, and praise. But the very first step of real progress consists in freeing our thoughts from dependence on the fact of the present sensation, and in rising to the apprehension of some abiding truth, which does not cease to exist when we cease to observe it, or perversely turn away from it, but abides unchanged amidst the confusion and uncertainty of our human experience. The analogy of the moral perceptions with those of the eye and the ear, though it needs to be carefully limited, is real and important. But in either case the path of true wisdom is to rise from the subjective sensation to the perception of abiding realities; and then to dwell upon these in quiet thought, till they are freed more and more from transient and accidental circumstances, and stand revealed to us in the calm grandeur of eternal truth.

Others, again, see in conscience only a faculty of prudential calculation, which has to deal with a large problem of the consequences of actions, and learns by habit to associate particular lines of conduct with the fear of punishment and the hope of praise and reward. But while such an estimate of probable future results may supply the materials to guide our actions, as well as our feelings of moral desire and approval, it must still be plain to those who reflect on the course of their own thoughts, or who study carefully the reasonings of utilitarian theorists, that the moral element in all these cases has to be supplied from some other source, and cannot be created by a process of calculation alone. The duty of seeking the greatest good, whether of ourselves or the whole family of mankind, must first be assumed, before we can enter on the addition and subtraction of pains and pleasures, and propose to ourselves, as an aim and object of desire, "the greatest happiness of the greatest number." Once assume benevolence, on the widest scale, to be an imperative duty, a voice of heaven, in some way or other, to the heart of man, and then the laborious attempt to decide what on the whole is best to be done, and ought to be done, may be entered upon with real earnestness, however imperfect the success may be. But until this principle has been assumed, we may have, instead of world-wide benevolence, the mere self-conceit of cold-hearted theorists, who deceive themselves into the notion that they are moral reformers, and are bestowing great benefits on mankind by their fancied skill in a new arithmetic, when they are really indulging the pride of a false philosophy, and undermining the foundations of all genuine morality.

The fourth and last view of conscience is that which looks upon it as no separable faculty, but simply as a name for reason, or the mind itself, when it is occupied with truths of one especial kind. Its supremacy will thus be no arbitrary gift, but result directly from the perceived supremacy of those laws of right and wrong and moral obligation with which it has to deal. It is well defined by Dr Calderwood: "Conscience is that power of mind, by which moral law is discovered to each individual for the guidance of his conduct. It is the reason, as that which discovers to us absolute moral truth, having the authority of sovereign moral law. It is an essential requisite for the direction of an intelligent agent, gifted with free will, and affords the basis for moral obligation and responsibility in human life. In discovering truth, it is seen to be a cognitive or intellectual power. Either it does not discover truth, or if it does, it is not a form of feeling, or combination of feelings, emotions, or desires. Truth is that which we see, and implies seeing power. Moral law is that which we can know, and implies knowing power. The authority of conscience is an abbreviated form for expressing the authority which is common to all the laws of morality. In affirming its authority over the other powers of the mind, we merely indicate that moral law is authoritative for the regulation of all the other motives and restraining forces which operate within our human nature."

The same view of the nature of conscience has been already affirmed by me in another work.

"It may be allowable, as a figure of rhetoric, to speak of conscience as a judge, which holds its court within the soul, and pronounces its judgment on all the lower faculties. But such metaphors, when constantly used, are liable to create a serious delusion. Conscience is simply the mind itself, exercising its judgment on the moral relations of right and wrong, on its own actions and the actions of others. Its supremacy over other faculties is merely a varied expression for the truth, that the relations the mind contemplates, when its acts receive this name, are in their own nature of binding authority, and claim allegiance and submission. In its other actings the mind contemplates things equal or inferior to itself, or superior beings, irrespective of any claim to actual dominion and supremacy. But the laws of moral duty are royal laws in their own nature, and speak with the voice of a king; and the judgments of the mind, in which it recognizes them, must partake of the same character. Thus the supremacy of conscience depends entirely on the distinctive nature of moral truth; but its defects, weakness, and error, are due to the mind itself, and are one form of its moral guilt and infirmity. Its dictates are binding so far as they are genuine reflections of eternal truth, or of real moral relations perceived by the soul. But the mistakes of conscience have no more real authority than any other kind of error. They have this peculiar nature, that they make sin inevitable. In obeying them, man sins against the laws of God; in disobeying them, against his own convictions of duty, and the internal harmony of his moral being."

On a just view of the nature of conscience must depend the answer to the question, what are the extent and proper limits of its authority? Is it supreme in any sense? And if so, is it absolutely or only relatively supreme?

"The high honour" has been claimed for Bp. Butler "of establishing the supremacy of conscience." And he certainly lays it down with great clearness and force in these well-known words.

"That principle by which we survey and either approve or disapprove our own heart, temper and actions, is not only to be considered as what is in its turn to have some influence, which may be of every passion, and the lowest appetites; but likewise as being superior, as from

its very nature manifestly claiming superiority over all the
others; insomuch that you cannot form a notion of this
faculty, conscience, without taking in judgment, direction,
superintendency. This is a constituent part of the idea
of the faculty, and to preside and govern, from the very
constitution of men, belongs to it. Had it strength as it
has right, had it power as it has manifest authority, it
would absolutely govern the world." (Serm. II. p. 36.)

This claim, however, of conscience to the governing
office, and a rightful authority over all the powers and
actions of mind and body, seems too plainly involved
in its nature, and too elementary a truth, to be rightly
assigned to any modern author as his own discovery.
All that Bp. Butler could do was to reassert a familiar
truth, involved in the very conception of a moral law,
and its apprehension by the mind of man. He has unfolded it in contrast with one special form of immoral
reasoning, which would set up a democratic equality of
all the desires of the mind, or appetites of the body,
simply because they exist. Such a republication of old
truths in some varied aspect, to meet fresh phases of
error, may be very important in its place. But we honour
the moralist at the expense of the great science with
which he deals, when we represent its fundamental data
to be so obscure as to have been first discovered in modern
times. These truths are old as the creation. The supremacy of the moral law, on which that of conscience
wholly depends, is revealed in the books of Moses, long
ages ago, more clearly and powerfully than in the sermons
of Butler, or in the treatises of heathen or Christian
moralists of later times.

The authority, it has been well observed, "is not
found in the nature of the faculty itself. The faculty is

a power of sight, such as makes a perception of self-evident truth possible to man, and contributes nothing to the truth which is perceived.   To the truth itself belongs inherent authority, that is, absolute right to command, not force to constrain."

The supremacy, then, of conscience is limited and relative, not absolute.   The eye does not create the landscape on which it gazes.   Neither does the individual conscience create the moral truths it contemplates, or clothe them with their claim to obedience and honour. The precepts of genuine morality, natural or revealed, are of direct and immediate obligation.   They bind, because they exist, and are the voice of God.   They can be felt to be binding, and guide the practice, only so far as their authority is accepted, and their true meaning discerned. A personal conviction with regard to our own duty neither adds to their authority, nor creates the obligation to obey; just as an image on the retina does not really intervene between the eye and the landscape, but is only the necessary condition, from the structure of the eye, on which healthy vision depends.

Is the conscience, as a faculty of the mind, capable of education and training?   To this question Dr Calderwood, whose definition I have quoted, gives a negative answer. In this he dissents, as he owns, from many authors with whom he substantially agrees in other things, as Reid, Dugald Stewart, and Dr Whewell, but quotes Kant on the other side.   Conscience, he says, from its very nature, cannot be educated.   Education in the sense of training is impossible.   As well propose to teach the eye how and what to see, and the ear how and what to hear, as teach reason how to perceive the self-evident, and what truths are of this nature.   All this has been provided for in the human constitution. And he then quotes with approval the strange dictum of Kant, that "an erring conscience is a chimera." (Cald. *Handbook*, p. 81.)

The assertion of Dr Whewell, here condemned, is perfectly true, and the opposite statement an error surprising in an author of such clear good sense and ability. No doubt, if we begin by confining the name of conscience to the sound and healthy conclusions of the mind on moral questions, to its clear and distinct vision of spiritual truth, or its perfect insight into the course of practical duty, then all need of training is excluded by the definition. But the definition itself will then degenerate into a barren truism. The mind needs no training to judge rightly, wherever right judgment is already attained. It needs no increase of light, where it already sees clearly. But this is neither the popular, nor yet the scientific meaning of the word. We certainly do not mean by conscientious convictions those which are infallibly right, but simply those which are honestly entertained. A person follows his conscience when he does what he sincerely thinks to be his duty, though he may have mistaken his duty, and acted on a wrong judgment. To the authority of Kant, whose paradoxes on this subject are many, we may oppose the far higher authority of the inspired Apostle, himself the most intensely conscientious of men,—"To them that are defiled and unbelieving is nothing pure, but even their own heart and conscience are defiled."

The illustration to which the appeal is made proves the exact converse. The eye does need to be trained, as in the case of the sailor, to discern distant objects, or as with the artist and his disciples, to catch the features of some magnificent landscape; and the ear is capable of and needs much training, to receive the more delicate distinctions and harmonics of sound. Neither organ would admit of training at all, if the sense were wholly wanting, as in the deaf and the blind. But those who are dim of sight and dull of hearing may do much, by artificial helps, to remedy, and in some cases to remove, their natural infirmity, while careful training how and what to observe is an apprenticeship required in almost every field of scientific inquiry.

I venture, then, with all confidence, to reverse the statement I have quoted above, which rests only on a deceptive limitation in the use of a familiar term. Conscience is a faculty which, like the eye and the ear, does require education, but for more urgent reasons, and to still nobler ends. The Apostle speaks of those who "by reason of use have their senses exercised to discern good and evil." Eyes, which are suddenly brought out of thick darkness, cannot at once bear the full light of clear noonday. They must first be shielded from excess of light, and gradually taught to use their newly acquired possession. For sight, though we speak of it under the name of intuition, to denote what is most immediate and spontaneous in the action of the mind, is really the integral of an immense number of experiences gradually acquired. We see the book, the room, the landscape before us. The perception is swift, like the motion of that light which is the medium of vision, with its billions of vibrations in a single second. But it is really the summation of countless elements of knowledge, in which form, colour, perspective, distance, natural properties, the indications of sight, sound, touch, smell, are all fused and blended into one harmonious whole. And in each direction the sense is capable, by diligent use, of further development. The geologist sees much in every

stone, or layer of earth, or mountain escarpment, the
naturalist in every plant, or beast, or bird, which does not
meet the eye of the common observer. Rich and various
associations of every kind gather around the objects, on
which the eye rests with fond and deepening interest.
Our minds, taught through the senses, lend to nature
its wedding garment or its shroud, while they perceive
the sad and joyful associations with which every scene
is peopled by thoughtful and intelligent observers. The
senses do not create, as the bee does not create the honey
which it sucks from innumerable flowers. But they lay
in growing stores by constant diligence of observation.

Conscience is the eye of the soul. If it be single and
upright, the whole moral being will be filled with light.
By wakeful vigilance it makes continual accessions to
the soul's perception of truth. The landscape is wide
and various. Every part of it yields new treasures to
the observer, in proportion as he gazes more thoughtfully
on the objects submitted to his view. In its first and
early stage of activity, when it is like a child still ignorant
of the outward world, or a prisoner just escaped from
some dark cell, it may scarcely be able to see at all, and
may need the help of others more experienced, or higher
in moral attainment, before it can detect a thousand
features of the objects which lie plainly before it. But
the truths contemplated are real, fixed, and abiding truths.
The power of the mind, by which it discerns them, is a
noble gift of God, a faculty which may be dulled and
clouded by vice and sensuality, but is never wholly and
hopelessly withdrawn. And the constant training of that
faculty, by use and exercise, to fulfil the solemn duties
confided to it, is not only possible, but highly expedient,
and itself a primary moral duty of ceaseless obligation.

Whoever has no longing for clearer insight into the laws of righteousness, and does not strive at all for their fuller apprehension and practical attainment, must be sinking into a moral lethargy, the dangerous precursor of disease and death.

But if the conscience is capable of education, and requires to be exercised and trained, how is this great end to be secured? Where shall we find a standard, to which the appeal can be made? How are we to detect deviations from this standard, and raise the conscience, when subject' to illusion, distortion, or paralysis, to a higher level? This is clearly a question of the greatest practical importance. For though Kant may have uttered the paradox, that "an erring conscience is a chimera," unless the laws of language deceive us on the one side, or the lessons of universal experience on the other, an erring conscience has been, in every age of the world, the most fruitful parent of strife, passion, warfare, and every variety of human folly and crime.

That school of ethical teachers, who would lay the foundations of morals in some recent discoveries or guesses of modern anatomy and physiology, call loudly on the independent or ideal moralist to produce a standard, which on their principles it is impossible to find. Where, they ask, is this rule to be found? "What is the standard conscience? That must be got at, or morality is not a subject to be reasoned or written about...We have standards of length, of weight, of measure, which, even though embodied in material objects, can hardly be said to have the independence contended for...When we are called upon to set our watches by Greenwich time, it is not a standard beyond humanity. The collective body of astronomers have agreed on a mode of reckoning, founded on the still more general recognition of the solar day as the principal unit. At Greenwich observatory observations are made, which determine the standard of this country; and the population, in accepting that standard, know or may know that they are following the Astronomer Royal, and the body of astronomers generally."

To this challenge Professor Maurice gives a partial and indirect reply by an appeal to two fictitious characters, Tennyson's *Northern Farmer*, haunted by strange death-bed scruples, and Tito in *Romola*. He infers from these excursions of fancy, in its truest and most faithful pictures of human life, that conscience is a fact and not a fiction, however hard its proper standard may be to find. But I think we may go considerably further and find, in those very illustrations from science to which the objector appeals, some real help to remove the phantoms of hopeless doubt and uncertainty which are raised by the necromancy of false theories, to crowd around our path, and hinder our clear perception of moral truths.

And first, how is it that, even in the business of daily life, we need standards of length, weight, and measure? Surely this is a sign, in itself, that men in all their social activity need some common, objective truth, to which all may appeal. They must have measures free from the caprice, the ignorance, and the perverted selfishness, of the individual buyer or seller, or else the wheels of commerce would stick fast in the mire, and the business of life come almost to an end. We thus escape from the vague guess-work of barbarous times, in which every man's arm or foot was his own standard, and attain something firmer, more definite, and more exact. And the standard is better, not because many conspire to receive it, but for a more solid reason. Patient skill and thought have been employed,

to get rid, as far as possible, of the sources of error, to
secure the best materials for the rod with which other
lengths are compared, to guard against possible flexure, to
allow for changes of temperature, and approach nearer and
nearer to an ideal of fixity, which science teaches us, after
all, we have not perfectly attained, while it no less plainly
assures us of the reality and closeness of the approximation.

But these standards, it is objected, are arbitrary in
their own nature, however superior to the rules and measures they may have displaced. And the reason is plain.
Length, solid capacity, weight and time, have no absolute
unit. They are matters, not of pure reason, but of practical observation and experiment. They stretch out con-
tinuously between zero and the infinite. Before we can
compare them, a unit must be assumed in every case, and
the choice is a matter of convenience, custom, and usage
alone. The relation of the series of numbers to the dimensions of space, the force of gravity, and the sequence of
time, is not fixed but variable. . It belongs to the province,
not of absolute reason, but of intelligent will. The relations of numbers, in themselves, are fixed and unalterable.
We cannot even conceive them to be reversed. So are
also the relations of space and figure, of force and time.
But the link which connects the first with all the rest
does not belong to the category of pure reason, but is borrowed from the domain of positive appointment, and of
human choice and will.

Even here, when once the choice has been made, there
is a ceaseless effort of science to eliminate error, and attain
a standard of ideal perfection. The first aim is to secure
that every copy shall agree with the original standard,
at least within limits practically insensible in the business of life. This could not be done, if lengths, weights,

measures, intervals, because each involves one arbitrary
unit, were in themselves capricious and arbitrary things.
The yard, the metre, the pound, the gramme, and in fresh
branches of science the units of work and of electric ten-
sion, are, if possible, to be everywhere the same; and
all secondary measures are tested, corrected, and improved, from time to time, by comparison with the ori-
ginals of which they bear the name.

But the effort proceeds still further. The primitive
measure of length or capacity, in its concrete form, is seen
and known to be liable to various changes, which interfere
with its use as a perfect standard. The rod may bend, and
the flexure, though slight, will cause a real variation of
length. It enlarges with heat and contracts with cold.
The measure of weight is still more variable. It is affected
by every change in the unit of length to which it is referred, and has other weaknesses of its own. It is affected
by the buoyancy of the air, which varies with temperature
and other changes, and still more by the latitude on
the earth's surface. Thus every standard ceases to be an
external, physical reality. One arbitrary element must
remain from the nature of the objects to be measured, but
all beside is scientific and ideal. The rod, by which length
is measured, is the unit under ideal conditions of temperature, seldom or never realized in the actual measurement. Or else it is a fixed, ideal ratio to some ideal pen-
dulum, vibrating in an ideal latitude, and at an ideal level,
in a given part of the time of the earth's revolution; or is
some decimal fraction of an ideal elliptic quadrant of the
surface of the earth.

In the standards of time this progressive effort is still
more striking and instructive. The loose impressions,
which vary with every mood and phase of individual

17—2

thought, are first replaced by a general reference to that universal standard, the natural day. But the sunrise and sunset vary widely with the times of the year; and the hour-glass and clepsydra are invented to divide more exactly the hours and intervals of each day, which were more rudely guessed before from the place of the sun in the sky. Clocks and watches are invented, and these are successively tested and verified by the growing exactness of celestial observations. The earliest and most popular unit of time, the natural day, when completed by the night, or reckoned from noon to noon or midnight to midnight, is found by science to be more stedfast than the other celestial cycles. But, to secure fuller accuracy, one important change has to be made, and the solar is turned for popular use into the mean solar, and for observations into the still more perfect standard, the sidereal day. And even here the striving after a perfect standard does not cease. However stedfast the earth's rotation, it has been lately inferred that, from tidal friction, some slight change may still occur in the course of ages. And an attempt has therefore been made, by ascertaining the rotation of Mars to the fraction of a second, to eliminate, by a comparison of the days of two neighbouring planets, the errors that might possibly arise from accepting either of them, alone, for an invariable measure.

Now all this process, by which standards of length, weight, measure and time, are first constituted, and then verified and improved, tends not to confirm but to disprove the dogma of those whom Plato calls "flowing philosophers," by the latest of whom this appeal is made. These facts lend no countenance to the ignoble theory that distinctions of right and wrong are the creations of human fancy, or the result of artificial associations of thought, due solely to the positive appointment of rules by human lawgivers, and to the dread of social punishment alone. Arbitrary units do not enter into the domain of pure science. In arithmetic, geometry, and mechanics, our reasoning is wholly independent of the yard, the pound, the metre, the gramme, which may be needful in the business of actual life. The conclusions depend either on the numerical series itself, or on proportions of distance, weight, force, and figure only. In all practical science these units are needful, and link the truths of pure reason with the realities of the actual world. Actual weights, lengths, and intervals, can all be conceived to have been different, and are to be learned by observation alone. But when once the transition is made, the whole aim and struggle of science is to restrict, within its narrowest limits, the uncertainty which attends the entrance of this arbitrary element. A separate science has been devised, to eliminate the errors of observation in the most effectual way, and to combine the separate data of the experiments in such intimacy of relation to each other, that the result may approach as nearly as possible to the character of pure and scientific truth.

The astronomers in our observatories do not create either the solar or the sidereal day. The accurate measure of time, which the nation obtains through their labours, is no creation of the scientific observer. He merely gains, by careful experiment, a more exact knowledge of that diurnal rotation of the earth, which was a settled fact of nature before observatories were built, or telescopes and transit instruments were made. The natural standard exists, not fixed in its own nature, but by the present constitution of our system. The task of the man of science is to dis-

cern it clearly, and to correct, by means of its evidence,
carefully observed, the various errors which attach to
looser reckonings of time by mankind at large.

The principle in Ethics is the same, and is only varied
in its application. Pure morals, like arithmetic and
geometry, involve no arbitrary unit, but occupy a higher
level of fixed and absolute truth. The great laws of
duty, and the contrast of moral good and evil, are inseparable from the nature and existence of agents endowed with reason and free will, who are capable of
mutual injury or blessing. They are firm and sure, like
the properties of number and space, and like these, open
a wide and immense field for the attainment of certain
truth. A round square is not more inconceivable than
the union of causeless and malicious hate, or of deceit and
treacherous cunning, with the attribute of perfect goodness. But when we pass from the great law of love to
the realities of moral action in the world around us, an
arbitrary element begins to appear. That law, as divinely
revealed, includes a reference to the actual powers and
constitution of those who are subject to its authority.
Where the strength is greater, and the heart and mind
and soul are more largely gifted, the precept of duty, to love
with all the mind and strength, must assume a larger
compass, and range over a wider field. And when we
descend lower, and enter on the complex relationships of
life, the positive and variable elements become still more
numerous. In every circle of human society, whether
more narrow or comprehensive, in the family, the church,
and the state, secondary standards, the product of local
custom or national legislation, need to be extensively
employed, and these may vary more or less from each
other. The principle of obedience to laws ordained by a .

just authority is the same, but the laws may be varied
to meet the varying circumstances of national and social
life. Yet this is no proof or sign that they are founded
on caprice and the selfishness of power alone. We might
infer, with equal truth and wisdom, that the labours
of our royal astronomers had created the stedfast order
of the earth's revolution, and of the celestial movements.
A perfect standard, wholly free from arbitrary and positive
elements, is only possible in that highest department of
morals, where it dwells in the light of heaven, and leaves
behind it all the specialties of earthly life in the presence
of God's eternal throne. But even where such perfection is
not attainable, a ceaseless effort to approach nearer to its
attainment is the first instinct of all genuine science. The
lazy and the dissolute may abandon the search, and resign
themselves, either in wilfulness or despondency, to the
loose guesses of capricious ignorance, or the blind impulses
of self-will. But true morality, like all genuine science,
strives ever to ascend from the fleeting, variable phe-.
nomena, where no rule or law is seen, to the perception
of a law that abides in the midst of perpetual change,
and a standard pure and absolute, on which the secondary
copies, useful for the guidance of daily life, depend for
all their real worth, by which they must also be tested,
when they are found to vary and contradict each other.
For even human standards of length or measure are not
mere arbitrary inventions. They point silently and secretly
to a fixed relation in the nature of things, without
which the attempt to provide them for general use, and
then to correct their errors, would be impossible. The
words of Cudworth include a reply, by anticipation, to
the sceptical inference falsely drawn from human reckonings of time.

"A horologe is not mere silver and gold, brass and steel, any way mingled or confounded together. It is such an apt and proportionable disposition of these materials as may harmoniously conspire to make up one equal and uniform motion; which runs parallel, as it were, with the motion of time, and, passing round the horary circle, and measured by it, may also measure out that silent and successive flux, which, like a still and deep river, carries down all things along with it indiscernibly and without any noise; and which in its progressive motion, treads so lightly and softly that it leaves no traces, prints, or footsteps at all behind it."

Thus all human standards of weight and time and measure imply a deeper law or fact of nature on which they depend. And human conscience, in like manner, in all its diversities and partial errors, points upward silently to a law of eternal and unchanging righteousness, whose seat is the bosom of God, and whose voice is the harmony of the world, the music of the celestial spheres.

LECTURE XIII.

THE DOCTRINE OF UTILITY.

A THIRD element, which must enter into all inquiries concerning the foundations of Moral Science, consists in the relation between moral acts themselves and the results or consequences to which they lead. The tree is known and tested by its fruit; and the nature of the fountain, by the streams which flow from it, and the verdure or barrenness of the territory through which they flow. When this element is wholly set aside, as in some schemes of "intuitive morals," ethical teaching will be likely to assume a vague, dreamy, and unreal character, and will awaken natural distrust in practical minds. On the other hand, when this view of the subject is made the one sufficient key to unlock all the secrets of conscience, and the mysteries of human life, all the highest and noblest aspirations of the soul are liable to be lost and buried in a quagmire of calculations impossible to be performed, from which extrication is hopeless. Such is the fundamental defect of all purely utilitarian theories.

Every moral action has a threefold relation, to a precedent law of right and duty, to which the agent owes allegiance,—to a present faculty of the agent himself, whether called conscience, the moral sense, or the practical reason, by which the law is perceived, and becomes applied to his own heart and life,—and to the results in his own later experience, and in the happiness or unhappiness of others, to which right or wrong conduct, a virtuous or a vicious life, is sure to lead. And this triple character of all human action is only the reflection of that higher truth, which sums up the noblest conceptions of Christian Theology:—"For of Him, and through Him, and to Him are all things, to whom be glory for ever. Amen."

The doctrine which makes utility the exclusive test of right and wrong, and decides on the moral character of actions by their supposed or expected consequences alone, may assume very different forms. The first is the theological, in which it borrows, but in borrowing distorts and partially degrades, some great truths of the Christian revelation. God wills the happiness of mankind. He commands us to practise universal beneficence. His will is sanctioned by promises and threatenings, that are to be fulfilled in a future life. Therefore self-love requires us to obey His command, and to practise works of social kindness, in hope of gaining the promised reward. But in applying the principle we are left to our own judgment; and the known tendencies of actions, deduced from experience, are said to be our chief guide.

The second form of the doctrine is the philanthropic or benevolent. All the motives of religious faith are either formally set aside, or silently disappear from view. In their place there is borrowed from the rival doctrine of intuitive morality a vast *à priori* maxim, the supreme, essential obligation, needing no proof, and assumed to be self-evident, of universal philanthropy or benevolence. But this great principle, whether borrowed from Christianity or from philosophic idealism, is no

sooner assumed, than it is disguised, concealed, and con-
substantiated, under the form and accidents of a complex
process of experiment and calculation. The whole business of morals is to calculate results, and work out problems of maxima from imperfect premises; while the one
element which alone has a truly ethical character, the
deliberate, earnest, conscientious aim to do good to our
fellows, and in so doing to please and serve the common
Creator and Preserver of mankind, is left habitually out
of sight, lest it should embarrass and disturb that process of arithmetic on which the whole science is made to
depend.

The third form is the philosophically selfish, or that of
Epicurus and his later disciples. It recognizes no religious
faith in its scheme of morals, nor any need for motives
drawn from the Christian message of a life to come. Neither does it purloin from the Scriptures the second great
commandment, and then conceal the precious treasure, as
Achan hid the talent of gold in the soil of his tent, burying
it in the heart of a system of pleasure-seeking arithmetic,
with which it has no natural connection. It lays down
the principle, based on certain animal instincts, that the
attainment of personal pleasure is the main end and
business of life. And then it proceeds to mitigate the
harshness, and prune away the grossness, of the naked
theory, by insisting on the need of a wise and thoughtful
prudence, grounded on the lessons of experience, to free
men from the pursuit of vicious indulgence, and to prove
the superior gain of temperance, kindness, the restraint of
passion, and the cultivation of private friendship. And
there can be no doubt that the laws of prudence, when
really studied and observed, may form the first steps in an
upward progress, from which the mind must, soon or late,

gain clear glimpses of higher and holier laws of action than the pursuit of selfish and personal pleasure alone.

The fourth and last form is that of political selfishness. Virtue, on this view, consists in a habit of submission to outward laws, created and sustained by the fear of human punishment.   Instead of rising above the love of fame,

That last infirmity of noble mind,

it consists rather in one of the worst infirmities of minds both feeble and ignoble; that is, in the animal fear of physical suffering, engrained and engrafted in the heart by cultivating the habits and instincts of a slave.

The attraction of all these theories lies in the desire to escape from the caprices of individual conscience, and uncertain standards that may pass current in society from time to time, and to obtain for morals some firm and solid basis, which does not vary with the fashions of the day.   From the ethics of common sense and instinctive feeling we may either rise towards the stars, or descend to find safer footing on the solid earth below.   Thus we are told that "utility sets up an outward standard in the room of an inward, being the substitution of a regard to consequences for a mere unreasoning sentiment or feeling." And again, that "the contest between the morality which appeals to an external standard, and that which grounds itself on internal conviction, is the contest of progressive morality against stationary, of reason and argument against the deification of mere opinion and habit."   In reality, it is needful both to rise and to descend ; to gaze on the skies above, and also to tread firmly on the ground beneath our feet.   But when philosophy would teach us that, to attain certainty, we must not only tread on the ground, but that our eyes must "be always downward bent," to explore the buried riches of the soil beneath us, we may remind it that the discoveries of genuine science often reverse the too hasty conclusions of the senses, and that fixity is rather to be found in the laws of the starry heavens than in the swiftly moving, ever-changing surface of that earth on which our feet seem to rest so firmly below.

The principle, which forms the basis of the utilitarian doctrine, has been laid down by Bentham, in his *Theory of Legislation,* in these words :—

" A principle is a first idea, which is made the beginning or basis of a system of reasonings. To illustrate it by a sensible image, it is a fixed point to which the first link of a chain is attached. Such a principle must be clearly evident. To illustrate and explain it must secure its acknowledgment. Such are the axioms of mathematics: they cannot be rejected without falling into absurdity.

" The logic of utility consists in setting out, in all the operations of the judgment, from the calculation or comparison of pains and pleasures, and in not allowing the interference of any other idea.

" I am a partizan of the principle of utility, when I measure my approbation or disapprobation of a public or private act by its tendency to produce pleasure or pain; when I employ the words *just, unjust, moral, immoral, good, bad,* simply as collective terms, including the ideas of certain pains or pleasures; it being always understood that I use the words, *pain* and *pleasure,* in their ordinary signification, without inventing any arbitrary definition for the sake of excluding certain pleasures, or denying the existence of certain pains. In this matter we want no refinement, no metaphysics. It is not necessary to consult Plato or Aristotle. Pain and pleasure are what every one feels to be such, the peasant and the prince, the unlearned and the philosopher.

" He who adopts the principle of utility esteems virtue
to be a good, only on account of the pleasures which result from it; he regards vice as an evil, only because of
the pains which it produces. Moral good is *good* only by
its tendency to produce physical good. Moral evil is *evil*,
only by its tendency to produce physical evil."

This geocentric theory of morals, however captivating
to some minds by its appeal to the senses, and its air of
simplicity, will be found, when closely examined, beset with
difficulties of the most formidable kind. It does not really
secure that certain and solid footing, to which it sacrifices
some of the noblest instincts of the soul. Utility in
morals, like fire in the domestic economy, is an excellent
servant, but a bad master. Its enthronement as supreme
is the destruction of the science which it pretends to adorn
and improve.

The first defect, its merely external character, meets
us in the outset of the theory. It deals only with the
outward actions themselves, and professes to dispense,
almost entirely, with a reference to the inward motives
and feelings of the heart. "There is no point," it has been
said, "which utilitarian thinkers have taken more pains to
illustrate than the difference between motive and intention. The morality of the act depends entirely on the
intention, that is, upon what the agent wills to do. The
feeling which makes him will so to do, when it makes no
difference in the act, makes none in the morality, though
it makes a great difference in our moral estimation of the
agent." (Mill's *Util.* p. 27.)

Here, then, we have an attempt to build a scheme of
moral action, from which all respect to the motives of the
agent is excluded as a superfluous element. But the
attempt is deceptive and vain. Moral elements are need-

ful to constitute a moral or immoral act, and these elements are to be found in the motives and feelings of the
agent, and in these alone. The contrast of motive and
intention is only that between a more immediate object,
and one more remote. He who intends to do good to
another, and harms him in the attempt, may be guilty of
a serious wrong. But the wrong thus inflicted is wholly
different, in a moral point of view, from similar acts done
in deliberate malice. There may be perhaps a criminal
rashness, a blind and erring superstition, or a disgraceful
ignorance. The act may thus be worthy of moral blame.
The laws of the land may sentence it to a just punishment. They may even, from the act itself, infer a con-
structive malice. But the moral distinction, wide and
deep in itself, still remains. The motive is the soul on
which the true nature of every act mainly depends. But
if there be grievous negligence in forming the judgment,
so as to inflict injury where kindness was meant, this
fault is a moral evil of another kind. And when this
neglect is wilful and aggravated, the man may be justly
held responsible, almost as much as for malicious wrong,
for evils which his ignorance and rashness may have caused
to the objects of a well-meaning, but misguided, thought-
less, and perverse benevolence.

The doctrine, which makes the moral good or evil of
actions depend only on their consequences, is open to an
objection at the outset of a very fatal kind. Acts, viewed
merely as physical changes, can have only physical
consequences. A sword is drawn, a pistol is fired, and
death ensues. Set aside all reference to the human will,
the motive of the agent, and in either case there is a
physical result alone. So much matter is moved, slowly
or swiftly, from place to place. Chemical elements enter

into new combinations. Light, heat, and sound are generated, swift and sudden motion is given to a ball of solid
metal, muscles or nerves are shattered, the conditions of
vital action are violated, and there is a lifeless corpse,
instead of a living man. But in all this there is no moral
consequence or result whatever. Once introduce the idea
of will and choice, and all is altered. The agent is no
longer a mere automaton in a vast engine-house of nature,
full of machines. He has acted rightly or wrongly. He
has done good or evil. He has committed an act of lawful self-defence, or of patriotic effort, or has been guilty
of a culpable homicide, or even of a deliberate and malicious murder. The motives of the agent, and his relation
to the person slain, alone give the act its moral colouring,
and render it the fit object of approval or blame.

All actions are thus morally sterile and unproductive,
unless moral features, prior to any later result, are assumed and pre-supposed. They can never, when these
are wanting, rise above the level of physical changes,
morally indifferent. We must recognize in them some
working of free choice, of a responsible and intelligent
will, of the desire to injure or benefit others, to do good or
to do evil. Then the dead corpse receives a new and
higher life. They become moral acts, out of which moral
consequences without number may be expected to flow.
A blow, in itself, is only one insensible element in a vast
problem of molecular change and planetary perturbation.
But let it be an act of wilful and deliberate insult, and it
may lead to some fatal duel, or possibly wrap a whole
kingdom in the flames of civil strife, or carry war and destruction to countless families and unborn generations.

Again, the moral tendency of actions presupposes and
requires moral laws of right and wrong, which affect not

the agent only, but those who are the objects of his
activity. The phrase sums up briefly all the effects that
follow, when injuries or benefits awaken various emotions
of gratitude or ingratitude, of indignation, resentment, or
forgiveness, in those who have been affected by them.
It would be a vain attempt to trace dynamical consequences, if we first assume a universe of particles wholly
inert, in which the forces of gravitation and cohesion and
electric affinity have no power. The persons acted upon
must have capacities of moral discernment, before moral
results, worthy of the name, can follow. It is the
perception, whether true or false, of some moral character
in the act, by those whom it directly or remotely
affects, on which the nature of the consequences will
almost entirely depend. And hence, in a world where
ignorance, error, and falsehood prevail, the estimate of
actions by their immediate and apparent consequences is
liable to be most deceptive. The clouds will hide the sun.
The drifting meteors project their own vagrancy, in parallax, on the orbs which are stedfast; and virtues which
cross the current of popular vice, and awake the opposition and hate of the corrupt and selfish, may be mistaken, like ancient prophets and apostles, for guilty
troublers of society, criminals that turn upside down the
peace of the world.

There is a further disproof of the doctrine that a calculation of consequences is the only source of morals, from
reflection upon the nature of the calculation itself. It is
a moral act, and subject to moral laws. The power to
foresee consequences, to remember the results of past
experience, to compare and analyse the causes of events,
and to trace the probable effects of a particular course on
the mind and feelings of others, is a high and noble faculty.

B. L.   18

Man did not create it for himself, it is the gift of God.
If actions themselves need moral rules to be calculated
for them, how much more the faculty by which these
calculations are to be made! But who can learn, by
calculating alone, the methods and principles on which
all right calculation must depend? *Quis custodiet ipsos
custodes?* Surely the gift is one of which the exercise
needs some guidance, since on its right or wrong performance, by the hypothesis, a life of vice or virtue, of wisdom
or guilt and folly, must naturally ensue.

The doctrine which assumes that pleasures are to be
courted simply because they please, and suffering to be
avoided simply because it is painful, turns a mere animal
instinct into a fundamental rule of moral arithmetic.
On what warrant is this rule assumed? First principles,
we are told, must be clear and evident, like the axioms
of mathematics. And then it is assumed, in the next
paragraph, that pleasures of disease, of vice, and malevolence, are to enter into our calculation side by side
with the pleasures of Christian piety or social kindness,
and must weigh equally in the scale, if their amount
or quantity be the same. But a calculation of results,
based on such a confusion of moral opposites, is immoral
in its own nature. Instead of founding a system of
genuine ethics, it may be said to involve a guilty and
fatal apotheosis of vice, disease, and folly. All reckoning of moral consequences is the use of a high and noble faculty of man's being. It is not a lawless process,
to be conducted by the capricious decisions of an erring
philosophy, when it confounds or denies distinctions on
which the foundations of morality depend. It is subject
to laws of moral duty. The pleasures to be compared
must be tried by a higher standard than of their

seeming intensity alone. Factors introduced by human vice and folly must be thrown aside, since they only tend to lower the tone of thought, and to prevent any true solution of a hard problem. For surely it is no less immoral to accept the diseased pleasures of others, their corrupt and malevolent passions, or their gross and sensual practices, for positive elements to guide my actions by an attempt to increase and enlarge them, than to indulge the like pleasures in my own person.

Again, the process of calculation, so far as it is lawful and desirable, is subject to limitations of a moral kind. There are cases in which it may be right and wise to delay immediate action, in order to gain a clearer judgment on the course which is best to pursue. But there are many others, in which prompt and immediate action, even with risk of partial mistake, is better than protracted deliberation. Now if the moral rightness of an action depends entirely on a correct estimate of all its consequences, in all such cases to act rightly must be impossible, because the requisite conditions could never be fulfilled. There is a time to speak, and to keep silence. There is also a time to calculate probable results, and a time when it is needful to act promptly and speedily, and long deliberation would be a fatal error. In the great majority of the practical duties of life, it is far better to use our eyes at once, or to correct their known defects with such glasses as are at hand and in constant use, than to spend months and years in constructing some moral telescope or microscope, which, after all, we may never be able to employ, because the season for action has passed away. When the conscience is well trained, and dwells in an atmosphere of purity and light, it is safer to act on its first and simplest impulses, than to submit them to a process of laborious and intricate calculation, which may serve, too often, for a chemical freezing mixture to all the warmer emotions and more generous instincts of the human heart.

Actions, then, can have no traceable moral results, unless moral laws, affecting the agent himself and the objects of his action, are presupposed. They sink to the lower level of a mere physical change, the proper subject neither of praise nor blame. The calculation, if made, must itself be subject to moral laws, and restrained by moral limitations. It is wrong to calculate and plan for the increase of such pleasures in others as it is criminal to indulge in our own person. It is foolish and wrong to go on calculating possible and remote results, when prompt and speedy action is the plain requirement of duty. But the difficulties of the theory are greater still. The calculation of consequences, when set up for the true foundation of morals, and the test of right conduct, is impossible. It is capricious and uncertain in the elements ou which it depends. In the form in which it has usually been proposed, it is degrading and immoral. And while the professed aim is to gain a clear and intelligible basis for morality, by such a process we sink in miry clay, and can never arrive at firm and solid ground.

And first, the calculation, viewed on the side of science, is impossible. It requires the summation of an infinite series. And the series is one of which the laws, as borrowed from experience only, are so immensely complex, that we cannot be sure even of a rude approach to its total value, by attempting to add together a few of its nearest terms. We cannot tell, by such means, whether it may not prove divergent, so that negative terms of greater amount may render futile our poor attempts to find its approximate value. And the infinity is not of a single, but of a double and triple kind. We have to trace out the results of the proposed action, not for a few hours or days only, but through a whole lifetime, or to distant generations, and throughout the life to come. We have to sum them up, by the theory, not with regard to ourselves alone, but to the whole family of mankind, and even to the countless numbers of generations still unborn. We must further trace them in connection with the immense variety of possible pains and pleasures, and their degrees of intensity. Each of the fifteen classes, which Bentham has enumerated, admits clearly of an almost countless diversity, not only in the strength of each conceivable form of pain and pleasure, but in the elements out of which they arise, and which must vary, more or less, with the moral antecedent which the problem requires us to determine.

The summation required is not only of an infinite series, with a threefold infinity of time, of persons, and of elements. It is also one of quantities wholly incommensurable. In geometry we may form a sum of numbers, or of lines, or of surfaces, or of cubical space. But we cannot form a sum of numbers with lines, or of lines with surfaces, or of surfaces with solid space of three dimensions. In each case a wide chasm of unlikeness or infinitude separates the proposed elements from each other. And in the moral problem, as proposed by utilitarian theories, the difficulty is just the same. It is owned, by one of the latest advocates and revisers of the system, that pleasures may differ in quality as well as quantity, and the admission is said to be quite consistent with the maintenance of the general system. The concession is candid and just. But the apology which attends it, for a master and teacher of logic, is most illogical. The essence and foundation of the theory is that the rightness or wrongness of actions must be determined by a summation of all the pains and pleasures which they generate, or to which they lead. But if these pleasures are owned to differ in quality as well as mere amount, the problem is either owned to be impracticable, or else completely changes its form.

Incommensurables are of two classes. The first is of things of the same kind, when the ratio cannot be strictly given by finite numbers, but we can approach to it as near as we please. In such cases, though scientific exactness is not reached, we can approach nearer and nearer to the truth, and a practical solution is possible. The other case is of things incommensurable in kind, as of lines and surfaces, or surfaces and solids. And here summation is strictly inconceivable. The gulf cannot be passed, and the only summation possible is by leaving the less important out of the calculation altogether. Now if the animal pleasures of sense, which swine may share, are owned to be distinct in quality from those of reason, thought, and intelligence, which are proper to men, the same principle clearly applies. And again, if the pleasures of lust, of selfish ambition, and of malevolent passion, the first and sixth and ninth in the utilitarian catalogue, are distinct in kind from those of justice, piety, and benevolence, here also a process of mere summation is impossible, and the attempt delusive. The pleasures and joys of a pure conscience are higher and holier than those of mere intellect, where no directly moral element appears ; and these, in their turn, are nobler than mere animal pleasures. Hence it follows that the moral elements of the problem must first be proved to be in equilibrium, before we have any right to compare the merely intellectual gain or loss ; and these, again, must be strictly equal, and disappear from the problem, before we

can lawfully introduce the pleasures of sense to turn the
scale. Such a conclusion results demonstrably from the
concession that is made, and it is fatal to the utilitarian
theory. The addition table, before supreme, comes to
occupy a very secondary place in this great problem of
life; and the old distinctions of higher and lower aims,
and the duty of choosing the highest, recognized by the
best schools of heathen philosophy, as well as by the
maxims of Christian faith, but set aside almost contemptuously by some modern writers, vindicate their reality and
importance, and stand out in full relief once more.

But the problem proposed has still another fault,
which is incurable. The calculation required is not only
of infinites and incommensurables, but also of indeterminates. We are called upon to solve an equation of a
degree which almost transcends the power of numbers to
express, and of which not only the quantity itself to be
determined, but nearly all the coefficients by which we
must determine it, are unknown. Our calculation is
to be of the supposed results of each act, as it will affect
the experience of ten thousand thousand moral agents
or sentient beings. And first we have to assume, in
each instance, that they also calculate a like problem
in each successive act, or else that they are guided by
impulse, habit, or some lower motive, without calculation.
In the former case the problem is clearly insoluble, and
the mere attempt to resolve it is a childish folly. Each of
a thousand unknown quantities is to be determined, by
first assuming all the others to be already known. A is
to decide whether a course of conduct is right by its
beneficial effect on the experience of all from B to Z.
And B, in turn, is to act on a similar calculation of the
future feelings and experiences of A, C &c. to Z, as be-

fore. If we assume that others do not calculate, but act
on mere impulse, the difficulty is only increased. We
have not merely to determine, in this case, the future
course and orbit of ten thousand moral planets, of all
degrees of size, and with no common centre, under laws of
high complexity; we have rather to decide, by calculation, the best course for one of the atoms of Epicurus,
from the future effects on a wide chaos of like atoms,
all assumed to move to and fro by mere caprice, or of
which the secret laws for their movements are quite
unknown.

But the calculation has still another fault. Instead
of providing a sure and firm foundation on which the
science of morals may rest, it builds plainly on the sand.
It assumes that, while the voice of conscience may deceive,
and common sense be merely a disguised name for despotic and arbitrary decisions of mere local or transient
prejudice, this appeal to pleasures and pains, produced by
certain acts, and the attempt to reckon up their amount,
can provide us with a clear and fixed standard, free from
the parallax and distortion of individual minds. But this
is an entire illusion. It is a fact of experience, no doubt,
in each case, and for each separate person, that such and
such things have been liked and given pleasure, and that
such others have been disliked, and caused an emotion of
pain. But how many steps have to be taken, before this
limited fact can be changed into a basis of scientific, or even
of practical and approximate calculation! The pleasure
or pain of the moment passes away, as soon as it has been
felt, and can never return. How are we to infer future
pleasures, through long years to come, from those of
previous days? The circumstances will not be the same.
The scene will have wholly changed. Every person af-

fected by the acts which are still in suspense will be in
a different natural, intellectual, moral position, and the
change is in progress hourly, even while the deliberation is
made. Man, as we have been told long ago by the patriarch, "never continueth at one stay." The pleasures of infancy, of early childhood, of youth and manhood, are not the
same. The choice of one is the dislike of another. The
preference of to-day is often reversed to-morrow. Fulness
breeds satiety. Vicious indulgence perverts the faculties
themselves. And thus to build a theory of morals on a
process of calculation, which assumes the nature and
extent of future pleasures, in ten thousand persons, from
our own experience, through a few days or months or
years, of pleasures that are now gone for ever, is the same
as to rear a stately and imposing structure on a foundation of ever-shifting heaps of sand.

To obtain anything like solid footing, we must turn
our thoughts from the mere fact of some past pain or
pleasure, of the liking or disliking, enjoyment or suffering, to the causes out of which it grows, and on
which its recurrence must depend. The pleasure or pain
results from a certain relation between the sentient
being or the moral agent, and the conditions, natural
or moral, in which he is placed. If there be such a
thing as a right or wrong state both of body and mind,
of natural or moral health, and of natural or moral
sickness and disease, then the future pain and enjoyment
must depend on both elements, the acts themselves,
with their own proper tendencies when perceived by
those who are in health, and those abnormal and unnatural
results which flow from the presence of disease and
moral evil alone. The first step of genuine science must
be to distinguish these two elements, instead of blending

them confusedly together. It must sever between consequences which properly belong to the action itself, and
those which are due to the disease, ignorance, vice or
folly, of those who come within the range of its influence.
And when these last have been separated and put aside,
as foreign factors which only obscure the real problem,
those which remain must be classed under their three
main heads, distinct in kind from each other, and also incapable of being fused into a process of arithmetic, because
they are incommensurable. There are the pleasures of
bodily health, in the exercise of all the outward senses
and corporeal powers; the higher enjoyments of intellect
and mental activity; and the highest of all, which include
a moral and spiritual element, the delights of a conscience
at peace within, and of a heart enlarged with love to
mankind, and still tending upward to lose itself in the
ocean of a love which is infinite and divine.

There is one further truth, familiar to every Christian
mind, which places an insurmountable barrier in the way
of any theory of morals, based upon consequences and
results alone. We are thrown at once upon two alternatives. We must strive to determine, either the natural
tendencies of the action, which may be thwarted and
opposed, and partially reversed, by the wrong conduct, the
error and ignorance of others, or else the results, which, in
the light of former experience, are most likely to follow.
If we are to deal only with tendencies, and not actual or
probable results, we have then to decide what is the
tendency which belongs to the act from its own nature,
apart from those deflecting influences from other sources,
which may turn it aside from its proper aim. And these
tendencies must be of the nature of internal laws or moral
forces. They must imply moral features of the act, and

depend upon these, and can exist on no other condition.
Kindness tends to beget kindness. But if the act of seeming kindness ceases to be really kind, the moral power is
wanting. If it ceases to be felt as kind, the moral power
is there, but ceases for the time to operate, through the
ignorance, misconception, or ingratitude, of those from
whom thanks are due. Instead of groping our way along
the countless terms of an infinite series, we thus detect the
secret law on which its development is mainly suspended,
though temporary causes may obscure it for a moment,
and introduce foreign terms that disguise its nature.
To borrow the language of pure science, we deal no longer
with the series itself, but with some generating function on
which it depends, in which moral features are already
present, and where spiritual laws shine out clearly, so as
to rule over the consequences which flow from them even
to distant generations.

But if we accept the other alternative, that our aim
must be to determine the actual results, and not the tendency alone, then the doctrine must be set aside for an
opposite reason. The improper results of actions, from
the error and vice of others beside the moral agent himself, are various, confused, and infinite in our actual world.
The attempt to trace them out in detail must defy the
efforts of the most powerful and intelligent mind. But
the process fails in another way. The world, in the faith
of the Christian, and of every Theist, is not abandoned to
chance or fate. It is under a scheme of moral government. The actions, then, of evil men are overruled by an
Almighty Power. They are thus compelled, even against
their own tendency, to minister to some great and worthy
end of the Divine government.

Astronomy has supplied us, of late, with an expressive
illustration and parable of this great moral truth. The
comets, those wandering and unformed stars, like truants
of our system, have been seen repeatedly, as they approach the sun, to suffer violent agitation. Jets of vapor-
ous light have been thrown out from them, as if in weak
rivalry or vain defiance of the mighty luminary which
controls their motion. But these, however violent their
agitation, are soon turned backward by a mightier force
than caused their first eruption, and only increase the
magnificence of the spectacle, while the whole obeys the
central force that draws it nearer and nearer to the sun.
So all evil actions, in their own proper tendency, seem to
fight with the order and laws of the Divine government,
and threaten to reverse them. They burst forth, in the
form of violent and hateful passions and appetites, from
that weak and errant centre of evil thoughts in which
they are born, the human heart. But no sooner do they
escape, and enter on the vast open range of Providence,
than a mightier Power seizes upon them, in spite of their
reluctance and opposition, and compels them to do its
will. They no longer obey the impulse of the evil passion in which they had their birth, but are strangely overruled by far-reaching might and far-seeing wisdom, and
minister to the action and abiding dominion of All-perfect
Love.

Now this great fact, dimly taught even by natural
reason, and more clearly revealed in the whole course of
Scripture, that evil is overruled for good, and that nothing
can escape from the counsel of One who is infinite in wisdom and goodness, destroys all contrast between good and
evil actions, as soon as we adopt the false principle which

would decide on their character by actual results and consequences alone. In this sense the words of the poet are true:

> All discord, harmony not understood,
> All partial evil, universal good.

All good actions, in their own nature, tend to results which are good. And this tendency, inherent in them from their moral nature, is ripened and perfected by the concurrent action of a superintending providence. All evil actions, in their own nature, tend to evil. But this evil, the result of their moral nature in the hour of their birth, is so controlled by that higher law of Divine wisdom, under control of which they come as soon as they are born, that they also lead to actual issues worthy of Him whose decrees they fulfil,

> Whose work is without labour, whose designs
> No flaw deforms, no difficulty thwarts.

How, then, can it be possible to discriminate the moral character of actions by their outward results, when all alike, though in a manner deeply mysterious, are known to minister to a work which is perfect; and when God was pleased to accomplish, by means of an act which on man's part was one of the worst and foulest crimes, His own good and excellent purpose, the redemption and spiritual recovery of a sinful and evil world?

When, however, instead of making the tendencies of actions, which is a silent paralogism, or their actual results, which is a fatal error, the ground of their moral nature for good or evil, we use the lessons of experience as a secondary guide for settling the wisest forms and true limits of human law, then the principle of utility, so applied and limited, must hold an important place in all applied Ethics, and needs to be borne in view by all those who

have to frame laws for the guidance of human society.
Or when we rise still higher, to contemplate the Providence of God and the great system of His moral government on a wider scale, and seek to define good and
evil by the harmony and consent of all those contrasted
elements on which their nature depends, the principle
holds a place of still higher importance. We cannot sever
actions from their consequences. If the tree be good,
its fruit will be good, and if the tree be corrupt and evil,
so must be the fruit also. A perfection, wholly apart
from consequences and effects of every kind, is inconceivable.

Actions that are really good must have a threefold
character. They must be good in the fountain from
which they spring, the channel through which they flow,
and the ocean to which they tend. They must be con-
formed, in their origin, to eternal laws of righteousness, on
harmony with which their real character depends. They
must be in harmony with a pure and upright conscience,
which recognizes the law of right, and strives to obey it.
And they must tend naturally, in their later progress, to
reproduce themselves. They are moral plants, endued
with a prolific virtue, and of each of them it may be said
with perfect truth, that "its seed is in itself upon the
earth."

Heroic virtue wakens emulation in noble minds. Holy
examples awaken the desire and thirst for holiness. Righteous government kindles instincts of justice, and diffuses
them through the whole nation. Kindness breeds kindness,
and love is the fruitful parent of love. And though
actions could have no moral tendencies, if ethical distinctions were set aside in the vain search after some
simpler theory, and right or wrong doing were to be

defined by visible success, and measurable results alone, still it is often through careful observation of results that our perception of their moral nature becomes more full and clear. Like sunlight reflected from the countless dewdrops of morning, the laws of righteousness, while they can gain no new force, shine with more conspicuous beauty, when they are seen in their combination with all the innumerable events of Providence and human history in this lower world. Actions do not assume a moral character, and become right or wrong, purely because of the results that follow after them in the near or distant future. But the great fact of an all-wise Providence secures that, soon or late, their moral tendency, from their own nature, shall prevail over every adverse and evil influence;—" so that men shall say, Verily there is a reward for the righteous: doubtless there is a God that judgeth in the earth."

THE ANALOGY

OF

MATHEMATICAL AND MORAL CERTAINTY,

A Commemoration Prize Essay

READ IN TRINITY COLLEGE CHAPEL,
DECEMBER, 1833.

AN ESSAY

ON

MATHEMATICAL AND MORAL CERTAINTY.

AMONG the votaries of Mathematical Science there have never been wanting voices to celebrate largely its numerous excellencies. The simplicity of its principles, the variety of its results, the certainty of its demonstrations, the beauty and harmony of its truths, and its wide command over the secrets of external nature, have all in their turn been the themes of frequent eulogy. Regarding it as the parent region of discovery, not only its native children, but many of the sons of tributary sciences, have been ready to pay their homage to its superior claims. By all who have journeyed in quest of physical truth its praises have often been sung, as mistress of those winding seas they have had to traverse; and in the unknown lands of science which have risen on their view, its flag has been the first to wave in triumph upon every shore. Others have claimed for it a higher merit; they have enlarged, and justly, on its influence upon the mind itself —on the habits it tends to induce of connected reasoning and patient thought—the strict rein it places on the loose wanderings of the fancy, and that stern discipline of the mental powers, which nerves them equally, whether with strength for the combat, or with swiftness for the race.

But here the topics of praise seem to be exhausted, and the strain, so full hitherto, dies away suddenly on the strings. To those, who, deaf to its lower claims, inquire into its moral virtues; who adhere to the golden rule of the reviver of philosophy, and measure the value of science, not by the false standard of that power over the elements, which spirits of darkness may wield as well as spirits of light, but by its use in the conduct of life; who ask, what higher truth it even indirectly teaches, what light it sheds on the mysteries of our being, what lessons of wisdom it has power to furnish, what sympathies to cherish, what kindly affections to revive, what lofty purposes of excellence to animate and sustain, the reply, if any reply be given, is faint and low. Its more just and candid admirers will excuse, perhaps, by the greatness of its other merits, its defect in these, as alien from its nature; while some of a bolder school, the idolaters of science, who dream that wisdom itself may in time be reduced to a formula, and virtue to a refined and subtle problem of chance, will treat the inquiry with contempt and silent scorn. The truth, however, of the charge would probably be at once admitted by both; and while all other fields of natural knowledge, to those who have learned to pursue them aright, yield in abundance the fruits of lofty poetry and of heavenly contemplation, it seems to be deemed utterly hopeless that any such plants of Paradise should be reared in this primitive region of granite rock and eternal snow.

The source of this wide-spread impression seems to lie in the opinion, which has taken deep root, of an entire contrast between the nature of mathematical and moral truth. They have been generally viewed as not more separate in their objects than in the kind of evidence on

which they severally rest. The claim of demonstrable
certainty has been granted to the former alone, while the
latter has been placed on the looser ground of induction
and cumulative proof. The great and leading distinction,
which obtains, by a close analogy, in things moral as well
as natural, between facts and truths, the floating phenomena apprehended by the senses, and the fixed laws or
ideas contemplated by the reason, has been transferred,
by a strange confusion of terms, if not of thought, to the
subjects themselves, till the very phrase, 'moral certainty,'
has come to denote what is in some measure uncertain,
and not capable from its nature of the strictness of demonstration. Between things regarded as so different in
kind it is no wonder that little analogy should be felt to
obtain. On this view the only lesson that could be drawn
from the truths of science was one of contrast, to seek for
such evidence only in moral subjects, as their nature
admits; to balance where we cannot prove, to creep where
we may not soar, and steer our winding course along the
coasts of experience, where there is no fixed loadstar seen,
to guide us freely across the trackless ocean.

There is something in this opinion, when entertained,
which must, to a reflecting mind, suggest itself at once as
strange and unnatural. Is it possible, then, that nature,
which in every other province has a temple, an oracle,
and a voice of wisdom, in this alone, the highest of all,
is mute and silent? Her smaller streams and fountains,
amidst their perpetual dance and play, may be seen lit
up continually with the beams of some loftier truth; and
this ocean, wide as space, and lasting as time, which en-
circles and sustains every realm of the universe with its
vast and eternal laws—has this alone no clear heavens
bending over it, whose image it may reflect in its deep

and tranquil bosom? Is Truth, as distinguished from
Presumption, her shadow, to be exiled from the spirit of
man, and the nobler aims and purposes of his being, to
seek an uneasy shelter, entrenched within the lines of the
geometer, or couched in mystic retreat beneath the letters
of the analyst, there to busy herself with many things,
and all needless, ministering only to bodily convenience,
and outward luxury and ease.

Let us briefly inquire, then, whether we may not with
safety take a nobler view; whether, in examining into the
nature of moral certainty, we may not find, in the certainty
of geometry, an attendant to guide us, instead of a rival
to discourage; whether we may not rest their claims on
a common footing; observing only that along with the
mental discipline they both require, in the former a moral
discipline is further needed, answerable to its greater
dignity; and thus rise to the conviction that, in the range
of moral as of natural truth, there is no need to be tossed
on the uncertain waves of opinion, but that in each alike
there are principles to be found, fixed and sure in themselves, and whose light streams far into the caverns of
nature, and the still more unfathomable depths of the
human heart. And although the remoteness of this view
from those of the schools of modern philosophy, with
a few bright exceptions, may give it the air of paradox,
it is not on that account the less likely to be true. For
what is paradox, indeed, but another name for that deepest
truth, which veils itself from a passing and careless gaze
in the inner shrine of this world's solemn temple?

At the very entrance, however, of our comparison,
a host of difficulties encompass us, and threaten to ob-
struct our path, like the clamorous shapes which beset
the knight of old, when forcing his toilsome way to the

palace of Truth. Their form and voice may be various, but their challenge is the same; and as they point to the countless train of varying thoughts, adverse schools, contending creeds, and clashing opinions, they ask with triumph where are the signs of this fancied certainty, the doctrines of this science, the waymarks of its progress, and the treasury of its results; and setting before us the trophies of physical research, demand an equally undisputed array of moral and spiritual discoveries.

It cannot be denied that, at first sight, this difficulty seems great and almost insurmountable. The analogy appears buried under a total contrast. And so it must appear, as long as the eye rests only on the passing surface, unmindful of the still deeps of thought that are slumbering below. To such an observer, and such are most, the history of the world presents only a waste of opinions, where wave and tide and current blend their effects confusedly, hopeless to the feet, and cheerless to the view. And even when the voice of Truth is heard to welcome him amidst its waves, his spirit must be calm and his faith be strong, who can walk forth in thought, without some secret misgiving, over this wide and wildering sea. Yet, however formidable the difficulty may appear at first, further reflection will greatly weaken its force, and supply us with a double answer, resting in part on the analogy in question, and partly on the difference between the circumstances of scientific and moral research.

Let us suppose the case of a simple observer of the heavens, a Chaldean shepherd on the plains of Dura, who had watched night by night, the moon, the planets, and the starry courses; and that in the midst of his laborious observation, still finding fresh aspects in the ever-moving.

sphere, he were told that all these varied appearances were linked by one simple law, from which they might be deduced with infallible certainty. We may imagine how he would start at such a statement, how he would appeal to their complex and still varying motions; and gazing on the mystic dance of those wandering fires, "excentric, intervolved"—be ready to seat some wayward Genius in each separate sphere, and hard would be it to persuade him that they were "regular then most, when most irregular they seem." But if by comparing with other observers, he were to learn that with each the appearances were different—that stars which to him rose and set continually, by another were never seen, and with a third were circling as constantly, unwet by the ocean wave, the discordance of the appearances with every observer would appear to give him a tenfold warrant for rejecting the statement altogether, as rash and visionary.

Thus it fares with higher truth. Habit and prejudice, the pride of intellect, and a selfish will, furnish to every man a continual parallax of thought; and till these are taken away, or account is had of their presence, we need not wonder that the results appear discordant, and no light of certainty pierces through the gloom. Remove these, and what before appeared the most complex may be found perhaps the most simple. In this view it is worthy of notice that the first triumph of applied analysis has been over those bodies, whose very name marked them out to us as truant wanderers in the sky. And if Light, the playmate of the changing clouds, be the next to bow to that potent spell, what presumption can hereafter be raised, from the complex and tremulous emotions of the heart, the web of opinions, or the tangled maze of the world's history, against the simplicity of those eternal truths on which the whole scheme reposes, or the sureness of the building reared on those foundations?

There is, however, a further key to this apparent contrast. The geometer never dreams of discovering afresh the whole train of science: he receives it advanced by the united labors of all who have gone before, and seeks only to supply what may be wanting, or explain what may be obscure, and so to pass on to further discoveries. He would smile at any one, who would advise him to ensure freedom from prejudice, by flinging aside the treasures that others have left, and raise the structure afresh by his own unaided powers. If this had been the course pursued by even the most favoured sons of Science, the walls on which she now hangs their trophies would still have been bare. Yet something like this has been too often advised, and too often practised, in themes of far more difficulty and moment, and it is no wonder that the progress, in such cases, should appear small and uncertain.

Above all, the difference lies mainly in the number of willing learners, rather than in the subjects themselves. There is something in the pursuit of pure science not a little flattering to the mind, and tending to leave on it a simple impression of its own power. With moral truth it is the reverse; it humbles that it may exalt, and reproves first, in order to restore. There is a sacrifice always involved in its reception, a surrender of selfish desires, a deadness to passing pleasures, which bars the avenues of its approach, though it only confirms it the more when once received. This, while detracting nothing from its intrinsic certainty, which it rather doubles by the joint testimony of the judgment and the will, clouds greatly the marks of its evidence from the superficial eye.

Thus many turn altogether from its portals; and even with those who enter in, it is frequently only after laying afresh, in their own experience, the foundation of a wisdom taught and proved long before.

It is true that this view of Moral Science, as in its own nature fixed and sure, like the laws of number or of space, however familiar with our elder writers, and ably sustained by some kindred spirits in our own day, accords ill with the stream of modern opinion, or the self-flatteries of an age, which, whatever may be its other intellectual claims, shews small signs of the unity which springs from conscious truth, or the meekness of a pure and living wisdom. And while its merely physical students or ephemeral writers keep within their proper bounds, they may well be borne with, and even justly admired. But if they would intrude, with insect doubts, into the still chambers of meditation and faith, to question the existence and reality of that higher knowledge, which they may never have sought for, and therefore have never found, their pretensions must be examined, and the intrusion repelled. And it may easily be seen that the causes which obscure the evidence of moral truth, though always acting, act most strongly in times of intellectual excitement and social luxury.

We may observe then, first, that a state of accumulated facts, multiplied opinions, enlarged materials of thought, diffused intelligence, and various reading, is of itself the most unfavourable to fixedness of views, and manliness of character, unless it be attended with an answering depth of inward research and silent meditation. Truth, and the facts which it knits together and explains, like law and its subjects in the social state, or flesh and spirit in man's mysterious being, are of themselves antagonist prin-

ciples; noblest indeed in their union, but still that very
union is not effected without a struggle, and the harmony
which results partakes always the nature of a triumph.
The appearances which flit around us in every field of
nature are of themselves a vagrant and lawless band, till
the idea, in full panoply, springs to birth in some master-
mind, which may reduce into unwilling obedience their
roving and scattered tribes. And hence, in every case,
the greater the amount of facts amassed, before a sound
theory has arisen to explain them, the greater the obstacles which such a theory will have to encounter. The
only reason why this is not perceived more commonly, is,
that facts and theory usually grow up side by side, and
advance together towards perfection. But if, as in the
formation of opinions on moral subjects, where the exercise of a private judgment, though sincere in its search,
will too often set aside authority both human and divine,
principles have to be formed and matured amidst the
pressure and excitement of intellect, in its most busy and
active forms, then the difficulty exists in all its power.
To persuade this moving and infinite world of thought
to own the jurisdiction, and bow to the authority of a
higher law, fixed and stable as those of number and space,
is a task which grows the more arduous, the more populous
that empire of thought becomes. Let us suppose no
longer a shepherd on the plains, but a modern observer of
the heavens, who had collected the observations of former
astronomers, and added his own, with every refinement of
minutest accuracy, before the first dawn of a true theory.
It is plain that with such a person the difficulties, which
a later Kepler or Newton would have had to encounter,
would be far greater than those which met them at the
time when they actually appeared. Few and loose com-

paratively as were the materials then, and rapid as the
advance of science had been in the preceding century,
the latter had to task its power to the utmost, to achieve
that first great victory, in the natural world, of law over
experience, and reason over the illusions of sense. How
much harder would it have afterwards become, when a
thousand disturbances then unnoticed and unmeasured,
rebel genii of air and earth and heaven, would have been
added to the array, and have seemed to mock every effort
to bring them under the yoke of theory! And perhaps
at last the results themselves might perish, from the want
of any principle to knit them into union, and give them
a voice prophetic of future changes.

This, which is true of the laws of matter, is true also
of the laws of mind. Each alike has its region of pure
and applied science, the one, sure in itself, and the other
scarce less so, while by the aid of some simple fact assumed, it explains, in strict consequence, the varied forms
of nature, and the forms, as various, of providence and of
human life. And it can be no presumption against the
equal evidence attainable in the latter case, that it may
seem to be seldom reached, even in an age of great mental
development. The man of various reading, if a man of
various reading only,—the able and practised statesman,
if versed only in the subtleties of state affairs, the traveller
in many climes, if his own heart and conscience have been
left unvisited, the citizen of the world in every form, if
a citizen of this world alone, is the least likely to apprehend the evidence, realize the depth, or trace the far-
spreading consequences, of those laws of judgment and
righteousness, which are the foundation even of the throne
of God. Every rule in their mind is clogged with exceptions, which leave it worthless, every maxim with

questions and doubts which destroy its power; and each guiding star, that might beam down benignant influence, meets there with some gross medium of earth, to distort at least, and perhaps entirely to quench its ray. And thus an intellectual age, from the multitude and weight of its materials of outward knowledge, is only in danger of sinking the deeper into the quicksands of scepticism and doubt on every truth of the conscience and reason, beyond the boundary-walls of time. On the first whisper that here too the certainty of demonstration may be gained—the troops of its jarring opinions, which, under their several factions, have striven long and in vain for mastery, muster at once on their frontiers to resent this intrusion of glimmering light into regions sacred to strife and dusky gloom. Freed then, in some measure, from the fear of this objection, which flings its shadow across our path, we may pursue our inquiry with less doubt of success, and trace rapidly the leading steps of demonstration in either case, illustrating by comparison the difficulties that arise as we proceed.

Every stream must have its fountain, and every course of demonstration some higher principle, out of which it springs. These, which are the ἀρχαί of Aristotelian philosophy, form the root of science—the postulates with which all reasoning begins, and without which, indeed, a single step cannot be taken. They are of two kinds, primitive, or dependent; according as they spring from the intuitive laws of thought, or are the result of a laborious induction. The former are the source of pure, the latter of mixed science, and the certainty to which they tend may in like manner be termed pure or mixed, as the principles on which it rests are absolute or dependent. That amusing travesty of logical forms, which,

Dr Brown has copied from Pope to raise our mirth at the
Stagyrite's expense, contains in it, as with ridicule is often
the case, the germs of a deeper wisdom than either seems
to have suspected. Truths, as language itself may teach,
have their families, their order and succession, their
parentage and their offspring: the child cannot usurp the
place of the parent, nor the parent of the child. Unlike
the shadowy forms of mere opinion, they are endued with
an intense vitality, and their incorruptible life multiplies
itself a thousand fold. But as there can be no family
without its patriarch, and no race without its founder,
whose breath of life is the immediate gift of heaven, so
have all the applied sciences their respective parent
truths, and the pure science from which they spring its
intuitive principles undemonstrated and underived. And
thus is man taught everywhere the same lesson of looking upward, and the only tenure by which he can till
the fields of science, is the silent acknowledgment that
Mystery is empress of the soil.

Overlooking, or strangely forgetting this simple and
evident maxim, some writers on mental philosophy have
perplexed themselves at the very threshold of their inquiries, one class attempting to set aside as incapable of
proof, and others as idly seeking to prove, principles,
which, whether they were willing or not, they were compelled silently to recognize in every page. And perhaps
even the labour might have been spared, however ingenious, which others have spent in proving that no proof is
needed, and that the lecturer may safely assume the
mental identity and bodily presence of those whom he
is addressing. Discussions of this kind of themselves may
seem curious and harmless; but the habit they foster of
questioning what is unquestionable, and perplexing the

consciousness with the attempt to contradict itself, tends greatly to induce a palsy of the soul; in which it grasps no truth firmly, has nerve for no manly purpose, but trembles with a general uneasiness of doubt; and the sense of duty is lulled asleep, while it is gravely resolving the question of its own existence, and of the living, moving world around it.

The principle, then, which lies at the basis of mathematical science, is this consciousness, which our senses furnish, of the existence of an outward and material world. On this simple postulate, it rears its various discoveries. Thought and reflection may suggest on this subject numerous inquiries; many curious, and some perplexing questions may be started, on the process by which the mind learns to clothe one object with the perceptions gleaned from differing senses. But these inquiries can never shake, nor even modify the conviction itself. It is just as strong in the sceptic philosopher, who strives to melt away his own consciousness in a *deliquium* of ideas, as in the merest peasant, and thus gives us a sure footing on which to rest in every further course of reasoning.

And yet this conviction, however simple and sure, may serve to remove the objections which have sometimes presented themselves in the parallel case of moral consciousness. For it is one which we hold in spite of many seeming difficulties. Even in the fields of nature, and, still more, in the chambers of art, we meet with visual images that mock us with an unreal form; and sleep too has its own world, filled with sights of beauty that own no outward archetype, and vocal with sounds of love or friendship that were never uttered.

All moral science, in like manner, springs from a fountain-truth, as simple, and even more deep in its in-

tuitive certainty—the inward consciousness of Will, and
that fixed sense of responsible being, which at once proclaims the soul a denizen of the world of spirits. It is,
like the former, a primary law of thought, which needs
no proof and requires no comment, but has its quiet and
undisturbed abode in the inmost chambers of the heart.
It embodies itself in the pronouns of every language,
breathes in every desire of the soul, lives in the memories
of the past and hopes of the future; and its voice is
heard with equal clearness, in the infant's lisping confession, or whispered prayer on its mother's knee, as in
the profoundest maxims of grave and hoary wisdom.

It is true that here also there are difficulties, which
only patient reflection can overcome, and which shade the
truth though it will not suffer itself to be buried. Even
when in its most wakeful hours and purest contempla-
tions, the mind may sometimes gaze, Narcissus-like, on
the images of its own creative fancy, till it is ready to
confound the shadowy with the true. Still worse, the soul
too has its sleep, and like the hero of Italian song, in the
enchanted isle of pleasure, with witcheries of delusion on
every side, lies too often a dreaming and inglorious cap-
tive, deaf to the sounds of wisdom, and dead to the visions
of immortality, that solicit an entrance to its ear and its
eye. In such a case, it would be as vain to look for any
certain discernment of moral truth, or any clear insight
into its lessons, as to expect the theorems of geometry to
evolve themselves spontaneously in the slumbers of the
peasant. Rather may we well imagine that a dim and
uncertain haze will creep gradually over the whole subject, till first principles themselves are obscured, and a
darkened understanding 'makes one blot of all the air,'
with its subtle spells. As one who has long been drugged

with opiates, and seldom opened his eyes to the light
of day, might almost learn to doubt the evidence of his
waking senses; so by such dreamers as these the very
existence of moral distinctions, of right and wrong, of good
and evil, comes at last to be mooted. Yet even here, the
unconquerable majesty of Truth asserts its power. In the
midnight haunts of dissipation, where riot holds its loudest
orgies of uneasy laughter and hollow mirth, the roar and
revelry will sometimes be hushed and still, and a voice be
heard of clear and solemn music, that bespeaks something
nobler than 'any mortal mixture of earth's mould'—the
plaining of a spirit parted from its guide, and lost in the
entangling wildernesses of the world.

There is no reason, then, in the nature of its first principles why the evidence of morals should be placed on
a lower footing, or regarded as less purely demonstrative,
than that of geometry. Each rests on its own firm and
simple basis, in the instincts and intuition of sense and of
conscience; and their difficulties are similar, though not
impairing the certainty in either case, for sense has its
illusions, and conscience may often be obscured with
clouds. With advancing knowledge, however, these difficulties, which were perplexing or startling at an earlier
stage, yield fresh confirmation to the realities, which they
seemed before to involve in doubt. The distorted vision,
and spectral image, are thus traced to the same laws of
light, which serve to link us with outward matter; and
false and varying standards of human morality confirm us
the more in that which is pure and divine, when once we
have learned the mysterious power of a fallen will, to
bend with its mist the light of conscience from that un-
broken course which it holds in mild regions of serene and
heavenly contemplation.

When, indeed, we pass from the nature of Moral Science in itself to its practical reception and growth, we can scarcely allow too largely for this last influence. The doctrine that belief is unconnected with the will may pass current with those whose horizon is bounded by the rules of arithmetic; in moral subjects it will not hold. And hence it arises that the outward marks of certainty or progression are, to the casual observer, so widely different from those of natural science. The strong sense of this actual disparity, has perhaps led a well-known living author, in his aphorisms, in some degree to overstate the real distinction, when he says: "The postulates of Geometry are such as no man *can* deny; the postulates of Moral Science such as no good man *will*." And this is the view which does seem most directly to suggest itself, upon observation of the wayward forms of human thought; but perhaps a closer reflection would lead us rather to state the difference thus—that the postulates of Geometry, no one denies or wishes to deny—those of Moral Science, they who wish it most earnestly cannot always. This view will explain the practical distinction as fully as the former, and the parallel is seen to hold with undiminished clearness.

In pursuing the course of demonstration, the next step is to separate the abstract relations which present themselves from the varying circumstances in which they are involved. To effect this, simple and precise definition is required. And here the need of patient attention begins to be felt, and we tread close on the verge of mystery. We have now to contemplate the relations of space, apart from the forms of matter, by which space itself becomes known to us, and the nature of number, distinct from the qualities of those units by which our ideas of number have been gained. The figures defined by Geometry cannot be viewed as merely states of the mind, without losing their objective character; and yet we cannot ascribe to them objective existence, without encumbering the idea with the addition of specific size. They seem rather to be viewed as the expression of general relations which the mind apprehends in external objects—relations fixed and unchanging, though the objects vary, and which the thoughts invest with a subjective or ideal unity. But though the process is not the most easy to explain, it is one which every mind, whose attention has been closely fixed, pursues naturally, and without difficulty. And when once the relation, whatever it be, has been strictly defined, its properties are felt to depend no longer on the object or diagram that may aid our conception, but to be conclusions of pure reason, resting solely on what the terms of the definition include.

The path which opens into the fields of ethical knowledge is of the same kind. The actions of human life, the varied emotions of the heart, and all the shifting scenes of thought and passion, are set before us; and the first impression, as in the natural world, is that of a multitude that distracts, and an immensity that confounds. The unthinking turn away discouraged, and live, as the rustic amidst the scenes of nature, but with a more dangerous ignorance—convenience or custom their only guide, their thoughts cooped always within the little horizon of their own narrow aims; and if ever they raise their eyes, as at times they must, to the blue heavens, yet soon turning them down again to earth, contented strangers to the meaning of all those high mysteries, whose silent majesty is encircling them evermore. But those who with persevering attention continue to gaze, will ere long perceive

20—2

ideas of the good, the fair, the lovely, and the pure, offering themselves unbidden to the view, and amidst the innumerable play of life's changing scenes, rising, like the
nymphs from the countless rippling of the ocean waves,
in forms of immortal and unfading beauty. And though
writers of an older school, whose thoughts dwelt much
and long in this sphere of contemplation, have naturally
used words answering to the vividness of their own impressions, and spoken of good and evil, of vice or virtue,
in terms that might imply a separate actual existence, it
would be wrong on that account to charge them with
entangling themselves in the empty fictions of a creative
fancy. Language, in spite of ourselves, will clothe the
most abstract thought with some floating drapery; and
the same objection which would discard the certainty of
moral relations, or dim the impression of their simple
power, because always enveloped in varying circumstances, must fling aside the conclusions of the geometer,
till he can set an abstract triangle or circle before our
eyes.

It is in this stage of comparison, that the inquiry into
the source and character of moral distinctions, which has
employed so many writers, and been the theme of so
many discussions, ancient and modern, would naturally
present itself to our notice. For the practical guidance
of life, the inquiry is happily superfluous : this temple,
sacred to the charities and the graces, will not be less sure
for the feet, or less goodly to the eye, because its foundations may be concealed in the bosom of the earth. Conscience has its voice for every ear that is open to receive
it, and misleads none, who have not first been more or
less willing to be deceived. But still the subject is in
itself one of the greatest interest, and especially after

furnishing the theme for such various disputes and not
a few specious falsehoods, a just view of its nature may
be deemed almost the first essential for all who would
pass beyond the sphere of individual action and accept
the more perilous office of the championship of truth, and
vindication of the ways of Providence. Of secondary
aids in pursuing this research, there is perhaps none so
sure and simple as the light which arises from keeping
the present analogy steadily in view. To attempt this
generally, would lead us too far; it may be enough to
illustrate briefly in a single instance; and the philosophical lectures of a recent author (Dr T. Brown) as among
the latest who have treated the subject, may serve as
a ground for the observation.

Agreeing then, with that luminous writer in most of
his statements, there is one principle in which he appears
to be still defective, and the error, though less obvious in
its consequences, to be as truly dangerous as those which
he has opposed. Laying his foundation more deeply than
some of his immediate precursors, he had yet to dig
a course deeper to find the rock on which the building
might rest securely. He has swept aside with a masterly
hand the cobwebs of the selfish theories—those fair-
seeming Florimels of ice and snow, which but for the
charmed girdle that subtle thought had placed around
them, the first warm feeling of the heart would have
melted away. He has further remarked that selfishness
loses nothing of its nature by reaching from time into
eternity, and seems only more heartless, when it stands
unmoved in the presence of Infinite Goodness, and even
in the hope of immortality thinks only of the gifts, and
forgets the Giver. He has even gone further, and traced
clearly the evil results of ascribing the source and ground

of obligation to an outward expression of the Divine Will,
instead of an inward feeling of the soul; however true it
be that those feelings when unperverted, must secretly
recognize that Will's supreme authority. Otherwise, indeed, it could possess no moral goodness, and the sole
attribute of the Divinity would be Almighty Power. But
when he proceeds, as he does continually, to speak of
these principles and feelings, as purely of positive Divine
appointment, which the same hand that implants them
may change or reverse, he fails to observe that he is
secretly retreading the steps of his own argument, and
the giant falsehood he had just exposed, which strips
even the throne of heaven of its glory, rears itself from
its fall with recovered force.

The sense of good and evil, it is true, are prior to the
expression of the Divine Will, which does not create, but
only awakens them. This conviction, always felt, though
sometimes a mistaken zeal may have sought to obscure it,
alone leaves any meaning to that earnest enquiry, 'shall
not the Judge of all the earth do right?'—That which
defines cannot, from its very nature, become a property;
and thus we cannot justly speak of that Will as good, so
long as we regard it as constituting of itself the final
standard of right and wrong. But it is plain that we are
brought equally to such a conclusion, whether we view it
as directly propounding itself as such a standard, or implanting feelings arbitrarily to which it afterwards refers.
The path leads us by a longer circuit, but the issue is the
same: indeed, when searched narrowly, the difference is
only this, that a secret sense of deception, painful even
to entertain for a moment, aggravates the evil of the
former view. The contrast is the same as would be felt
between the sway of an arbitrary sovereign, who should

claim obedience to his commands on the sole ground of
power; and one who should further claim the praise of
his subjects for governing with the sanction of a senate
of his own appointing, and tamely subservient to his will.
Yet surely this would be a faithful emblem of the divine
government, could we conceive the moral emotions as of
arbitrary appointment, and liable to be reversed at will
so that what we now condemn as evil, we might in such
a case have been taught to praise as good. From such
a view the mind recoils even more than from the former,
and takes refuge in the parallel expostulation, 'Shall the
throne of iniquity have fellowship with Thee, which
frameth mischief by a law?'

Now if we accept the illustration afforded by geometry, the mist clears from around us, and these spectral
difficulties haunt us no longer. The relations which there
present themselves, as soon as perceived, suggest the feeling of unchangeableness. Though both the forms of
matter from which they have been abstracted, and the
mind which perceives them, readily acknowledge a creative will, with these the thought cannot be associated,
without the sense of an entire disparity. The only aspect
in which we can regard them, is as the objects of an all-
including intuition, but not as the objects of arbitrary
power. And in meditating closely on Moral Truth, we
shall find the same conviction equally strong. It is as
easy to conceive the laws of space inverted as the laws of
conscience, and to grant that the properties of the circle
might change, as that treachery should become a virtue,
and compassion a crime. So rooted is this conviction of
good and evil as anterior to choice, and law, as in
thought at least earlier than will, that reason and revelation unite in tracing it even up to the throne of God, and

He who sits thereon himself accounts it his glory, that
He delights in judgment, justice, and loving-kindness.
And thus, in the words of Hooker, the "perfection which
God is, giveth perfection to that He doeth," and that
Eternal Law, whose voice is the harmony of the world,
and to whom all creatures in heaven and earth do homage,
finds in His bosom her seat and surest resting-place.

If any, however, shrink from this view, as seeming to
affix bounds to Infinite Power, they will do well to reflect
that, by rejecting it, the still nobler attribute of wisdom
is entirely excluded. Wisdom lies in the choice of the
highest ends, and the best means to ensure their accomplishment; and the idea of means and of an end alike
involves a fixed relation, so that without the former the
latter could not equally be ensured. Exclude this, and
a series of effectless and unconnected acts comes in the
room of moral government, and a cold and iron fate
usurps the place in the thoughts of a widening and still
progressive Providence.

There is another subject of much practical importance,
which the present comparison may assist in explaining,
and which will serve to account for much of the uncertainty often associated with moral science. In the
barrenness of imperfect definitions, which describe loosely,
without defining, we may learn the effect of a low and
variable standard of right and wrong in impairing the
vitality of truth, and blocking up the avenues of wisdom.
It is not enough, for instance, that a triangle were defined
as a figure bounded by three sides, unless we imply that
the sides are strictly right lines. A single consequence
could not be else deduced, and the figure might pass by
insensible change into a tortuous curve. And very similar
is the result, when we would bend in our reasonings the

rule of integrity, however lightly, to meet some purpose of passing convenience. No further lesson can then be learned: the key is twisted from its natural shape, and will no longer open the mysteries of Providence, or move freely in the wards of the heart.

The last step which requires notice in all demonstrations is that course of deduction, which, starting from previous definitions, passes into all the varied theorems of science. To define is to lay the foundation, but this rears the superstructure. There are two modes of arriving at truth, 'induction,' and 'deduction,' or syllogism. In the former we rise from instances to general maxims, in the latter we re-descend, whether from the maxims of induction, or the intuitive truths of reason, to remoter results. And the figure has further propriety, for in rising, the course, though safe, is laborious and slow, while the descent is easy, but a single false step may prove dangerous to the whole.

It is amusing to observe, how in the schools of modern philosophy, as in other schools where the master has lost his authority, reprisals have been taken for former bondage, and it seems felt as the greatest triumph of their young liberty, to pull Aristotle or Plato by the beard. The treatment which the syllogism has received at their hands is a striking instance. It appears to haunt them with the memory of past subjection. Every folly of the schools, not to say every crime of the middle ages, has been laid at its door; and the vehemence with which they have exorcised it might lead us to suspect that this was the triple knot of darkness, which so long had shrouded learning in its gloom.

On a calm examination, we find little ground for this indignant contempt with which it has been greeted. The syllogism, as a recent encyclopedist has justly stated, was never designed by Aristotle for a new and peculiar degree of argument, and still less, as the rather flippant remark of Locke would imply, as a means for making men rational, but simply as an expression of the course which the mind silently pursues in all its reasonings. It is a method for spelling out distinctly the steps of an argument. A reader, who should spell every word at length, it is true, might make us first laugh. and soon grow weary. But though in correct and tasteful reading many letters are always silent, and even many words passed over lightly, still it can scarcely be doubted that he who would read without danger of mistake must at some time or other have learned to spell. And so it is in the case before us. A train of reasoning, as expressed, may usually be only a series of minor propositions issuing in the conclusion; and in the readiness of the mind to invent, and its strength to retain these, resides mainly its reasoning power; but the major must always be silently implied, or fallacy creeps in, and the argument fails. And hence, though in point of expression a syllogism might be called a redundant enthymeme, in point of thought it must be found that an enthymeme, as its name implies, is only a secret and mental syllogism.

Against the course of syllogistic reasoning, the writer before alluded to, in common with several others of equal note, brings forward a more important charge. They accuse it of entire and necessary barrenness. And as this perhaps is the most common source of the opinion that the certainty of science is not attainable in morals, it will require to be briefly examined. The charge is, simply, that a syllogism begs the point in debate, and assumes the very thing it is wanted to prove; and that, since the

major involves the conclusion, the latter must be felt to
be true, before the former can be justly admitted.

It is easy to see that this triumphant charge, which is
brought with the air of a valuable discovery, does not lie
against the forms of logic, but against the very nature of
deductive reasoning. To deduce is not to create or to
invent, but merely to unfold. The fallacy lies in supposing that when a proposition is felt and granted to be
true, all its various consequences must also be felt and
known. In a separate syllogism this may seem to be the
case, and here is the secret of that fancied leanness to
which Reid and Brown allude; but to denounce, on this
ground, the whole process of deduction as unnecessary
and superfluous, is as reasonable as to persuade a man
that his legs are useless, because he appears just where
he was after a single stride.

The present analogy, however, more palpably sets
aside this objection, and places the importance of deduction in its fullest light. The demonstrations of geometry
are simply a course of syllogistic reasoning; and though
to throw the whole into mood and figure would be absurd,
yet, on suspicion of a lurking fallacy, any part might be
presented in a syllogistic form. Do we then speak of the
process as idle, or the results as useless or uncertain, because they must all have been included, as truly they
must, in the principles from which they have been derived? Or rather, is it not the greatest boast of this
science, that from definitions so simple, and axioms so
few, it brings to light conclusions innumerable, that spread
into all the fields of nature, and supply all the arts of
society with ceaseless inventions? For, to use again the
figure which a misplaced ridicule supplies, it is not so
much the elder sons of truth's immortal family, as its

younger descendants, that stoop to intermarry with the
dying phenomena around us, and yield the offspring of arts
that minister to the comforts, or lessons that aid in the
guidance, of daily life.

Now there is nothing in the nature of moral subjects
to preclude our offering the same answer. The spirit of
man has its own self-evidence, conscience its own definitions, and those not cold and silent, as in geometry, but
vocal with strong emotion, and endued with a living
power; its truths are in their nature as prolific; the
opening for deduction is the same; and why should it not
lead to certainties as sure, and conclusions as various?
Even were we to speak of a person as knowing whatever
is involved in a truth which he admits, and thus with
Socrates in the *Meno* regard all reasoning as a calling to
memory things already known, however forced and unnatural such a style of expression would be, this could not
affect the practical importance of the course of deduction
we are considering. The acorn may be said to contain
the oak, but certainly will neither roof a palace, nor build
a navy: still less could that implicit knowledge, which on
such a view we may all be fancied to possess, supply the
place of expanded wisdom. The colours of the spectrum
must have been at first in the sunbeam, but are we therefore to speak of the prism as useless? Deduction is the
prism of the reason; and why should we prize it more
lightly, or place less faith in its power to unfold those
various hues of unknown beauty, which lie veiled beneath
the simplicity of truth?

But however complete the parallel between the nature
of Mathematical and Moral Science, in their postulates,
their definitions, their reasonings, and the certainty to
which they lead, we shall be in great danger of questioning

the whole, unless we bear in mind the great difference
which exists in the comparative ease of their attainment.
The path to the latter is encompassed with many obstacles
and dangers from which the former is free. Giant forms
of prejudice, the idols of the market, the theatre and the
cave, beset its approaches, with passion to bewilder, and
pleasure to betray. It is not merely as in the other case,
that the mind must be freed from distraction, and brought
into the attitude of patient attention—though even this
is no easy task. There is a moral atmosphere also needed,
clear from the cold damps of interest, with a kindly mixture of sunshine and shower, before the germs which may
have been sown in the conscience can grow up into full
conviction or ripened knowledge, or root themselves firmly
against the passing storm.

These observations, which are rather hints that might
lead to thought, than thoughts themselves, may be found,
perhaps, if pursued into their further bearings, to remove
the blank which has been so often felt, and which was
alluded to before. They would thus lead us to see the
great moral purpose to be fulfilled, when rightly understood, by mathematical truth, as one wide emblem of the
sureness of those unchanging laws, which, whether remem-
bered or forgotten, whether honoured or despised, rule
with unfailing might in the destinies of men and of kingdoms. Thus might we learn that this wand of science,
which has been used with fatal force by unblest hands,
to freeze the spirit into moral apathy, and bind down its
powers to earth, needs only to be reversed to break the
spell, and to rear it once more from the dust into the
mild and stately dignity which befits the assured possessor
of eternal truth. Once taught to understand this his

appointed office, even the Genius of the severer sciences, blinded almost by poring continually on his figures traced in the sand, might be brought to turn his countenance heavenward, and with silent and upward eye do homage to faith's calm and moonlight beam.

A remark on this subject, in closing, may not be un-suited to the time-hallowed walls of this retreat of learning and nursery of the Christian church.

There is something in the memory of departed ages, which lends a tender and solemn feeling to every theme with which it is mingled, and flings a twilight grandeur wherever it falls. And never perhaps does the high dignity of the pursuits of science strike the soul with deeper power, than when we thus view them as a charge bequeathed by past generations, and see its signal lights thus handed onward, and still onward, over the hills of time. It is then by degrees that we are wakened into the sense of its imperishableness; and while we reflect how many, that have sought to decipher this book of nature, have long since passed away, and these mysterious charac-ters remain unchanging and unchangeable, we gaze on it with a thrill of livelier interest, and feel that the names, which have engraven themselves on its truths, have gained a more lasting record than pillars of brass or iron. A feeling of awe thus mingles with our inquiries, as if we were searching into the archives of eternity; and if pri-vileged to pass onward a single step in these pleasant paths, the high consciousness awakens that we are now communing with truth, which from the beginning has had its dwelling in the temple of nature, but had ever before been veiled, in still retirement, from every mortal eye.

But if such be the direct interest of natural science, when viewed as the deposit left us by the fathers of a former age, how far deeper does it become, when we learn to see in it the reflected image of truth, immutable like itself, but nobler in its objects, and loftier in its aims; a truth mingled with all the mysteries of the soul's inmost consciousness, and which the same hands have entrusted to our charge! The porch itself is worthy of all admiration —how much more the temple into which it leads! And though we may see too many who enter the former, and admire its beauty, refusing to press into the inner shrine, and even turning their backs in contempt when they ought to adore, to worship nature in her forms of eastern splendor, forgetful of Him who has robed her in the garments of light, we shall not from this feel tempted to doubt the harmony of the whole building, or the veiled glory that dwells within. The pride of an exclusive pursuit may lead the sceptic analyst to grasp all certainty as his peculiar claim, and to look with scorn upon truths too living, and too mighty, for an enfeebled conscience and a palsied heart. But those who enter into the spirit of the fathers of our church, who have here left their memory at least to their children, will read the lessons of science with a different eye. And while they train their thoughts by its severe and wholesome discipline, they will also see in it a monitor that is ever pointing them onward to holier aims. Amidst the busy scenes of life, in all their farthest and most inland wanderings, they will hear its voice, like the mystic shell from the caves of ocean, breathe in their ears its soft and solemn warning. It will thus recall their thoughts to 'that immortal sea,' towards which the spirit yearns continually, till they dwell once more in

the presence of truths, unchanging and eternal, although
forsaken and unvisited by the passing throng,

> "And see the children sport upon the shore,
> And hear the mighty waters rolling evermore."

June 1872.

A Catalogue of Theological Books,
with a Short Account of their
Character and Aim,

Published by

MACMILLAN AND CO.

Bedford Street, Covent Garden, London.

Abbott (Rev. E. A.)—BIBLE LESSONS. By the Rev. E. A. Abbott, M.A., Head Master of the City of London School. Second Edition. Crown 8vo. 4s. 6d.

> *Among the subjects treated in this volume are:—"The Times of Christ," "The Life of Christ," "Christ's Miracles," "Christ's Sacrifice," "Love," "Forgiveness," "Faith," and "Prayer." The book is written in the form of dialogues carried on between teacher and pupil, and its main object is to make the scholar think for himself. "Wise, suggestive, and really profound initiation into religious thought."*—Guardian. *The Bishop of St. David's, in his speech at the Education Conference at Abergwilly, says he thinks " nobody could read them without being the better for them himself, and being also able to see how this difficult duty of imparting a sound religious education may be effected."*

1

Ainger (Rev. Alfred).—SERMONS PREACHED IN
THE TEMPLE CHURCH. By the Rev. ALFRED AINGER,
M.A. of Trinity Hall, Cambridge, Reader at the Temple Church.
Extra fcap. 8vo. 6s.

*This volume contains twenty-four Sermons preached at various times
during the last few years in the Temple Church, and are charac-
terised by such qualities as are likely to make them acceptable to
cultivated and thoughtful readers. The following are a few
of the topics treated of:—" Boldness;" " Murder, Ancient and
Modern;" "The Atonement;" " The Resurrection;" " The Fear
of Death;" " The Forgiveness of Sins, the Remission of a Debt"
(2 Sermons); "Anger, Noble and Ignoble;" "Culture and
Temptation;" " The Religious Aspect of Wit and Humour;"
"The Life of the Ascended Christ." " It is," the British Quarterly says, "the fresh unconventional talk of a clear independent
thinker, addressed to a congregation of thinkers . . . . Thoughtful
men will be greatly charmed by this little volume."*

Alexander.—THE LEADING IDEAS of the GOSPELS.
Five Sermons preached before the University of Oxford in 1870—
71. By WILLIAM ALEXANDER, D.D., Brasenose College; Lord
Bishop of Derry and Raphao; Select Preacher. Cr. 8vo. 4s. 6d.

*Each of these Sermons is on a characteristic text taken successively
from each of the four Gospels, there being two on that from St.
John; viz.—St. Matt. i. 1; St. Mark i. 1; St. Luke i. 3; St. John
i. 1, 14. " Dr. Alexander is eminently fitted for the task he has
undertaken. He has a singular felicity of style, which lights up
the discourse and clothes it with great beauty and impressiveness."*
—Nonconformist.

Arnold.—A BIBLE READING BOOK FOR SCHOOLS.
THE GREAT PROPHECY OF ISRAEL'S RESTORATION (Isaiah,
Chapters 40—66). Arranged and Edited for Young Learners. By
MATTHEW ARNOLD, D.C.L., formerly Professor of Poetry in the
University of Oxford, and Fellow of Oriel. 18mo, cloth. 1s.

Mr. Arnold has undertaken this really important task, on account

*of his conviction "of the immense importance in education of what
is called letters; of the side which engages our feelings and imagination." Mr. Arnold in this little volume, attempts to do for the
Bible what has been so abundantly done for Greek and Roman,
as well as English authors; viz.—to take "some whole, of admirable literary beauty in style and treatment, of manageable
length, within defined limits; and present this to the learner in an
intelligible shape, adding such explanations and helps as may enable
him to grasp it as a connected and complete work." Mr. Arnold
thinks it clear that nothing could more exactly suit the purpose
than the last twenty-seven chapters of the Book of Isaiah, beginning
"Comfort ye" &c. He has endeavoured to present a perfectly correct text, maintaining at the same time the unparalleled balance
and rhythm of the Authorized Version. In the copious notes every
assistance is given to the complete understanding of the text. There
is nothing in the book to hinder the adherent of any school of interpretation or of religious belief from using it. The Preface
contains much that is interesting and valuable on the relation of
"letters" to education, of the principles that ought to guide the
makers of a new version of the Bible, and other important matters.
Altogether, it is believed, the volume will be found to form a text-
book of the greatest value to schools of all classes.*

Baring-Gould.—LEGENDS OF OLD TESTAMENT
CHARACTERS, from the Talmud and other sources. By the
Rev. S. BARING-GOULD, M.A., Author of "Curious Myths of
the Middle Ages," "The Origin and Development of Religious
Belief," "In Exitu Israel," etc. In two vols. crown 8vo. 16s.
Vol. I. Adam to Abraham. Vol. II. Melchizidek to Zechariah.

*Mr. Baring-Gould's previous contributions to the History of Mytho-
logy, and the formation of a science of comparative religion are
admitted to be of the highest importance; the present work, it is
believed, will be found of equal value. He has collected from the
Talmud and other sources, Jewish and Mahommedan, a large
number of curious and interesting legends concerning the principal
characters of the Old Testament, comparing these frequently with
similar legends current among many of the peoples, savage and*

civilised, all over the world. "These volumes contain much that is strange, and to the ordinary English reader, very novel."—
Daily News.

Barry, Alfred, D.D.—The ATONEMENT of CHRIST.

Six Lectures delivered in Hereford Cathedral during Holy Week, 1871. By ALFRED BARRY, D.D., D.C.L., Canon of Worcester, Principal of King's College, London. Fcap. 8vo. 2s. 6d.

In writing these Sermons, it has been the object of Canon Barry to set forth the deep practical importance of the doctrinal truths of the Atonement. "The one truth," says the Preface, "which, beyond all others, I desire that these may suggest, is the inseparable unity which must exist between Christian doctrine, even in its more mysterious forms, and Christian morality or devotion. They are a slight contribution to the plea of that connection of Religion and Theology, which in our own time is so frequently and, as it seems to me, so unreasonably denied." The Guardian calls them "striking and eloquent lectures."

Binney.—SERMONS PREACHED IN THE KING'S WEIGH HOUSE CHAPEL, 1829—69. By THOMAS BINNEY,

D.D. New and Cheaper Edition. Extra fcap. 8vo. 4s. 6d.

*In the earnestness and vigour which characterise the sermons in this volume the reader will find a clue to the vast influence exerted by Mr. Binney for forty years over a wide circle, particularly young men. In the concluding sermon, preached after the publication of the first edition, he reviews the period of his ministry as a whole, dwelling especially on its religious aspects. "Full of robust intelligence, of reverent but independent thinking on the most profound and holy themes, and of earnest practical purpose."—*London Quarterly Review.

Burgon.—A TREATISE on the PASTORAL OFFICE.

Addressed chiefly to Candidates for Holy Orders, or to those who have recently undertaken the cure of souls. By the Rev. JOHN W. BURGON, M.A., Oxford. 8vo. 12s.

The object of this work is to expound the great ends to be accomplished by the Pastoral office, and to investigate the various means by which these ends may best be gained. Full directions are given as to preaching and sermon-writing, pastoral visitation, village education and catechising, and confirmation. Under the heading of "Pastoral Method" the author shows how each of the occasional offices of the Church may be most properly conducted, as well as how a clergyman's ordinary public ministrations may be performed with the greatest success. The best methods of parochial management are examined, and an effort is made to exhibit the various elements of the true pastoral spirit. "The spirit in which it approaches and solves practical questions is at once full of common sense and at the same time marked by a deep reverential piety and a largeness of charity which are truly admirable."—Spectator.

Butler (G.)—Works by the Rev. GEORGE BUTLER, M.A., Principal of Liverpool College :

FAMILY PRAYERS. Crown 8vo. 5s.

The prayers in this volume are all based on passages of Scripture—the morning prayers on Select Psalms, those for the evening on portions of the New Testament.

SERMONS PREACHED in CHELTENHAM COLLEGE CHAPEL. Crown 8vo. 7s. 6d.

These Sermons, twenty-nine in number, were delivered at intervals from the opening of Cheltenham College Chapel in 1858, to the last Sunday of the year 1861, and contain references to the important events which occurred during that period—the Indian mutiny, the French campaign in Italy, the liberation of Sicily and Naples, the establishment of the kingdom of Italy, the American Civil War, and the deaths of many eminent men. "These sermons are plain, practical, and well adapted to the auditors. . . . . We cordially recommend the volume as a model of pulpit style, and for individual and family reading."—Weekly Review.

Butler (Rev. H. M.)—SERMONS PREACHED in the CHAPEL OF HARROW SCHOOL. By H. MONTAGU BUTLER, Head Master. Crown 8vo. 7s. 6d.

Whilst these Sermons were prepared to meet the wants of a special class,

Butler (Rev. H. M.)—*continued.*

there is a constant reference in them to the great principles which underlie all Christian thought and action. They deal with such subjects as "Temptation," "Courage," "Duty without regard to consequences," "Success," "Devout Impulses," and "The Soul's need of God." "These sermons are adapted for every household. There is nothing more striking than the excellent good sense with which they are imbued."—Spectator.

A SECOND SERIES. Crown 8vo. 7s. 6d.

"Excellent specimens of what sermons should be,—plain, direct, practical, pervaded by the true spirit of the Gospel, and holding up lofty aims before the minds of the young."—Athenæum.

Butler (Rev. W. Archer).—Works by the Rev. WILLIAM ARCHER BUTLER, M.A., late Professor of Moral Philosophy in the University of Dublin:—

SERMONS, DOCTRINAL AND PRACTICAL. Edited, with a Memoir of the Author's Life, by THOMAS WOODWARD, Dean of Down. With Portrait. Eighth and Cheaper Edition, 8vo. 8s.

This volume contains twenty-six Sermons by one of the most earnest, thoughtful, and eloquent preachers of his time, treating of almost every point of evangelical doctrine and Christian practice. The following selections from the titles of the sermons will give a fair idea of the contents of the volume:—"The Mystery of the Holy Incarnation;" "The Daily Self-Denial of Christ;" "The Power of the Resurrection;" "Self-Delusion as to our Real State before God;" "The Faith of Man and the Faithfulness of God;" "The Wedding-Garment;" "Human Affections Raised, not Destroyed by the Gospel;" "The Rest of the People of God;" "The Divinity of our Priest, Prophet, and King;" "Church Education in Ireland" (two Sermons). The Introductory Memoir narrates in considerable detail and with much interest, the events of Butler's brief life; and contains a few specimens of his sweet and tender poetry, and

Butler (Rev. W. Archer.)—*continued.*

a few extracts from his thoughtful addresses and essays, including a long and eloquent passage on the Province and Duty of the Preacher.

A SECOND SERIES OF SERMONS. Edited by J. A. JEREMIE, D.D., Dean of Lincoln. Sixth and Cheaper Edition. 8vo. 7s.

In this volume are contained other twenty-six of the late Professor Butler's Sermons, embracing a wide range of Christian topics, as will be seen by the following selection from the titles:—" Christ the Source of all Blessings;" " The Hope of Glory and the Charities of Life;" "The Holy Trinity;" " The Sorrow that Exalts and Sanctifies;" " The Growth of the Divine Life;" " The Folly of Moral Cowardice;" "Strength and Mission of the Church;" " The Blessedness of Submission;" " Eternal Punishment." The North British Review says, " Few sermons in our language exhibit the same rare combination of excellencies; imagery almost as rich as Taylor's; oratory as vigorous often as South's; judgment as sound as Barrow's; a style as attractive but more copious, original, and forcible than Atterbury's; piety as elevated as Howe's, and a fervour as intense at times as Baxter's. Mr. Butler's are the sermons of a true poet."

LETTERS ON ROMANISM, in reply to Dr. Newman's Essay on Development. Edited by the Dean of Down. Second Edition, revised by Archdeacon HARDWICK. 8vo. 10s. 6d.

These Letters contain an exhaustive criticism, written in the author's most vigorous and polished style, of Dr. Newman's famous " Essay on the Development of Christian Doctrine." An attempt is made to shew that the theory is opposed to the received doctrine of the Romish Church; that it is based on purely imaginary grounds, and necessarily carries with it consequences in the highest degree dangerous both to Christianity and to general truth. Whilst the work is mainly polemical in its character, it contains the exposition of many principles of far more than mere temporary interest. "A work which ought to be in the Library of every student of Divinity."—BP. ST. DAVID'S.

LECTURES ON ANCIENT PHILOSOPHY. *See* SCIENTIFIC CATALOGUE.

Cambridge Lent Sermons. — SERMONS preached during Lent, 1864, in Great St. Mary's Church, Cambridge. By the BISHOP OF OXFORD, Revs. H. P. LIDDON, T. L. CLAUGHTON, J. R. WOODFORD, Dr. GOULBURN, J. W. BURGON, T. T. CARTER, Dr. PUSEY, Dean HOOK, W. J. BUTLER, Dean GOODWIN. Crown 8vo. 7*s*. 6*d*.

The names of the preachers of these Sermons are a guarantee that they are worth reading. They were preached on the Wednesdays and Fridays during Lent 1864, and treat of the following among other subjects:—"God in His Perfections the Measure of the Sinfulness of Sin in the Creature," by the Bishop of Oxford; "Adam hiding himself from the Presence of the Lord," by the Rev. H. P. Liddon; "God the Hope and Joy of the Penitent," by the Rev. T. T. Carter; "David in his Sin and his Penitence," by the Rev. Dr. Pusey; "God the Consolation of the Afflicted," by the Very Rev. Dean Hook; "God the Reward of the Faithful," by the Rev. W. J. Butler.

Campbell. — Works by JOHN M'LEOD CAMPBELL :—

THE NATURE OF THE ATONEMENT AND ITS RELATION TO REMISSION OF SINS AND ETERNAL LIFE. Third Edition, with an Introduction and Notes. 8vo. 10*s*. 6*d*.

Three chapters of this work are devoted to the teaching of Luther on the subject of the Atonement, and to Calvinism, as taught by Dr. Owen and President Edwards, and as recently modified. The remainder is occupied with the different aspects of the Atonement as conceived by the author himself, the object being partly to meet the objections of honest inquirers, but mainly so to reveal the subject in its own light as to render self-evident its adaptation to the spiritual wants of man. The book has been found richly suggestive by many of the profoundest minds in the Church. Professor Rolleston, in quoting from this book in his address to the Biological Section of the British Association (Liverpool, September, 1870), speaks of it as "the great work of one of the first of living theologians." "Among the first theological treatises of this generation." — Guardian.

Campbell (J. M'Leod.)—*continued.*

CHRIST THE BREAD OF LIFE. An Attempt to give a profitable direction to the present occupation of Thought with Romanism. Second Edition, greatly enlarged. Crown 8vo. 4s. 6d.

In this volume the Doctrines of the Infallibility of the Church and Transubstantiation are regarded as addressed to real inward needs of humanity, and an effort is made to disengage them from the truths whose place they usurp, and to exhibit these truths as adequate to meet human cravings. The aim is, first, to offer help to those who feel the attractions to Romanism too strong to be overcome by direct arguments addressed to sense and reason; and, second, to quicken interest in the Truth itself. "Deserves the most attentive study by all who interest themselves in the predominant religious controversy of the day."—Spectator.

Cheyne.—Works by T. K. CHEYNE, M.A., Fellow of Balliol College, Oxford :—

THE BOOK OF ISAIAH CHRONOLOGICALLY ARRANGED. An Amended Version, with Historical and Critical Introductions and Explanatory Notes. Crown 8vo. 7s. 6d.

The object of this edition is to restore the probable meaning of Isaiah, so far as can be expressed in appropriate English. The basis of the version is the revised translation of 1611, but alterations have been introduced wherever the true sense of the prophecies appeared to require it. The Westminster Review *speaks of it as "a piece of scholarly work, very carefully and considerately done." The* Academy *calls it "a successful attempt to extend a right understanding of this important Old Testament writing."*

NOTES AND CRITICISMS on the HEBREW TEXT OF ISAIAH. Crown 8vo. 2s. 6d.

This work is offered as a slight contribution to a more scientific study of the Old Testament Scriptures. The author aims at completeness, independence, and originality, and constantly endeavours to keep philology distinct from exegesis, to explain the form without pronouncing on the matter. Saad Yah's Arabic Version in the Bod-

lsian has been referred to, while Walton and Buxtorf have been carefully consulted. The philological works of German critics, especially Ewald and Delitsch, have been anxiously and repeatedly studied. The Academy *calls the work "a valuable contribution to the more scientific study of the Old Testament."*

Choice Notes on the Four Gospels, drawn from Old and New Sources. Crown 8vo. 4s. 6d. each Vol. (St. Matthew and St. Mark in one Vol. price 9s.).

These Notes are selected from the Rev. Prebendary Ford's Illustrations of the Four Gospels, the choice being chiefly confined to those of a more simple and practical character. The plan followed is to go over the Gospels verse by verse, and introduce the remarks, mostly meditative and practical, of one or more noted divines, on the verses selected for illustration. The names of the writers from whom the remarks are taken are invariably appended to the extracts, and amongst others to be met with, are the following:—J. Ford, Bonaventura, William Law, Pascal, Austin, Dr. Donne, Bonnell, Flavel, Bishop Hall, Dr. John Scott, Thomas Scott, R. Cecil, St. Ambrose, Bengel, Bishop Reynolds, J. H. Newman, George Herbert, Bishop Jewel, Jeremy Taylor, Cardinal Bellarmine, Quarles, St. Augustine, Archbishop Trench, Archbishop Leighton, Lord Bacon, Dr. Pusey, St. Chrysostom, Dr. Arnold, Thomas Fuller. Thus the selection is made in a catholic spirit, and the reader will find it a safe and useful companion in his meditations.

Church.—SERMONS PREACHED BEFORE the UNIVERSITY OF OXFORD. By the very Rev. R. W. CHURCH, M.A., Dean of St. Paul's. Second Edition. Crown 8vo. 4s. 6d.

Sermons on the relations between Christianity and the ideas and facts of modern civilized society. The subjects of the various discourses are:—" The Gifts of Civilization," " Christ's Words and Christian Society," " Christ's Example," and " Civilization and Religion." " Thoughtful and masterly . . . We regard these sermons as a landmark in religious thought. They help us to understand the latent strength of a Christianity that is assailed on all sides."— Spectator.

Clay.—THE POWER OF THE KEYS. Sermons preached
in Coventry. By the Rev. W. L. CLAY, M.A. Fcap. 8vo. 3s. 6d.

*In this work an attempt is made to shew in what sense, and to what
extent, the power of the Keys can be exercised by the layman, the
Church, and the priest respectively. The* Church Review *says the
sermons are "in many respects of unusual merit."*

Clergyman's Self-Examination concerning the
APOSTLES' CREED. Extra fcap. 8vo. 1s. 6d.

*"These Confessions have been written by a clergyman for his own use.
They speak of his own unbelief. Possibly they may help some of
his brethren, who wish to judge themselves that they may not be
ashamed before the Judge of all the earth." He takes each clause
of the Creed and examines it in the light of common sense, in order
to obtain its real meaning; searching at the same time his own
heart to discover to what extent he really believes the statements so
frequently uttered by him. Not only is it calculated to afford
material aid to a proper understanding of the Creed, but will also
be found extremely useful as a manual of devotion.*

Collects of the Church of England. With a beautifully Coloured Floral Design to each Collect, and Illuminated
Cover. Crown 8vo. 12s. Also kept in various styles of morocco.

*In this edition of the Church Collects, the paper is thick and hand-
some, and the type large and beautiful, each Collect, with a few
exceptions, being printed on a separate page. The distinctive characteristic of this edition is the coloured floral design which ac-
companies each Collect, and which is generally emblematical of the
character of the day or saint to which it is assigned; the flowers
which have been selected are such as are likely to be in bloom on the
day to which the Collect belongs. From the variety of plants
elected and the faithfulness of the illustrations to nature, the
volume should form an instructive and interesting companion to
all devout Christians, who are likely to find their devotions assisted
and guided by having thus brought before them the flowers in their
seasons, God's beautiful and never-failing gifts to men. The*

*Preface explains the allusions and the table of contents gives both
the popular and scientific name of each plant. There are at least
one hundred separate plants figured. "Carefully, indeed lovingly
drawn and daintily coloured," says the* Pall Mall Gazette. *The*
Guardian *thinks it "a successful attempt to associate in a natural
and unforced manner the flowers of our fields and gardens with
the course of the Christian year."*

Cotton.—Works by the late GEORGE EDWARD LYNCH
COTTON, D.D., Bishop of Calcutta:—

SERMONS PREACHED TO ENGLISH CONGREGA-
TIONS IN INDIA. Crown 8vo. 7s. 6d.

*These Sermons are selected from those which were preached between
the years 1863 and 1866 to English congregations under the varied
circumstances of place and season which an Indian Bishop encounters. "The sermons are models of what sermons should be,
not only on account of their practical teachings, but also with
regard to the singular felicity with which they are adapted to times,
places, and circumstances."—*Spectator.

EXPOSITORY SERMONS ON THE EPISTLES FOR
THE SUNDAYS OF THE CHRISTIAN YEAR. Two
Vols. Crown 8vo. 15s.

*These two volumes contain in all fifty-seven Sermons. They were
all preached at various stations throughout India, and from the
nature of the circumstances which called them forth, the varied
subjects of which they treat are dealt with in such a manner as is
likely to prove acceptable to Christians in general. Each sermon,
furnishes some account of the context and general scope of the epistle
for the day, with a careful paraphrase of it, and with an explanation of any important difficulties occurring in it; and in conclusion, draws out the main truths or precepts of the epistle. The
Preface contains some sensible remarks on "Complaints against
Modern Sermons," "Expository Preaching," "Plan of the Sermon," and other topics.*

Cure.—THE SEVEN WORDS OF CHRIST ON THE CROSS. Sermons preached at St. George's, Bloomsbury. By the Rev. E. CAPEL CURE, M.A. Fcap. 8vo. 3s. 6d.

These seven Sermons were preached at St. George's, Bloomsbury, during the season of Lent, each having for its text one of the seven last sayings of Christ while He hung on the Cross, as they are recorded in the following places:—(1) *Luke xxiii.* 34; (2) *Luke xxiii.* 43; (3) *John xix.* 26; (4) *Matthew xxvii.* 46; (5) *John xix.* 28; (6) *John xix.* 30; (7) *Luke xxiii.* 46. *Of these Sermons the* John Bull *says,* "*They are earnest and practical;*" *the* Nonconformist, "*The Sermons are beautiful, tender, and instructive;*" *and the* Spectator *calls them* "*A set of really good Sermons.*"

Curteis.—DISSENT in its RELATION to the CHURCH OF ENGLAND. Eight Lectures preached before the University of Oxford, in the year 1871, on the foundation of the late Rev. John Bampton, M.A., Canon of Salisbury. By GEORGE HERBERT CURTEIS, M.A., late Fellow and Sub-Rector of Exeter College; Principal of the Lichfield Theological College, and Prebendary of Lichfield Cathedral; Rector of Turweston, Bucks. 8vo. 14s.

In these Bampton Lectures the Author has endeavoured to accomplish three things:—I. To shew those who are in despair at the present divided aspect of Christendom, that from the Apostles' time downwards there has never been an age of the Church without similar internal conflicts; that if well managed, these dissensions may be kept within bounds, and made to minister to the life and movement of the whole polity; but if ill-managed, they are always liable to become a wasting fever instead of a healthy warmth. II. To present materials by which Churchmen might be aided in forming an intelligent and candid judgment as to what precisely these dissenting denominations really are; what it is they do, and what they claim to teach; and why it is they are now combining to bring the Church of England, if possible, to the ground. III. To point out some few indications of the wonderful and every way deplorable misapprehensions which have clothed the Church of England to their eyes in colours absolutely foreign to her true character; have ascribed to her doctrines absolutely contrary to her meaning; and have interpreted her customs in a way repellant to the Christian Common-sense of her own people.

Davies.—Works by the Rev. J. LLEWELYN DAVIES, M.A., Rector of Christ Church, St. Marylebone, etc. :—

THE WORK OF CHRIST ; or, the World Reconciled to God. With a Preface on the Atonement Controversy. Fcap. 8vo. 6s.

The reader will here find, amongst others, sermons on " The forgiveness of sins," " Christ dying for men," " Sacrifice," " The Example of Christ," " The Baptism of Christ," " The Temptation of Christ," "Love, Divine and Human," " Creation by the Word," " Holy Seasons," and " The Coming of the Son of Man." The Preface is devoted to shewing that certain popular theories of the Atonement are opposed to the moral sense of mankind, and are not imposed on Christians by statements either in the Old or New Testaments.

SERMONS on the MANIFESTATION OF THE SON OF GOD. With a Preface addressed to Laymen on the present Position of the Clergy of the Church of England; and an Appendix on the Testimony of Scripture and the Church as to the possibility of Pardon in the Future State. Fcap. 8vo. 6s. 6d.

The Preface to this work is mainly occupied with the distinction between the essential and non-essential elements of the Christian faith, proving that the central religious controversy of the day relates, not, as many suppose, to such questions as the Inspiration of Scripture, but to the profounder question, whether the Son of God actually has been manifested in the person of Jesus of Nazareth. The grounds on which the Christian bases his faith are also examined. In the Appendix the testimony of the Bible and the Anglican formularies as to the possibility of pardon in the future state is investigated. The sermons, of which the body of the work is composed, treat of the great principles revealed in the words and acts of Jesus. " This volume, both in its substance, prefix, and suffix, represents the noblest type of theology now preached in the English Church."—Spectator.

Davies (Rev. J. Llewelyn)—*continued.*

BAPTISM, CONFIRMATION, AND THE LORD'S
SUPPER, as Interpreted by their Outward Signs. Three Expository Addresses for Parochial use. Fcap. 8vo., limp cloth.
1*s.* 6*d.*

*The method adapted in these addresses is to set forth the natural and
historical meaning of the signs of the two Sacraments and of Confirmation, and thus to arrive at the spiritual realities which they
symbolize. The work touches on all the principal elements of a
Christian man's faith.*

THE EPISTLES of ST. PAUL TO THE EPHESIANS,
THE COLOSSIANS, and PHILEMON. With Introductions
and Notes, and an Essay on the Traces of Foreign Elements in
the Theology of these Epistles. 8vo. 7*s.* 6*d.*

*The Author believes the Epistles to the Ephesians and Colossians to
be specially adapted to the wants of the present age. The chief aim,
therefore, of the translations and notes in the present volume is
simply to bring out as accurately as possible the apostle's meaning.
The General Introduction, treats mainly of the time and circumstances in which Paul is believed to have written these Epistles.
To each Epistle there is a special critical introduction. The
Essay "On the Traces of Foreign elements in the Doctrine of
these Epistles" discusses the question how far the ideas in the
Epistles which resemble gnostical systems are to be found in books
and traditions to which St. Paul and his contemporaries had
access. "A valuable contribution to the literature of the Pauline
Epistles."—*Freeman.*

MORALITY ACCORDING TO THE SACRAMENT
OF THE LORD'S SUPPER. Crown 8vo. 3*s.* 6*d.*

*These discourses were preached before the University of Cambridge.
They form a continuous exposition, and are directed mainly against
the two-fold danger which at present threatens the Church—the
tendency, on the one hand, to regard Morality as independent of
Religion, and, on the other, to ignore the fact that Religion finds
its proper sphere and criterion in the moral life.*

Davies (Rev. J. Llewelyn)—*continued.*

THE GOSPEL and MODERN LIFE. Sermons on some of the Difficulties of the Present Day, with a Preface on a Recent Phase of Deism. Extra fcap. 8vo. 6s.

The "recent phase of Deism" examined in the preface to this volume is that professed by the "Pall Mall Gazette"—that in the sphere of Religion there are one or two "probable suppositions," but nothing more. The writer starts with an assumption that mankind are under a Divine discipline, and in the light of this conviction passes under review the leading religious problems which perplex thoughtful minds of the present day. Amongst other subjects examined are—"Christ and Modern Knowledge," "Humanity and the Trinity," "Nature," "Religion," "Conscience," "Human Corruption," and "Human Holiness." "There is probably no writer in the Church fairer or more thoroughly worth listening to than Mr. Llewelyn Davies, and this book will do more than sustain his already high reputation."—Globe.

De Teissier.—Works by G. F. DE TEISSIER, B.D.:—

VILLAGE SERMONS, FIRST SERIES. Crown 8vo. 9s.

This volume contains fifty-four short Sermons, embracing many subjects of practical importance to all Christians. The Guardian says they are "a little too scholarlike in style for a country village, but sound and practical." The following are a few of the titles of the Sermons:—"Death of the Prince Consort;" "Particular Providence;" "The Suffering Christ;" "Charity the Crown of Christianity;" "On Self-Deceit;" "On Hypocrisy;" "Christ Risen;" "The Comfort of Religion;" "Good Neighbourhood;" "The Return of Spring;" "A Harvest Sermon;" "Heart-Religion."

VILLAGE SERMONS, SECOND SERIES. Crown 8vo. 8s. 6d.

"This second volume of Parochial Sermons is given to the public in the humble hope that it may afford many seasonable thoughts for such as are Mourners in Zion." There are in all fifty-two Sermons embracing a wide variety of subjects connected with Christian faith and practice.

De Teissier (G. F.)—*continued.*

THE HOUSE OF PRAYER ; or, a Practical Exposition of the Order for Morning and Evening Prayer in the Church of England. 18mo. extra cloth. 4s. 6d.

"*There is in these addresses to the Christian reader,*" *says the Introduction, an attempt to set forth the* devotional *spirit of our Church in her daily forms of Morning and Evening Prayer, by shewing how all the parts of them may have a just bearing upon Christian practice, and so may have a deep influence upon the conduct of all our honest worshippers, under every possible relation and circumstance of life.*" "*For a certain devout tenderness of feeling and religious earnestness of purpose, this little book of Mr. De Teissier's is really noteworthy; and it is a book which grows upon you very much when you read it.*"—Literary Churchman.

Ecce Homo. A SURVEY OF THE LIFE AND WORK OF JESUS CHRIST. 23rd Thousand. Crown 8vo. 6s.

It is needless to say anything in recommendation of a book so widely known, and whose striking merit has been recognised by men and periodicals of all varieties of opinion. The following are a few selections from the very favourable notices with which the press has received it. "*A very original and remarkable book, full of striking thought and delicate perception; a book which has realised with wonderful vigour and freshness the historical magnitude of Christ's work, and which here and there gives us readings of the finest kind of the probable motive of His individual words and actions.*"— Spectator. *He bates not a jot of Christ's pretensions. Miracles he insists upon as an integral part of the history. With a generous-minded sceptic this book may lead him on to give earnest and persistent attention to Christianity. The best and most established believer will find it adding some fresh buttresses to his faith. Finally it traces the working of the great principles of Christian charity through all the ramifications of character and action.*"— Literary Churchman. *If we have not misunderstood him, we have before us a writer who has a right to claim deference from those who think deepest and know most.*"—Guardian.

2

Farrar.—Works by the Rev. F. W. FARRAR, M.A., F.R.S., Head Master of Marlborough College, and Hon. Chaplain to the Queen :—

THE FALL OF MAN, AND OTHER SERMONS.
Second and Cheaper Edition. Extra fcap. 8vo. 4s. 6d.

This volume contains twenty Sermons. No attempt is made in these sermons to develope a system of doctrine. In each discourse some one aspect of truth is taken up, the chief object being to point out its bearings on practical religious life. The Nonconformist says of these Sermons,—"Mr. Farrar's Sermons are almost perfect specimens of one type of Sermons, which we may concisely call beautiful. The style of expression is beautiful—there is beauty in the thoughts, the illustrations, the allusions—they are expressive of genuinely beautiful perceptions and feelings." The British Quarterly says,—"Ability, eloquence, scholarship, and practical usefulness, are in these Sermons combined in a very unusual degree."

THE WITNESS OF HISTORY TO CHRIST. Being the Hulsean Lectures for 1870. New Edition. Crown 8vo. 5s.

In these Lectures, Mr. Farrar endeavours to grapple with the most recent manifestations of infidelity, and endeavours to prove the divinity of Christ and the supernatural origin of Christianity on rational grounds, and by an appeal to the origin and progress of the Christian Religion itself. The copious notes contain many references which will be found of great use to the enquiring student. The following are the subjects of the Five Lectures:—I. "The Antecedent Credibility of the Miraculous." II. "The Adequacy of the Gospel Records." III. "The Victories of Christianity." IV. "Christianity and the Individual." V. "Christianity and the Race." The subjects of the four Appendices are:—A. "The Diversity of Christian Evidences." B. "Confucius." C. "Buddha." D. "Comte." "Here," the Standard says, "we have eloquence combined with abundant information on all points of importance, both as regards theology and classical accuracy. This renders the book one of lasting value."

SEEKERS AFTER GOD. The Lives of Seneca, Epictetus, and Marcus Aurelius. See SUNDAY LIBRARY at end of Catalogue.

Fellowship: LETTERS ADDRESSED TO MY SISTER MOURNERS. Fcap. 8vo. cloth gilt. 3s. 6d.

*The Seven Letters contained in this little volume are written by one who has herself been shrouded in the darkest shadow of affliction consequent on being bereaved of one in whom her whole life was built up. In these Letters she tells her own sorrowful tale in un-affected, tender, touching words, which cannot but appeal to all who are placed in a similar comfortless position. She does not attempt to preach or to aggravate the sorrow and sense of loss of mourners by administering advice which they cannot take, or quoting texts and sentiments calculated only to irritate. She speaks of her loss and consequent grief in such a way as only a genuine mourner can; of the well-meant but aggravating comfort and useless advice administered her by her many comforters, and shews her fellow-mourners by what means, in course of soothing time, she got consolation and arrived at calmness and resignation. "A beautiful little volume, written with genuine feeling, good taste, and a right appreciation of the teaching of Scripture relative to sorrow and suffering."—*Nonconformist.* "A very touching, and at the same time a very sensible book. It breathes throughout the truest Christian spirit."—*Contemporary* Review.*

Forbes.—THE VOICE OF GOD IN THE PSALMS. By GRANVILLE FORBES, Rector of Broughton. Cr. 8vo. 6s. 6d.

This volume contains a connected series of twenty Sermons, divided into three parts, the two first parts being Introductory. Part I. treats of the "Ground of Faith," and consists of four Sermons on "Faith in God," "God's Voice within us," "Faith in God the Ground of Faith in the Bible," and "God's Voice in the Bible." Part II. treats of "The Voice of God in the Law and the Prophets," on which there are four Sermons; and Part III., occupying the greater part of the volume, deals with "The Voice of God in the Psalms," and consists of twelve Sermons. The last Sermon is on "The Voice of God in History." The Literary Churchman *says these Sermons are "characterized throughout by a strong realisation of the Providence and Fatherhood of God, and by their vivid apprehension of the Voice of God within man as answering to and accepting the Revelation of God to Man."*

Gifford.—THE GLORY OF GOD IN MAN. By E. H. GIFFORD, D.D. Fcap. 8vo., cloth. 3s. 6d.

This is a connected sequence of four Sermons which treat of "The Unrighteousness of Man," "The Righteousness of God," "Life in Christ," and "The Love of the Spirit." Notes are appended in which the sentiments of various authors on the statements made are quoted or referred to. " The sermons are short, thoughtful, and earnest discussions of the weighty matter involved in the subjects of them."—Journal of Sacred Literature.

Golden Treasury Psalter. *See* p. 50.

Hardwick.—Works by the Ven. ARCHDEACON HARDWICK:

CHRIST AND OTHER MASTERS. A Historical Inquiry into some of the Chief Parallelisms and Contrasts between Christianity and the Religious Systems of the Ancient World. New Edition, revised, and a Prefatory Memoir by the Rev. FRANCIS PROCTER, M.A. Two vols. crown 8vo. 15s.

After several introductory chapters dealing with the religious tendencies of the present age, the unity of the human race, and the characteristics of Religion under the Old Testament, the Author proceeds to consider the Religions of India, China, America, Oceanica, Egypt, and Medo-Persia. The history and characteristics of these Religions are examined, and an effort is made to bring out the points of difference and affinity between them and Christianity. The object is to establish the perfect adaptation of the latter faith to human nature in all its phases and at all times. "The plan of the work is boldly and almost nobly conceived. . . We commend the work to the perusal of all those who take interest in the study of ancient mythology, without losing their reverence for the supreme authority of the oracles of the living God."- Christian Observer.

A HISTORY OF THE CHRISTIAN CHURCH. Middle Age. From Gregory the Great to the Excommunication of Luther. Edited by WILLIAM STUBBS, M.A., Regius Professor of Modern History in the University of Oxford. With Four Maps constructed for this work by A. KEITH JOHNSTON. Third Edition. Crown 8vo. 10s. 6d.

Although the ground-plan of this treatise coincides in many points

Hardwick (Archd.)—*continued.*

with that of the colossal work of Schröckh, yet in arranging the materials a very different course has frequently been pursued. With regard to his opinions the late author avowed distinctly that he construed history with the specific prepossessions of an Englishman and a member of the English Church. The reader is constantly referred to the authorities, both original and critical, on which the statements are founded. For this edition Professor Stubbs has carefully revised both text and notes, making such corrections of facts, dates, and the like as the results of recent research warrant. The doctrinal, historical, and generally speculative views of the late author have been preserved intact. "As a Manual for the student of ecclesiastical history in the Middle Ages, we know no English work which can be compared to Mr. Hardwick's book." —Guardian.

A HISTORY of the CHRISTIAN CHURCH DURING THE REFORMATION. New Edition, revised by Professor STUBBS. [*In the Press.*

This volume is intended as a sequel and companion to the "History of the Christian Church during the Middle Age." The author's earnest wish has been to give the reader a trustworthy version of those stirring incidents which mark the Reformation period, without relinquishing his former claim to characterise peculiar systems, persons, and events according to the shades and colours they assume, when contemplated from an English point of view, and by a member of the Church of England.

Hervey.—THE GENEALOGIES OF OUR LORD AND SAVIOUR JESUS CHRIST, as contained in the Gospels of St. Matthew and St. Luke, reconciled with each other, and shown to be in harmony with the true Chronology of the Times. By Lord ARTHUR HERVEY, Bishop of Bath and Wells. 8vo. 10s. 6d.

The difficulties and importance of the subject are first stated, the three main points of inquiry being clearly brought out. The Author then proceeds to shew that the genealogies of St. Matthew's and St. Luke's Gospels are both genealogies of Joseph, and examines the principle on which they are framed. In the following chapters the remaining aspects of the subject are exhaustively investigated.

Hymni Ecclesiæ.—Fcap. 8vo. 7s. 6d.

A selection of Latin Hymns of the Mediæval Church, containing selections from the Paris Breviary, and the Breviaries of Rome, Salisbury, and York.   The selection is confined to such holy days and seasons as are recognised by the Church of England, and to special events or things recorded in Scripture.   This collection was edited by Dr. Newman while he lived at Oxford.

Kempis, Thos. A.— DE IMITATIONE CHRISTI.

LIBRI IV.   Borders in the Ancient Style, after Holbein, Durer, and other Old Masters, containing Dances of Death, Acts of Mercy, Emblems, and a variety of curious ornamentations. In white cloth, extra gilt. 7s. 6d.

The original Latin text has been here faithfully reproduced.   The Spectator says of this edition, it "has many solid merits, and is perfect in its way."   While the Athenæum says, " The whole work is admirable; some of the figure compositions have extraordinary merit."

Kingsley.—Works by the Rev. CHARLES KINGSLEY, M.A.,

Rector of Eversley, and Canon of Chester.   (For other Works by the same author, *see* HISTORICAL and BELLES LETTRES CATALOGUES).

The high merits of Mr. Kingsley's Sermons are acknowledged. Whether preached to the rustic audience of a village Church or to the princely congregation of the Chapel Royal, these Sermons are invariably characterized by intense earnestness and magnanimity, combined with genuine charity and winning tenderness ; the style is always clear, simple, and unaffectedly natural, abounding in beautiful illustration, the fruit of a rich fancy and a cultivated taste.   They are emphatically practical.

THE WATER OF LIFE, AND OTHER SERMONS.

Second Edition. Fcap. 8vo. 3s. 6d.

This volume contains twenty-one Sermons preached at various places —Westminster Abbey, Chapel Royal, before the Queen at Windsor,

Kingsley (Rev. C.)—*continued*.

etc. The following are a few of the titles:—"The Water of Life;" "The Wages of Sin;" "The Battle of Life;" "Ruth;" "Friendship, or David and Jonathan;" "Progress;" "Faith;" "The Meteor Shower" (1866); *"Cholera"* (1866); *"The God of Nature."*

VILLAGE SERMONS. Seventh Edition. Fcap. 8vo. 3s. 6d.

The following are a few of the titles of these Sermons:—"God's World;" "Religion not Godliness;" "Self-Destruction;" "Hell on Earth;" "Noah's Justice;" "Our Father in Heaven;" "The Transfiguration;" "The Crucifixion;" "The Resurrection;" "Improvement;" "On Books;" "The Courage of the Saviour."

THE GOSPEL OF THE PENTATEUCH. Second Edition. Fcap. 8vo. 3s. 6d.

This volume consists of eighteen Sermons on passages taken from the Pentateuch. They are dedicated to Dean Stanley out of gratitude for his Lectures on the Jewish Church, under the influence and in the spirit of which they were written. "With your book in my hand," Mr. Kingsley says in his Preface, "I have tried to write a few plain Sermons, telling plain people what they will find in the Pentateuch. I have told them that they will find in the Bible, and in no other ancient book, that living working God, whom their reason and conscience demand; and that they will find that He is none other than Jesus Christ our Lord."

GOOD NEWS OF GOD. Fourth Edition. Fcap. 8vo. 3s. 6d.

This volume contains thirty-nine short Sermons, preached in the ordinary course of the author's parochial ministrations. A few of the titles are—"The Beatific Vision;" "The Life of God;" "The Song of the Three Children;" "Worship;" "De Profundis;" "The Race of Life;" "Heroes and Heroines;" "Music;" "Christ's Boyhood;" "Human Nature;" "True Prudence;" "The Temper of Christ;" "Our Deserts;" "The Loftiness of God."

Kingsley (Rev. C.)—*continued.*

SERMONS FOR THE TIMES. Third Edition. Fcap.
8vo. 3s. 6d.

*Here are twenty-two Sermons, all bearing more or less on the every-
day life of the present day, including such subjects as these:—
"Fathers and Children;" "A Good Conscience;" "Names;"
"Sponsorship;" "Duty and Superstition;" "England's Strength;"
"The Lord's Prayer;" "Shame;" "Forgiveness";" The True
Gentleman:" "Public Spirit."*

TOWN AND COUNTRY SERMONS. Second Edition.
Extra fcap. 8vo. 3s. 6d.

*Some of these Sermons were preached before the Queen, and some in
the performance of the writer's ordinary parochial duty. There are
thirty-nine in all, under such titles as the following:—"How to keep
Passion-Week;" "A Soldier's Training;" "Turning-points;"
"Work;" "The Rock of Ages;" "The Loftiness of Humility;"
"The Central Sun;" "Ex Torre Nuca;" "The Eternal Manhood;" "Hypocrisy;" "The Wrath of Love." Of these Sermons
the Nonconformist says, "They are warm with the fervour of the
preacher's own heart, and strong from the force of his own convictions. There is nowhere an attempt at display, and the clearness and simplicity of the style make them suitable for the youngest
or most unintelligent of his hearers."*

SERMONS on NATIONAL SUBJECTS. Second Edition.
Fcap. 8vo. 3s. 6d.

THE KING OF THE EARTH, and other Sermons.
a Second Series of Sermons on National Subjects. Second
Edition. Fcap. 8vo. 3s. 6d.

*The following extract from the Preface to the 2nd Series will explain
the preacher's aim in these Sermons:—"I have tried......to proclaim the Lord Jesus Christ, as the Scriptures, both in their*

Kingsley (Rev. C.)—*continued.*

> strictest letter and in their general method, from Genesis to Reve-
> lation, seem to me to proclaim Him; not merely as the Saviour of
> a few elect souls, but as the light and life of every human being
> who enters into the world; as the source of all reason, strength,
> and virtue in heathen or in Christian; as the King and Ruler of
> the whole universe, and of every nation, family, and man on
> earth; as the Redeemer of the whole earth and the whole human
> race...... His death, as a full, perfect, and sufficient sacrifice,
> oblation, and satisfaction for the sins of the whole world, by which
> God is reconciled to the whole human race.

DISCIPLINE, AND OTHER SERMONS. Fcp. 8vo. 3s. 6d.

> Herein are twenty-four Sermons preached on various occasions, some
> of them of a public nature—at the Volunteer Camp, Wimbledon,
> before the Prince of Wales at Sandringham, at Wellington College,
> etc. A few of the titles are—"Discipline" (to Volunteers);
> "Prayer and Science;" "False Civilisation;" "The End of
> Religion;" "The Humanity of God;" "God's World;" "Self-
> Help;" "Toleration;" "The Likeness of God." This volume
> the Nonconformist calls,—"Eminently practical and appropriate
> ...... Earnest stirring words." The Guardian says,—"There is
> much thought, tenderness, and devoutness of spirit in these Sermons,
> and some of them are models both in matter and expression."

DAVID. FOUR SERMONS: David's Weakness—David's
Strength—David's Anger—David's Deserts. Fcap. 8vo. 2s. 6d.

> These four Sermons were preached before the University of Cam-
> bridge, and are specially addressed to young men. Their titles are,
> —"David's Weakness;" "David's Strength;" "David's Anger;"
> "David's Deserts." The Freeman says—"Every paragraph
> glows with manly energy, delivers straightforward practical truths,
> in a vigorous, sometimes even passionate way, and exhibits an
> intense sympathy with everything honest, pure, and noble."

Lightfoot.—Works by J. B. LIGHTFOOT, D.D., Hulsean
Professor of Divinity in the University of Cambridge; Canon of
St. Paul's.

ST. PAUL'S EPISTLE TO THE GALATIANS. A Revised Text, with Introduction, Notes, and Dissertations. Third
Edition, revised. 8vo. cloth. 12s.

> *The subjects treated in the Introduction are—the Galatian people, the
> Churches of Galatia, the date and genuineness of the Epistle, and
> its character and contents. The dissertations discuss the question
> whether the Galatians were Celts or Tartars, and the whole subject
> of "The Brethren of the Lord," and "St. Paul and the Three."
> While the Author's object has been to make this commentary
> generally complete, he has paid special attention to everything re-
> lating to St. Paul's personal history and his intercourse with the
> Apostles and Church of the Circumcision, as it is this feature in
> the Epistle to the Galatians which has given it an overwhelming
> interest in recent theological controversy. The* Spectator *says
> "there is no commentator at once of sounder judgment and more
> liberal than Dr. Lightfoot."*

ST. PAUL'S EPISTLE TO THE PHILIPPIANS. A
Revised Text, with Introduction, Notes, and Dissertations. Second
Edition. 8vo. 12s.

> *The plan of this volume is the same as that of "The Epistle to the
> Galatians." The Introduction deals with the following subjects:
> —"St. Paul in Rome," "Order of the Epistles of the Captivity,"
> "The Church of Philippi," "Character and Contents of the Epistle,"
> and its genuineness. The Dissertations are on "The Christian
> Ministry," "St. Paul and Seneca," and "The Letters of Paul
> and Seneca." "No commentary in the English language can be
> compared with it in regard to fulness of information, exact
> scholarship, and laboured attempts to settle everything about the
> epistle on a solid foundation."—*Athenæum. *"Its author blends
> large and varied learning with a style as bright and easy, as telling
> and artistic, as that of our most accomplished essayists."—*Non-
> conformist.

Lightfoot (Dr. J. B.)—*continued.*

ST. CLEMENT OF ROME, THE TWO EPISTLES TO
THE CORINTHIANS. A Revised Text, with Introduction
and Notes. 8vo. 8s. 6d.

*This volume is the first part of a complete edition of the Apostolic
Fathers. The Introductions deal with the questions of the genuine-
ness and authenticity of the Epistles, discuss their date and character,
and analyse their contents. An account is also given of all the
different epistles which bear the name of Clement of Rome. "By
far the most copiously annotated edition of St. Clement which we
yet possess, and the most convenient in every way for the English
reader."—Guardian.*

ON A FRESH REVISION OF THE ENGLISH NEW
TESTAMENT. Second Edition. Crown 8vo. 6s.

*The Author begins with a few words on S. Jerome's revision of the
Latin Bible, and then goes on to shew in detail the necessity for
a fresh revision of the authorized version on the following grounds:
—1. False Readings. 2. Artificial distinctions created. 3. Real
distinctions obliterated. 4. Faults of Grammar. 5. Faults of
Lexicography. 6. Treatment of Proper Names, official titles, etc.
7. Archaisms, defects in the English, errors of the press, etc.
The volume is completed by (1) an elaborate appendix on the words
δικαίωσις and πειρασμός, (2) a table of passages of Scripture
quoted, and (3) a general index. "The book is marked by careful
scholarship, familiarity with the subject, sobriety, and circumspec-
tion."—Athenæum. "It abounds with evidence of the most extensive learning, and of a masterly familiarity with the best results
of modern Greek scholarship."—Standard.*

Luckock.—THE TABLES OF STONE. A Course of
Sermons preached in All Saints' Church, Cambridge, by H. M.
LUCKOCK, M.A., Vicar. Fcap. 8vo. 3s. 6d.

*Sermons illustrative of the great principles of morality, mostly based
on texts from the New Testament Scriptures.*

Maclaren.—SERMONS PREACHED at MANCHESTER. By ALEXANDER MACLAREN. Third Edition. Fcap. 8vo. 4s. 6d.

These Sermons, twenty-four in number, are well known for the freshness and vigour of their thought, and the wealth of imagination they display. They represent no special school, but deal with the broad principles of Christian truth, especially in their bearing on practical, every day life. A few of the titles are:—" The Stone of Stumbling," " Love and Forgiveness," " The Living Dead," " Memory in Another World," " Faith in Christ," " Love and Fear," " The Choice of Wisdom," " The Food of the World."

A SECOND SERIES OF SERMONS. Second Edition. Fcap. 8vo. 4s. 6d.

This 2nd Series, consisting of nineteen Sermons, are marked by the same characteristics as the 1st. The Spectator characterises them as "vigorous in style, full of thought, rich in illustration, and in an unusual degree interesting."

Maclear.—Works by G. F. MACLEAR, D.D., Head Master of King's College School, and Preacher at the Temple Church :—

A CLASS-BOOK OF OLD TESTAMENT HISTORY. With Four Maps. Sixth Edition. 18mo. 4s. 6d.

" The present volume," says the Preface, "forms a Class-Book of Old Testament History from the Earliest Times to those of Ezra and Nehemiah. In its preparation the most recent authorities have been consulted, and wherever it has appeared useful, Notes have been subjoined illustrative of the Text, and, for the sake of more advanced students, references added to larger works. The Index has been so arranged as to form a concise Dictionary of the Persons and Places mentioned in the course of the Narrative." The Maps, prepared by Stanford, materially add to the value and usefulness of the book: they are—1. A Map illustrating the Dispersion of Noah's Descendants. 2. A Map of Canaan, Egypt, and Sinai, to illustrate the Patriarchal History and the Exodus; with Mt. Sinai enlarged. 3. The Holy Land divided among the Twelve Tribes. 4. Solomon's Dominions, the Kingdoms of Judah and Israel, and the Lands of the Captivities. In the Appendix are

Maclear (G. F.)—*continued.*

given a variety of Tables of great interest and utility. The British Quarterly Review calls it "A careful and elaborate, though brief compendium of all that modern research has done for the illustration of the Old Testament. We know of no work which contains so much important information in so small a compass."

A CLASS-BOOK OF NEW TESTAMENT HISTORY.
Including the Connexion of the Old and New Testament. Fourth Edition. 18mo. 5s. 6d.

The present volume forms a sequel to the Author's Class-Book of Old Testament History, and continues the narrative to the close of St. Paul's second imprisonment at Rome. It is marked by the same characteristics as the former work, and it is hoped that it may prove at once a useful Class-Book and a convenient companion to the study of the Greek Testament. The work is divided into three Books—I. The Connection between the Old and New Testaments. II. The Gospel History. III. The Apostolic History. In the Appendix are given Chronological Tables. I. Of the Jews under the Empire. II. The Era of the Ptolemies and Seleucidæ. III. Rise of the Herodian Family. IV. The Gospel History. V. The Apostolic History. Appendix VI. is a Table of the Herodian Family. There are five Maps, viz.—1. A Map of the Holy Land to illustrate the Asmonean Period. 2. A Map of the Holy Land to illustrate the New Testament. 3. The Shores of the Sea of Galilee. 4. Jerusalem in the time of our Lord. 5. A Map to illustrate the Apostolic History. The Clerical Journal *says, "It is not often that such an amount of useful and interesting matter on biblical subjects, is found in so convenient and small a compass, as in this well-arranged volume."*

A CLASS-BOOK OF THE CATECHISM OF THE CHURCH OF ENGLAND. Second Edition. 18mo. cloth. 2s. 6d.

The present work is intended as a sequel to the two preceding books. "Like them, it is furnished with notes and references to larger works, and it is hoped that it may be found, especially in the higher

Maclear (G. F.)—*continued.*

> *forms of our Public Schools, to supply a suitable manual of in-*
> *struction in the chief doctrines of our Church, and a useful help*
> *in the preparation of Candidates for Confirmation."* The Author
> *goes over the Church Catechism clause by clause, and gives all*
> *needful explanation and illustration, doctrinal, practical, and*
> *historical; the Notes make the work especially valuable to the student*
> *and clergyman. After a brief Introduction on the Derivation,*
> *Division, and History of the Catechism, the book is divided into*
> *five Parts:—I. The Christian Covenant. II. The Creed.*
> *III. The Ten Commandments. IV. The Lord's Prayer.*
> *V. The Sacraments. Appended are a General Index, an Index*
> *of Greek and Latin Words, and an Index of the Words ex-*
> *plained throughout the book.* The Literary Churchman *says,*
> *"It is indeed the work of a scholar and divine, and as such, though*
> *extremely simple, it is also extremely instructive. There are few*
> *clergy who would not find it useful in preparing candidates for*
> *Confirmation; and there are not a few who would find it useful to*
> *themselves as well."*

**A FIRST CLASS-BOOK OF THE CATECHISM OF
THE CHURCH OF ENGLAND,** with Scripture Proofs for
Junior Classes and Schools. Second Edition. 18mo. 6d.

> *This is an epitome of the larger Class-book, meant for junior students*
> *and elementary classes. The book has been carefully condensed, so*
> *as to contain clearly and fully, the most important part of the*
> *contents of the larger book. Like it the present Manual is sub-*
> *divided into five parts, each part into a number of short chapters,*
> *one or more of which might form a suitable lesson, and each*
> *chapter is subdivided in a number of sections, each with a pro-*
> *minent title indicative of its contents. It will be found a valuable*
> *Manual to all who are concerned with the religious training of*
> *children.*

A SHILLING-BOOK of OLD TESTAMENT HISTORY.
18mo. cloth limp. 1s.

> *This Manual bears the same relation to the larger Old Testament*

Maclear (G. F.)—*continued.*

History, that the book just mentioned does to the larger work on the Catechism. As in it, the small-type notes have been omitted, and a clear and full epitome given of the larger work. It consists of Ten Books, divided into short chapters, and subdivided into sections, each section treating of a single episode in the history, the title of which is given in bold type. The Map is clearly printed, and not overcrowded with names.

A SHILLING-BOOK of NEW TESTAMENT HISTORY. 18mo. cloth limp. 1s.

This bears the same relation to the larger New Testament History that the work just mentioned has to the large Old Testament History, and is marked by similar characteristics.

THE ORDER OF CONFIRMATION. A Sequel to the Class-Book of the Church Catechism, with Prayers and Collects. 18mo. 3d.

The Order of Confirmation is given in full, after which the Manual is divided into seven brief chapters:—I. "The Meaning of Confirmation." II. "The Origin of Confirmation." III., IV., V. "The Order of Confirmation," treating, (1) of "The Interrogation and Answer," (2) "The Laying on of Hands," (3) "The Prayers and Benediction," VI. "The Holy Communion." Chapter VII. consists of a few suitable Prayers and Collects intended to be used by the candidate during the days of preparation for Confirmation. Valuable references and notes are added. The Manual will be found valuable both by candidates and by clergymen. The Literary Churchman *calls it "An admirable Manual. Thoroughly sound, clear, and complete in its teaching, with some good, clear, personal advice as to Holy Communion, and a good selection of prayers and collects for those preparing for Confirmation."*

Macmillan.—Works by the Rev. HUGH MACMILLAN.   (For other Works by the same Author, see CATALOGUE OF TRAVELS and SCIENTIFIC CATALOGUE).

THE TRUE VINE; or, the Analogies of our Lord's Allegory.   Second Edition.   Globe 8vo.   6s.

This work is not merely an exposition of the fifteenth chapter of St. John's Gospel, but also a general parable of spiritual truth from the world of plants.   It describes a few of the points in which the varied realm of vegetable life comes into contact with the higher spiritual realm, and shews how rich a field of promise lies before the analogical mind in this direction.   The majority of the analogies are derived from the grape-vine; but the whole range of the vegetable kingdom is laid under contribution for appropriate illustration.   Indeed, Mr. Macmillan has brought into his service many of the results of recent scientific and historic research and biblical criticism; as well as the discoveries of travellers ancient and modern.   The work will thus be found not only admirably suited for devotional reading, but also full of valuable and varied instruction.   The Nonconformist *says, "It abounds in exquisite bits of description, and in striking facts clearly stated."   The* British Quarterly *says, "Readers and preachers who are unscientific will find many of his illustrations as valuable as they are beautiful."*

BIBLE TEACHINGS IN NATURE.   Sixth Edition. Globe 8vo.   6s.

In this volume the author has endeavoured to shew that the teaching of nature and the teaching of the Bible are directed to the same great end; that the Bible contains the spiritual truths which are necessary to make us wise unto salvation, and the objects and scenes of nature are the pictures by which these truths are illustrated. The first eight chapters describe, as it were, the exterior appearance of nature's temple—the gorgeous, many-coloured curtain hanging before the shrine.   The last seven chapters bring us into the interior—the holy place, where is seen the very core of symbolical ordinances.   "He has made the world more beautiful to us, and unsealed our ears to voices of praise and messages of love that might

Macmillan (H.)—*continued.*

> *otherwise have been unheard.*"—British Quarterly Review. "*Mr. Macmillan has produced a book which may be fitly described as one of the happiest efforts for enlisting physical science in the direct service of religion.*"—Guardian.

THE MINISTRY OF NATURE. Second Edition. Globe 8vo. 6s.

> *Mr. Macmillan believes that nature has a spiritual as well as a material side,—that she exists not only for the natural uses of the body, but also for the sustenance of the life of the soul. This higher ministry, the author believes, explains all the beauty and wonder of the world, which would often be superfluous or extravagant. In this volume of fourteen chapters the Author attempts to interpret Nature on her religious side in accordance with the most recent discoveries of physical science, and to shew how much greater significance is imparted to many passages of Scripture and many doctrines of Christianity when looked at in the light of these discoveries. Instead of regarding Physical Science as antagonistic to Christianity, the Author believes and seeks to shew that every new discovery tends more strongly to prove that Nature and the Bible have One Author. "Whether the reader agree or not with his conclusions, he will acknowledge he is in the presence of an original and thoughtful writer."—*Pall Mall Gazette. "*There is no class of educated men and women that will not profit by these essays.*"—Standard.

M'Cosh.—For Works by JAMES McCOSH, LL.D., President of Princeton College, New Jersey, U.S., *see* PHILOSOPHICAL CATALOGUE.

Maurice.—Works by the late Rev. F. DENISON MAURICE, M.A., Professor of Moral Philosophy in the University of Cambridge.

> *Professor Maurice's Works are recognized as having made a deep impression on modern theology. With whatever subject he dealt he tried to look at it in its bearing on living men and their everyday surroundings, and faced unshrinkingly the difficulties which*

Maurice (F. D.)—*continued.*

occur to ordinary earnest thinkers in a manner that showed he had intense sympathy with all that concerns humanity. By all who wish to understand the various drifts of thought during the present century, Mr. Maurice's works must be studied. An intimate friend of Mr. Maurice's, one who has carefully studied all his works, and had besides many opportunities of knowing the Author's opinions, in speaking of his so-called "obscurity," ascribes it to "the never-failing assumption that God is really moving, teaching and acting; and that the writer's business is not so much to state something for the reader's benefit, as to apprehend what God is saying or doing." The Spectator *says—"Few of those of our own generation whose names will live in English history or literature have exerted so profound and so permanent an influence as Mr. Maurice."*

THE PATRIARCHS AND LAWGIVERS OF THE OLD TESTAMENT. Third and Cheaper Edition. Crown 8vo. 5s.

The Nineteen Discourses contained in this volume were preached in the chapel of Lincoln's Inn during the year 1851. The texts are taken from the books of Genesis, Exodus, Numbers, Deuteronomy, Joshua, Judges, and Samuel, and involve some of the most interesting biblical topics discussed in recent times. In his Preface to the First Edition, Mr. Maurice endeavours to explain the mission and justify the position of the Church of England against the attacks of Dissenters and others; in his Preface to the Second Edition he comments upon some remarks made by Mr. Mansel on the meaning given by Mr. Maurice to the word 'Eternal.' In the latter Preface the writer says,—"My chief object in preaching and writing upon the Old Testament has been to shew that God has created man in His image; that being so created he is capable of receiving a revelation from God,—of knowing what God is; that without such a revelation he cannot be truly a man; that without such knowledge he cannot become what he is always feeling that he ought to become."

Maurice (F. D.)—*continued.*

THE PROPHETS AND KINGS OF THE OLD TES-
TAMENT.   Third Edition, with new Preface.   Crown 8vo.
10*s.* 6*d.*

*The previous work brings down Old Testament history to the time of
Samuel.   The Sermons contained in the present volume—twenty-
seven in number, coming down to the time of Ezekiel—though they
commence at that point are distinct in their subject and treatment.
Mr. Maurice, in the spirit which animated the compilers of the
Church Lessons, has in these Sermons regarded the Prophets more
as preachers of righteousness than as mere predictors—an aspect
of their lives which, he thinks, has been greatly overlooked in our
day, and than which, there is none we have more need to contemplate.   He has found that the Old Testament Prophets, taken
in their simple natural sense, clear up many of the difficulties
which beset us in the daily work of life; make the past intelligible,
the present endurable, and the future real and hopeful.   In the
Preface to this Third Edition, Mr. Maurice propounds his views
with regard to the connection of Church and State, with special
reference to the recent disestablishment of the Irish Church, and
the wish in certain quarters to treat the Church of England in the
same way.*

THE GOSPEL OF THE KINGDOM OF HEAVEN.
A Series of Lectures on the Gospel of St. Luke.   Crown 8vo.   9*s.*

*Mr. Maurice, in his Preface to these Twenty-eight Lectures, says,
—"In these Lectures I have endeavoured to ascertain what is told
us respecting the life of Jesus by one of those Evangelists who proclaim Him to be the Christ, who says that He did come from a
Father, that He did baptize with the Holy Spirit, that He did rise
from the dead.   I have chosen the one who is most directly connected with the later history of the Church, who was not an Apostle,
who professedly wrote for the use of a man already instructed in
the faith of the Apostles.   I have followed the course of the writer's
narrative, not changing it under any pretext.   I have adhered to
his phraseology, striving to avoid the substitution of any other for
his."   This is necessary on account of the conventional notions*

Maurice (F. D.)—*continued.*

*which most people are apt to attach to the words of the Gospels;
and in the remainder of his Preface, Mr. Maurice points out some
of these conventional notions, 1. In relation to Miracles. 2. On
the question, Are the Gospels the announcement of a religion?
3. Concerning Eternal Punishment. 4. The Authenticity and
Inspiration of the Gospels.*

THE GOSPEL OF ST. JOHN. A Series of Discourses.
Third and Cheaper Edition. Crown 8vo. 6s.

*These Discourses, twenty-eight in number, are of a nature similar
to those on the Gospel of St. Luke, and will be found to render
valuable assistance to any one anxious to understand the Gospel of
the beloved disciple, so different in many respects from those of the
other three Evangelists. Appended are eleven notes illustrating
various points which occur throughout the discourses, such as,
" Baur's Theory of the Gospels;" "On the objections to a Revision
of the Scriptures;" "On the Resurrection of the Body and the
Judgment-day;" "On the doctrine of the Atonement—Scotch and
English Divinity;" "On Corporate Holiness," etc. The Literary
Churchman thus speaks of this volume:—"Thorough honesty,
reverence, and deep thought pervade the work, which is every way
solid and philosophical, as well as theological, and abounding with
suggestions which the patient student may draw out more at length
for himself."*

THE EPISTLES OF ST. JOHN. A Series of Lectures
on Christian Ethics. Second and Cheaper Edition. Cr. 8vo. 6s.

*These Lectures on Christian Ethics were delivered to the students of
the Working Men's College, Great Ormond Street, London, on
a series of Sunday mornings. There are twenty Lectures in all,
founded on various texts taken from the Epistles of St. John, which
abound in passages bearing directly on the conduct of life, the duty
of men to God and to each other. It will be found that a very
complete system of practical morality is developed in this volume,
in which the most important points in Ethics are set forth in an
unconventional and interesting manner. Mr. Maurice believes
that the question in which we are most interested, the question which*

Maurice (F. D.)—*continued.*

most affects our studies and our daily lives, is the question, whether there is a foundation for human morality, or whether it is dependent upon the opinions and fashions of different ages and countries. This important question will be found amply and fairly discussed in this volume, which the National Review *calls " Mr. Maurice's most effective and instructive work. He is peculiarly fitted by the constitution of his mind, to throw light on St. John's writings." Appended is a note on "Positivism and its Teacher."*

EXPOSITORY SERMONS ON THE PRAYER-BOOK.
The Prayer-book considered especially in reference to the Romish System. Second Edition. Fcap. 8vo. 5s. 6d.

" There are certain popular notions which," says the Preface, " assume that the Church of England is the result of a compromise; that the Articles embody the opinions of one party to the bargain, the Liturgy those of the other; that every time I put my hand to the former document I proclaim myself in the strictest sense a Protestant, that every time I use the latter I act as a Papist; that in fact, I am neither. . . . In delivering these Sermons [in Lincoln's Inn Chapel in 1848-9], I endeavoured to tell laymen why I could with a clear heart and conscience ask them to take part with me in this Common Prayer. In publishing them I would address myself with equal earnestness and affection to another class, to the younger part of the clergy, and to those who are preparing for Orders." After an Introductory Sermon, Mr. Maurice goes over the various parts of the Church Service, expounds in eighteen Sermons, their intention and significance, and shews how appropriate they are as expressions of the deepest longings and wants of all classes of men.

LECTURES ON THE APOCALYPSE, or Book of the
Revelation of St. John the Divine. Crown 8vo. 10s. 6d.

These Twenty-three Lectures on what is generally regarded as the most mysterious Book in the Bible, do not demand that extensive knowledge of ancient or modern history which it is necessary to possess to be able to judge of most modern commentaries on Prophecy. Mr. Maurice, instead of trying to find far-fetched allusions to great historical events in the distant future, endeavours to discover the

Maurice (F. D.)—*continued.*

plain, literal, obvious meaning of the words of the writer, and shews that as a rule these refer to events contemporaneous with or immediately succeeding the time when the book was written. At the same time he shews the applicability of the contents of the book to the circumstances of the present day and of all times. Here, as in his other expositions of Scripture, Mr. Maurice attempts to shew that the Bible authorises us to believe that the Kingdom of Heaven, instead of being some dull Utopia in the far-distant future, is not "far off from any one of us," is indeed in our very midst. "Never," says the Nonconformist, *"has Mr. Maurice been more reverent, more careful for the letter of the Scripture, more discerning of the purpose of the Spirit, or more sober and practical in his teaching, than in this volume on the Apocalypse."*

WHAT IS REVELATION? A Series of Sermons on the Epiphany; to which are added, Letters to a Theological Student on the Bampton Lectures of Mr. Mansel. Crown 8vo. 10s. 6d.

Both Sermons and Letters were called forth by the doctrine maintained by Mr. Mansel in his Bampton Lectures, that Revelation cannot be a direct Manifestation of the Infinite Nature of God. Mr. Maurice maintains the opposite doctrine, and in his Sermons explains why, in spite of the high authorities on the other side, he must still assert the principle which he discovers in the Services of the Church and throughout the Bible. In the Letters to a Student of Theology, he has followed out all Mr. Mansel's Statements and Arguments step by step. The subjects of the Sermons are:—I. The Magians. II. Christ among the Doctors. III. St. Paul at Athens. IV. The Miracles. V. Casting out the Evil Spirit. VI. Christ's Parables. VII. Practice and Speculation. Among the matters discussed in the Letters are:— Sir William Hamilton; Butler; the Atonement and Incarnation; the Criterion of Truth; Philosophy of Consciousness; the Scotch; Prayer; Knowing and Being; the Trinity; Miracles; Kant; Contents and Evidences of the Bible. The Nonconformist *says, "There will be found ample materials to stimulate Christian faith and earnestness, to quicken and give tenderness to charity, and to vivify conceptions of the 'things not seen which are eternal.'"*

Maurice (F. D.)—*continued.*

SEQUEL TO THE INQUIRY, "WHAT IS REVELA-
TION?" Letters in Reply to Mr. Mansel's Examination of
"Strictures on the Bampton Lectures." Crown 8vo. 6s.

*This, as the title indicates, was called forth by Mr. Mansel's Ex-
amination of Mr. Maurice's Strictures on his doctrine of the
Infinite.*

THEOLOGICAL ESSAYS. Third Edition. Crown 8vo.
10s. 6d.

"*The book,*" says Mr. Maurice, "*expresses thoughts which have
been working in my mind for years; the method of it has not been
adopted carelessly; even the composition has undergone frequent
revision.*" *There are seventeen Essays in all, and although meant
primarily for Unitarians, to quote the words of the Clerical
Journal, "it leaves untouched scarcely any topic which is in agitation in the religious world; scarcely a moot point between our
various sects; scarcely a plot of debateable ground between Christians and Infidels, between Romanists and Protestants, between
Socinians and other Christians, between English Churchmen and
Dissenters on both sides. Scarce is there a misgiving, a difficulty, an aspiration stirring amongst us now,—now, when men
seem in earnest as hardly ever before about religion, and ask and
demand satisfaction with a fearlessness which seems almost awful
when one thinks what is at stake—which is not recognised and
grappled with by Mr. Maurice.*"

THE DOCTRINE OF SACRIFICE DEDUCED FROM
THE SCRIPTURES. Crown 8vo. 7s. 6d.

*Throughout the Nineteen Sermons contained in this volume, Mr.
Maurice expounds the ideas which he has formed of the Doctrine
of Sacrifice, as it is set forth in various parts of the Bible. The
first five Sermons consider various sacrifices referred to in the Old
Testament, while in the remainder the death and resurrection of
Christ are looked at from different points of view. He has "tried
to speak of Sacrifice under every aspect in which the Bible presents
it." In the Dedicatory Letter (occupying fifty pages) to the*

Maurice (F. D.)—*continued.*

Members of the Young Men's Christian Association, Mr. Maurice animadverts on an attack made on his opinions and character, by the Rev. Dr. Candlish of Edinburgh, in an address to that Society in Exeter Hall. "The habitual tone," says the Christian Spectator, *"is that of great seriousness and calm,—a seriousness which makes an impression of its own, and a serenity which is only broken by some overpowering feeling forcing itself into expression, and making itself heard in most meaning and stirring words."*

THE RELIGIONS OF THE WORLD, AND THEIR RELATIONS TO CHRISTIANITY. Fourth Edition. Fcap. 8vo. 5s.

These Eight Boyle Lectures are divided into two parts, of four Lectures each. In the first part Mr. Maurice examines the great Religious systems which present themselves in the history of the world, with the purpose of inquiring what is their main characteristic principle. The second four Lectures are occupied with a discussion of the questions, "In what relation does Christianity stand to these different faiths? If there be a faith which is meant for mankind, is this the one, or must we look for another?" In the Preface, the most important authorities on the various subjects discussed in the Lectures are referred to, so that the reader may pursue the subject further.

ON THE LORD'S PRAYER. Fourth Edition. Fcap. 8vo. 2s. 6d.

In these Nine Sermons the successive petitions of the Lord's Prayer are taken up by Mr. Maurice, their significance expounded, and, as was usual with him, connected with the every-day lives, feelings, and aspirations of the men of the present time. They were delivered in the momentous year 1848, and frequent allusions are made and lessons drawn from the events of that year.

ON THE SABBATH DAY; the Character of the Warrior, and on the Interpretation of History. Fcap. 8vo. 2s. 6d.

This volume contains Three Sermons on the Sabbath-day, one of them being in reference to the proposed opening of the Crystal Palace on Sunday—one on the "Character of the Warrior,"

Maurice (F. D.)—*continued.*

suggested by the Death of the Duke of Wellington; the fifth being on "The Divine Interpretation of History," delivered during the Great Exhibition of 1851. In this last Mr. Maurice points out a few difficulties which, judging from his own experience, he thinks likely to perplex students of history, explaining how the Bible has anticipated and resolved them.

THE GROUND AND OBJECT OF HOPE FOR MANKIND. Four Sermons preached before the University of Cambridge. Crown 8vo. 3s. 6d.

In these Four Sermons Mr. Maurice views the subject in four aspects:—I. The Hope of the Missionary. II. The Hope of the Patriot. III. The Hope of the Churchman. IV. The Hope of Man. The Spectator *says, " It is impossible to find anywhere deeper teaching than this;" and the* Nonconformist, *"We thank him for the manly, noble, stirring words in these Sermons—words fitted to quicken thoughts, to awaken high aspiration, to stimulate to lives of goodness."*

THE LORD'S PRAYER, THE CREED, AND THE COMMANDMENTS. A Manual for Parents and Schoolmasters. To which is added the Order of the Scriptures. 18mo. cloth limp. 1s.

This book is not written for clergymen, as such, but for parents and teachers, who are often either prejudiced against the contents of the Catechism, or regard it peculiarly as the clergyman's book, but, at the same time, have a general notion that a habit of prayer ought to be cultivated, that there are some things which ought to be believed, and some things which ought to be done. It will be found to be peculiarly valuable at the present time, when the question of religious education is occupying so much attention. The book consists of four parts:—I. The Lord's Prayer. II. The Belief (Creed). III. The Commandments. IV. The Scriptures. Each part is divided into days, for each day a petition of the Prayer, a clause of the Creed, a Commandment, or a book or connected group of books of the Bible is taken, and a few words of exhortation, explanation, or reflection given on the sentiment suggested.

Maurice (F. D.)—*continued.*

THE CLAIMS OF THE BIBLE AND OF SCIENCE.

A Correspondence on some Questions respecting the Pentateuch. Crown 8vo. 4*s.* 6*d.*

This volume consists of a series of Fifteen Letters, the first and last addressed by a 'Layman' to Mr. Maurice, the intervening thirteen written by Mr. Maurice himself. In the Layman's first letter to Mr. Maurice, immediately called forth by the appearance of Bishop Colenso's work on the Pentateuch, the writer sets forth some of the difficulties likely to be suggested to an ordinary thinker and believer in Christianity, by recent criticisms on the Bible of the class to which the works of Colenso belong. Three questions especially he propounds, to which, he thinks, a layman may naturally at the present time ask for an answer:—1. Do not our faith in Christ, and our belief in the four Gospels as a real history, rest on grounds independent of the results of any critical inquiry into the authorship of the Pentateuch? 2. May we not continue to read the Pentateuch as the Word of God, speaking of man and to man, without putting a forced construction on the plain meaning of the words, and without imposing fetters on the freedom of scientific or critical investigation in any matters which God has given us the power to inquire into? 3. Is faith in Christ contingent on the proof or disproof of the existence of certain natural phenomena, which seem not to accord with the language of the Bible? Mr. Maurice, in his Thirteen Letters, takes up these and the other points suggested by the Layman, and endeavours to clear them up and to throw light on the all-important Biblical controversy generally.

DIALOGUES ON FAMILY WORSHIP. Crown 8vo. 6*s.*

"The parties in these Dialogues," says the Preface, "are a Clergyman who accepts the doctrines of the Church, and a Layman whose faith in them is nearly gone. The object of the Dialogues is not confutation, but the discovery of a ground on which two Englishmen and two fathers may stand, and on which their country and their children may stand when their places know them no more." Some of the most important doctrines of the Church are discussed, the whole series of dialogues tending to shew

Maurice (F. D.)—*continued.*

that men of all shades of belief may look up to and worship God as their common and loving Father. The key-words of the Dialogues are as follow:—I. A Layman's Perplexities. II. A Mother's Faith. III. Male Calvinism. IV. The Regenerate and the Unregenerate. V. The Natural and the Supernatural. VI. The Revelation and the Family of Abraham. VII. The Father and the Son. VIII. Repentance and Conversion. IX. Fathers in God. X. Heathen and Christian Devotion. XI. The Method of Prayer. XII. The Soul and the Spirit.

THE COMMANDMENTS CONSIDERED AS IN-STRUMENTS OF NATIONAL REFORMATION. Crown 8vo. 4s. 6d.

This is a book of practical morality and divinity. It was to some extent occasioned by Dr. Norman Macleod's Speech on the Sabbath, and his views of the Commandments. The author endeavours to shew that the Commandments are now, and ever have been, the great protesters against Presbyteral and Prelatical assumptions, and that if we do not receive them as Commandments of the Lord God spoken to Israel, and spoken to every people under heaven now, we lose the greatest witnesses we possess for national morality and civil freedom.

MORAL AND METAPHYSICAL PHILOSOPHY. Vol. I. Ancient Philosophy from the First to the Thirteenth Centuries. Vol. II. Fourteenth Century and the French Revolution, with a Glimpse into the Nineteenth Century. Two Vols. 8vo. 25s.

This is an edition in two volumes of Professor Maurice's History of Philosophy from the earliest period to the present time. It was formerly issued in a number of separate volumes, and it is believed that all admirers of the author and all students of philosophy will welcome this compact edition. In a long introduction to this edition, in the form of a dialogue, Professor Maurice justifies his own views, and touches upon some of the most important topics of the time.

Maurice (F. D.)—*continued.*

SOCIAL MORALITY. Twenty-one Lectures delivered in the University of Cambridge. Cheaper Edition. [*In the Press.*

*In this series of Lectures, Professor Maurice considers, historically and critically, Social Morality in its three main aspects:—I. "The Relations which spring from the Family—Domestic Morality." II. "Relations which subsist among the various constituents of a Nation—National Morality." III. "As it concerns Universal Humanity—Universal Morality." Appended to each series is a chapter on "Worship:" first, "Family Worship;" second, "National Worship;" third, "Universal Worship." "Whilst reading it we are charmed by the freedom from exclusiveness and prejudice, the large charity, the loftiness of thought, the eagerness to recognise and appreciate whatever there is of real worth extant in the world, which animates it from one end to the other. We gain new thoughts and new ways of viewing things, even more, perhaps, from being brought for a time under the influence of so noble and spiritual a mind."—*Athenæum.*

THE CONSCIENCE: Lectures on Casuistry, delivered in the University of Cambridge. Second and Cheaper Edition. Crown 8vo. 5s.

In this series of nine Lectures, Professor Maurice, endeavours to settle what is meant by the word "Conscience," and discusses the most important questions immediately connected with the subject. Taking "Casuistry" in its old sense as being the "study of cases of Conscience," he endeavours to show in what way it may be brought to bear at the present day upon the acts and thoughts of our ordinary existence. He shows that Conscience asks for laws, not rules; for freedom, not chains; for education, not suppression. He has abstained from the use of philosophical terms, and has touched on philosophical systems only when he fancied "they were interfering with the rights and duties of wayfarers." The Saturday Review says: "We rise from the perusal of these lectures with a detestation of all that is selfish and mean, and with a living impression that there is such a thing as goodness after all."

Maurice (F. D.)—*continued.*

LECTURES ON THE ECCLESIASTICAL HISTORY OF THE FIRST AND SECOND CENTURIES. 8vo. 10s. 6d.

The work contains a series of graphic sketches and vivid portraits, bringing forcibly before the reader the life of the early Church in all its main aspects. In the first chapter on "The Jewish Calling," besides expounding his idea of the true nature of a " Church," the author gives a brief sketch of the position and economy of the Jews; while in the second he points out their relation to " the other Nations." Chapter Third contains a succint account of the various Jewish Sects, while in Chapter Fourth are briefly set forth Mr. Maurice's ideas of the character of Christ and the nature of His mission, and a sketch of events is given up to the Day of Pentecost. The remaining Chapters, extending from the Apostles' personal Ministry to the end of the Second Century, contain sketches of the character and work of all the prominent men in any way connected with the Early Church, accounts of the origin and nature of the various doctrines orthodox and heretical which had their birth during the period, as well as of the planting and early history of the Chief Churches in Asia, Africa and Europe. Besides the Apostles, the work contains characteristic sketches of the lives, position, and influence of Justin Martyr, St. Ignatius, Melito, Polycarp, Marcion, Dionysius of Corinth, Clement of Alexandria, Clement of Rome, Irenaeus, Tertullian, and many others. The three concluding chapters treat of the relations of the Church to the Emperors, the Philosophers, and the Sects.

LEARNING AND WORKING. Six Lectures delivered in Willis's Rooms, London, in June and July, 1854.—THE RELIGION OF ROME, and its Influence on Modern Civilisation. Four Lectures delivered in the Philosophical Institution of Edinburgh, in December, 1854. Crown 8vo. 5s.

In the Dedication and Preface to this volume, Professor Maurice shows that these two sets of Lectures have many points of connection. In the first series of Lectures the author endeavours to explain to such an audience as was likely to meet in Willis's Rooms,

Maurice (F. D.)—*continued.*

> the scope and aims of the course of education established at the
> then recently founded Working Men's College, and at the same
> time expounds his notions of education in general, the pivot of his
> system being the truth that Learning and Working are not incom-
> patible. The title to the second series is a sufficient index to their
> nature.

Moorhouse.—Works by JAMES MOORHOUSE, M.A., Vicar
of Paddington :—

SOME MODERN DIFFICULTIES RESPECTING the
FACTS OF NATURE AND REVELATION. Fcap. 8vo.
2s. 6d.

> The first of these Four Discourses is a systematic reply to the Essay
> of the Rev. Baden Powell on Christian Evidences in "Essays and
> Reviews." The fourth Sermon, on "The Resurrection," is in
> some measure complementary to this, and the two together are
> intended to furnish a tolerably complete view of modern objections
> to Revelation. In the second and third Sermons, on the "Tempta-
> tion" and "Passion," the author has endeavoured "to exhibit the
> power and wonder of those great facts within the spiritual sphere,
> which modern theorists have especially sought to discredit." The
> British Quarterly says of them,—"The tone of the discussion is
> able, and throughout conservative of Scriptural truth."

JACOB. Three Sermons preached before the University of
Cambridge in Lent 1870. Extra fcap. 8vo. 3s. 6d.

> In these Three Sermons the author endeavours to indicate the course
> of that Divine training by which the patriarch Jacob was converted
> from a deceitful and unscrupulous into a pious and self-denying
> man. In the first Sermon is considered "The Human Subject,"
> or the nature to be trained ; in the second "The Divine Power,"
> the power by which that training was effected ; and in the third
> "The Great Change," or the course and form of the training.

Moorhouse (J.)—*continued.*

THE HULSEAN LECTURES FOR 1865. Cr. 8vo. 5s.

> *The following are the subjects of the Four Hulsean Lectures in this volume:—I. "Bearing of Present Controversies on the Doctrine of the Incarnation." II. "How far the Hypothesis of a real Limitation in our Saviour's Human Knowledge is consistent with the Doctrine of His Divinity." III. "The Scriptural Evidence of our Saviour's Sinlessness." IV. "What Kind and Degree of Human Ignorance were left possible to our Lord Jesus Christ by the fact of His Human Sinlessness." The three Sermons which follow elucidate many difficulties which in the Lectures could not be investigated with that degree of care and fulness which was desirable. "Few more valuable works have come into our hands for many years . . . a most fruitful and welcome volume."*—Church Review.

O'Brien.—AN ATTEMPT TO EXPLAIN and ESTABLISH THE DOCTRINE OF JUSTIFICATION by FAITH ONLY. By JAMES THOMAS O'BRIEN, D.D., Bishop of Ossory. Third Edition. 8vo. 12s.

> *This work consists of Ten Sermons. The first four treat of the nature and mutual relations of Faith and Justification; the fifth and sixth examine the corruptions of the doctrine of Justification by Faith only, and the objections which have been urged against it. The four concluding sermons deal with the moral effects of Faith. Various Notes are added explanatory of the Author's reasoning.*

Palgrave.—HYMNS. By FRANCIS TURNER PALGRAVE. Third Edition, enlarged. 18mo. 1s. 6d.

> *This is a collection of twenty original Hymns, which the Literary Churchman speaks of as "so choice, so perfect, and so refined,— so tender in feeling, and so scholarly in expression."*

Palmer.—THE BOOK OF PRAISE: From the Best English Hymn Writers. Selected and arranged by Sir ROUNDELL PALMER. With Vignette by WOOLNER. 18mo. 4s. 6d.

> *The present is an attempt to present, under a convenient arrangement, a collection of such examples of a copious and interesting branch of*

popular literature, as, after several years' study of the subject, have seemed to the Editor most worthy of being separated from the mass to which they belong. It has been the Editor's desire and aim to adhere strictly, in all cases in which it could be ascertained, to the genuine uncorrupted text of the authors themselves. The names of the authors and date of composition of the hymns, when known, are affixed, while notes are added to the volume, giving further details. The Hymns are arranged according to subjects. "There is not room for two opinions as to the value of the 'Book of Praise.'" —Guardian. *"Approaches as nearly as one can conceive to perfection."*—Nonconformist.

BOOK OF PRAISE HYMNAL. *See* end of this Catalogue.

Paul of Tarsus. An Inquiry into the Times and the Gospel of the Apostles of the Gentiles. By a GRADUATE. 8vo. 10s. 6d.

The Author of this work has attempted, out of the materials which were at his disposal, to construct for himself a sketch of the time in which St. Paul lived, of the religious systems with which he was brought in contact, of the doctrine which he taught, and of the work which he ultimately achieved. The Author's researches have been pursued with independence, candour, and ability, and it is confidently expected that the work will afford considerable assistance towards the solution of the important question,—By what means, and under what pressure, have the dogmas of later Christianity been developed from the Pauline original? "Turn where we will throughout the volume, we find the best fruit of patient inquiry, sound scholarship, logical argument, and fairness of conclusion. No thoughtful reader will rise from its perusal without a real and lasting profit to himself, and a sense of permanent addition to the cause of truth."—Standard.

Prescott.—THE THREEFOLD CORD. Sermons preached before the University of Cambridge. By J. E. PRESCOTT, B.D. Fcap. 8vo. 3s. 6d.

The title of this volume is derived from the subjects of the first three of these Sermons—Love, Hope, Faith. Their full titles are:—

I. "*Christ the Bringer of Peace—Love.*" II. "*Christ the Renovator—Hope.*" III. "*Christ the Light—Faith.*" *The fourth, an Assize Sermon, is on "The Divinity of Justice." The Sermons are an attempt to shew that Christian theology is sufficient for the wants of the present day. The Notes throughout the volume direct the reader to valuable sources of information. The* Churchman *says the volume " is evidently the production of a scholar. Eloquent and striking passages abound throughout."*

Procter.—A HISTORY OF THE BOOK OF COMMON PRAYER: With a Rationale of its Offices. By FRANCIS PROCTER, M.A. Tenth Edition, revised and enlarged. Crown 8vo. 10s. 6d.

The fact that in fifteen years nine editions of this volume have been called for, shews that such a work was wanted, and that to a large extent Mr. Procter's book has supplied the want. "In the course of the last thirty years," the author says, "the whole subject has been investigated by divines of great learning, and it was mainly with a view of epitomizing their extensive publications, and correcting by their help sundry traditional errors or misconceptions, that the present volume was put together." The Second Part is occupied with an account of "The Sources and Rationale of the Offices." The Athenæum *says:—" The origin of every part of the Prayerbook has been diligently investigated,—and there are few questions or facts connected with it which are not either sufficiently explained, or so referred to, that persons interested may work out the truth for themselves."*

Procter and Maclear.—AN ELEMENTARY INTRODUCTION TO THE BOOK OF COMMON PRAYER. Fourth Edition, Re-arranged and Supplemented by an Explanation of the Morning and Evening Prayer and the Litany. By F. PROCTER, M.A. and G. F. MACLEAR, D.D. 18mo. 2s. 6d.

This book has the same object and follows the same plan as the Manuals already noticed under Mr. Maclear's name. Each book is subdivided into chapters and sections. In Book I. is given a detailed History of the Book of Common Prayer down to the

4

Attempted Revision in the Reign of William III. Book II., consisting of four Parts, treats in order the various parts of the Prayer Book. Valuable Notes, etymological, historical, and critical, are given throughout the book, while the Appendix contains several articles of much interest and importance. Appended is a General Index and an Index of Words explained in the Notes. The Literary Churchman *characterizes it as "by far the completest and most satisfactory book of its kind we know. We wish it were in the hands of every schoolboy and every schoolmaster in the kingdom."*

Psalms of David CHRONOLOGICALLY ARRANGED.

An Amended Version, with Historical Introductions and Explanatory Notes. By FOUR FRIENDS. Second and Cheaper Edition, much enlarged. Crown 8vo. 8s. 6d.

One of the chief designs of the Editors, in preparing this volume, was to restore the Psalter as far as possible to the order in which the Psalms were written. They give the division of each Psalm into strophes, and of each strophe into the lines which compose it, and amend the errors of translation. In accomplishing this work they have mainly followed the guidance of Professor Henry Ewald. A Supplement contains the chief specimens of Hebrew lyric poetry not included in the Book of Psalms. The Spectator *calls it "One of the most instructive and valuable books that have been published for many years."*

Golden Treasury Psalter.—THE STUDENT'S EDITION.

Being an Edition with briefer Notes of the above. 18mo. 3s. 6d.

This volume will be found to meet the requirements of those who wish for a smaller edition of the larger work, at a lower price for family use, and for the use of younger pupils in Public Schools. The short notes which are appended to the volume will, it is hoped, suffice to make the meaning intelligible throughout. The aim of this edition is simply to put the reader as far as possible in possession of the plain meaning of the writer. "It is a gem," the Nonconformist *says.*

Ramsay.—THE CATECHISER'S MANUAL; or, the
Church Catechism Illustrated and Explained, for the Use of
Clergymen, Schoolmasters, and Teachers. By ARTHUR RAMSAY,
M.A. Second Edition. 18mo. 1s. 6d.

*This Manual, which is in the form of question and answer, is in-
tended to afford full assistance both to learners and teachers, to
candidates for Confirmation as well as to clergymen, in the
understanding of the Church Catechism, and of all the matters
referred to therein. It is divided into seven chapters:—I. "The
Church Catechism," in which the meaning and object of the
Catechism is explained, as well as the significance and object of
Confirmation. II. The various parts of the Catechism are
analysed and explained. III. The Creeds—the Apostles', the
Nicene, and the Athanasian. IV. The Apostles' Creed. V. The
Commandments. VI. The Lord's Prayer. VII. The Sacraments. The* English Journal of Education *says,—"This is by
far the best Manual on the Catechism we have met with, adapted
not only for the use of the national schoolmaster, but also for the
clergyman and the tutor.*

Rays of Sunlight for Dark Days. A Book of Selections for the Suffering. With a Preface by C. J. VAUGHAN, D.D.
18mo. Fifth Edition. 3s. 6d. Also in morocco, old style.

*Dr. Vaughan says in the Preface, after speaking of the general run
of Books of Comfort for Mourners, "It is because I think that
the little volume now offered to the Christian sufferer is one of
greater wisdom and of deeper experience, that I have readily con-
sented to the request that I would introduce it by a few words of
Preface." The book consists of a series of very brief extracts from
a great variety of authors, in prose and poetry, suited to the many
moods of a mourning or suffering mind. "Mostly gems of the first
water."—*Clerical Journal.

Reynolds.—NOTES OF THE CHRISTIAN LIFE. A
Selection of Sermons by HENRY ROBERT REYNOLDS, B.A.,
President of Cheshunt College, and Fellow of University College,
London. Crown 8vo. 7s. 6d.

This work may be taken as representative of the mode of thought and feeling which is most popular amongst the freer and more cultivated Nonconformists. "*The reader throughout,*" *says the* Patriot, "*feels himself in the grasp of an earnest and careful thinker.*" "*It is long,*" *says the* Nonconformist, "*since we have met with any published sermons better calculated than these to stimulate devout thought, and to bring home to the soul the reality of a spiritual life.*"

Roberts.—DISCUSSIONS ON THE GOSPELS. By the Rev. ALEXANDER ROBERTS, D.D. Second Edition, revised and enlarged. 8vo. 16s.

This volume is divided into two parts. Part I. "On the Language employed by our Lord and His Disciples," in which the author endeavours to prove that Greek was the language usually employed by Christ Himself, in opposition to the common belief that Our Lord spoke Aramæan. Part II. is occupied with a discussion "On the Original Language of St. Matthew's Gospel," and on "The Origin and Authenticity of the Gospels." The author propounds some novel views on the points discussed, the result of long and deep study and research. The volume abounds in valuable Notes, and in the Second Part is a chapter bearing chiefly on the proper authenticity of the Gospels as recently challenged by M. Renan. "The author brings the valuable qualifications of learning, temper, and an independent judgment. . . . It is but bare justice to affirm that his arguments render it [his proposition] extremely probable."—Daily News. "*This volume is of intense interest to every Biblical student. It enters a field of inquiry hitherto untrodden.*"—British Standard.

Robertson.—PASTORAL COUNSELS. Being Chapters on Practical and Devotional Subjects. By the late JOHN ROBERTSON, D.D. Third Edition, with a Preface by the Author of "The Recreations of a Country Parson." Extra fcap. 8vo. 6s.

These Sermons are the free utterances of a strong and independent thinker. He does not depart from the essential doctrines of his Church, but he expounds them in a spirit of the widest charity, and always having most prominently in view the requirements of practical life. "The sermons are admirable specimens of a practical, earnest, and instructive style of pulpit teaching."—Nonconformist.

Rowsell.—MAN'S LABOUR AND GOD'S HARVEST. Sermons preached before the University of Cambridge in Lent, 1861. Fcap. 8vo. 3s.

This volume contains Five Sermons, the general drift of which is indicated by the title. "We strongly recommend this little volume to young men, and especially to those who are contemplating working for Christ in Holy Orders."—Literary Churchman. "Mr. Rowsell's Sermons must, we feel sure, have touched the heart of many a Cambridge Undergraduate, and are deserving of a wide general circulation."—The Ecclesiastic.

Sanday.—THE AUTHORSHIP AND HISTORICAL CHARACTER OF THE FOURTH GOSPEL, considered in reference to the Contents of the Gospel itself. A Critical Essay. By WILLIAM SANDAY, M.A., Fellow of Trinity College, Oxford. Crown 8vo. 8s. 6d.

The object of this Essay is critical and nothing more. The Author attempts to apply faithfully and persistently to the contents of the much disputed fourth Gospel that scientific method which has been so successful in other directions. "The facts of religion," the Author believes, "(i. e. the documents, the history of religious bodies, &c.) are as much facts as the lie of a coal-bed or the formation of a coral-reef." It is believed that the work will prove of value to theologians, as well as to all who take an interest in the subject of which it treats.

Sergeant.—SERMONS. By the Rev. E. W. SERGEANT, M.A., Balliol College, Oxford; Assistant Master at Westminster College. Fcap. 8vo. 2s. 6d.

This volume contains Nine Sermons on a variety of topics, preached by the author at various times and to various classes of hearers. The First Sermon is on Free Inquiry.

Smith.—PROPHECY A PREPARATION FOR CHRIST. Eight Lectures preached before the University of Oxford, being the Bampton Lectures for 1869. By R. PAYNE SMITH, D.D., Dean of Canterbury. Second and Cheaper Edition. Crown 8vo. 6s.

The author's object in these Lectures is to shew that there exists in the

Old Testament an element, which no criticism on naturalistic principles can either account for or explain away: that element is Prophecy. The author endeavours to prove that its force does not consist merely in its predictions. The Bible describes man's first estate of innocency, his fall, and the promise given by God of his restoration. Virtually the promise meant that God would give man a true religion; and the author asserts that Christianity is the sole religion on earth that fulfils the conditions necessary to constitute a true religion. God has pledged His own attributes in its behalf; this pledge He has given in miracle and prophecy. The author endeavours to shew the reality of that portion of the proof founded on prophecy. "*These Lectures overflow with solid learning.*"—Record.

Smith.—CHRISTIAN FAITH. Sermons preached before the University of Cambridge. By W. SAUMAREZ SMITH, M.A., Principal of St. Aidan's College, Birkenhead. Fcap. 8vo. 3*s.* 6*d.*

The first two sermons in this volume have special reference to the Person of Christ; the next two are concerned with the inner life of Christians; and the last speaks of the outward development of Christian faith. "*Appropriate and earnest sermons, suited to the practical exhortation of an educated congregation.*"—Guardian.

Stanley.—Works by the Very Rev. A. P. STANLEY, D.D., Dean of Westminster.

THE ATHANASIAN CREED, with a Preface on the General Recommendations of the RITUAL COMMISSION. Cr. 8vo. 2*s.*

The object of the work is not so much to urge the omission or change of the Athanasian Creed, as to shew that such a relaxation ought to give offence to no reasonable or religious mind. With this view, the Dean of Westminster discusses in succession—(1) *the Authorship of the Creed,* (2) *its Internal Characteristics,* (3) *the Peculiarities of its Use in the Church of England,* (4) *its Advantages and Disadvantages,* (5) *its various Interpretations, and* (6) *the Judgment passed upon it by the Ritual Commission. In conclusion, Dr. Stanley maintains that the use of the Athanasian*

Stanley (Dean)—*continued.*

Creed should no longer be made compulsory. "Dr. Stanley puts with admirable force the objections which may be made to the Creed; equally admirable, we think, in his statement of its advantages."— Spectator.

THE NATIONAL THANKSGIVING. Sermons preached in Westminster Abbey. Second Edition. Crown 8vo. 2s. 6d.

These Sermons are (1) "Death and Life," preached December 10, 1871; (2) "The Trumpet of Patmos," December 17, 1871; (3) "The Day of Thanksgiving," March 3, 1872. It is hoped that these Sermons may recall, in some degree, the serious reflections connected with the Prince of Wales's illness, which, if the nation is true to itself, ought not to perish with the moment. The proceeds of the publication will be devoted to the Fund for the Restoration of St. Paul's Cathedral. "In point of fervour and polish by far the best specimens in print of Dean Stanley's eloquent style."—Standard.

Sunday Library. See end of this Catalogue.

Swainson.—Works by C. A. SWAINSON, D.D., Canon of Chichester:—

THE CREEDS OF THE CHURCH IN THEIR RE-LATIONS TO HOLY SCRIPTURE and the CONSCIENCE OF THE CHRISTIAN. 8vo. cloth. 9s.

The Lectures which compose this volume discuss, amongst others, the following subjects: "Faith in God," "Exercise of our Reason," "Origin and Authority of Creeds," and "Private Judgment, its use and exercise." "Treating of abstruse points of Scripture, he applies them so forcibly to Christian duty and practice as to prove eminently serviceable to the Church."—John Bull.

THE AUTHORITY OF THE NEW TESTAMENT, and other LECTURES, delivered before the University of Cambridge. 8vo. cloth. 12s.

The first series of Lectures in this work is on "The Words spoken by the Apostles of Jesus," "The Inspiration of God's Servants,"

*" The Human Character of the Inspired Writers," and " The Divine Character of the Word written." The second embraces Lectures on " Sin as Imperfection," " Sin as Self-will," " Whatsoever is not of Faith is Sin," " Christ the Saviour," and " The Blood of the New Covenant." The third is on "Christians One Body in Christ," " The One Body the Spouse of Christ," " Christ's Prayer for Unity," " Our Reconciliation should be manifested in common Worship," and " Ambassadors for Christ." "All the grave and awful questions associated with human sinfulness and the Divine plan of redemption are discussed with minute and painstaking care, and in the Appendix all the passages of Scripture referring to them are marshalled and critically reviewed."—*Wesleyan Times.*

Taylor.—THE RESTORATION OF BELIEF. New and Revised Edition. By ISAAC TAYLOR, Esq. Crown 8vo. 8s. 6d.

The earlier chapters are occupied with an examination of the primitive history of the Christian Religion, and its relation to the Roman government; and here, as well as in the remainder of the work, the author shews the bearing of that history on some of the difficult and interesting questions which have recently been claiming the attention of all earnest men. The book will be found to contain a clear and full statement of the case as it at present stands in behalf of Christianity. The last chapter of this New Edition treats of " The Present Position of the Argument concerning Christianity," with special reference to M. Renan's Vie de Jésus. *The* Journal of Sacred Literature *says,—" The current of thought which runs through this book is calm and clear, its tone is earnest, its manner courteous. The author has carefully studied the successive problems which he so ably handles."*

Temple.—SERMONS PREACHED IN THE CHAPEL of RUGBY SCHOOL. By F. TEMPLE, D.D., Bishop of Exeter. New and Cheaper Edition. Extra fcap. 8vo. 4s. 6d.

This volume contains Thirty-five Sermons on topics more or less intimately connected with every-day life. The following are a few of the subjects discoursed upon:—"Love and Duty;" "Coming to Christ;" "Great Men;" "Faith;" "Doubt;" "Scruples;"

Temple (F., D.D.)—*continued.*

"Original Sin;" "Friendship;" "Helping Others;" "The Discipline of Temptation;" "Strength a Duty;" "Worldliness;" "Ill Temper;" "The Burial of the Past." The Critic speaks of them thus:—"We trust that the tender affectionate spirit of practical Christianity which runs through every page of the volume will have its due effect. . . . desiring to rouse the youthful hearers to a sense of duty, and to arm them against the perils and dangers of the world against which they are so soon to battle."

A SECOND SERIES OF SERMONS PREACHED IN THE CHAPEL OF RUGBY SCHOOL. Extra fcap. 8vo. 6s.

This Second Series of Forty-two brief, pointed, practical Sermons, on topics intimately connected with the every-day life of young and old, will be acceptable to all who are acquainted with the First Series. The following are a few of the subjects treated of:—"Disobedience," "Almsgiving," "The Unknown Guidance of God," "Apathy one of our Trials," "High Aims in Leaders," "Doing our Best," "The Use of Knowledge," "Use of Observances," "Martha and Mary," "John the Baptist," "Severity before Mercy," "Even Mistakes Punished," "Morality and Religion," "Children," "Action the Test of Spiritual Life," "Self-Respect," "Too Late," "The Tercentenary."

A THIRD SERIES OF SERMONS PREACHED IN RUGBY SCHOOL CHAPEL IN 1867—1869. Extra fcap. 8vo. 6s.

This third series of Bishop Temple's Rugby Sermons, contains thirty-six brief discourses, characterized by "a penetrating and direct practicalness, informed by a rare intuitive sympathy with boy-nature; its keen perception of reality and earnestness, its equally keen sympathy with what is noblest in sentiment and feelings." The volume includes the "Good-bye" sermon preached on his leaving Rugby to enter on the office he now holds.

Thring.—Works by Rev. EDWARD THRING, M.A.

SERMONS DELIVERED AT UPPINGHAM SCHOOL.
Crown 8vo. 5*s.*

*In this volume are contained Forty-seven brief Sermons, all on
subjects more or less intimately connected with Public-school life.
"These Sermons," the author says, "are sent into the world as
parts of a system, and as exponents, in some degree, of the experience of working men, that it is possible to have a free and
manly school-life, complete in all its parts, neither lost in a crowd,
nor shut up in a prison, nor reared in a hot-bed."—"We desire
very highly to commend these capital Sermons which treat of a boy's
life and trials in a thoroughly practical way and with great
simplicity and impressiveness. They deserve to be classed with the
best of their kind."*—Literary Churchman.

THOUGHTS ON LIFE-SCIENCE.   New Edition, enlarged and revised. Crown 8vo. 7*s.* 6*d.*

*In this volume are discussed in a familiar manner some of the most
interesting problems between Science and Religion, Reason and
Feeling. "Learning and Science," says the Author, "are claiming
the right of building up and pulling down everything, especially
the latter. It has seemed to me no useless task to look steadily at
what has happened, to take stock as it were of man's gains, and to
endeavour amidst new circumstances to arrive at some rational
estimate of the bearings of things, so that the limits of what is possible at all events may be clearly marked out for ordinary readers.
. . . . This book is an endeavour to bring out some of the main
facts of the world."*

Tracts for Priests and People.   By VARIOUS
WRITERS.

THE FIRST SERIES. Crown 8vo. 8*s.*
THE SECOND SERIES. Crown 8vo. 8*s.*

The whole Series of Fifteen Tracts may be had separately, price
One Shilling each.

*A series of papers written after the excitement aroused by the publica-
tion of "Essays and Reviews" had somewhat abated, and designed,*

by the exposition of positive truth, to meet the religious difficulties of honest inquirers. Amongst the writers are Mr. Thomas Hughes, Professor Maurice, the Rev. J. Llewellyn Davies, and Mr. J. M. Ludlow.

Trench.—Works by R. CHENEVIX TRENCH, D.D., Archbishop of Dublin. (For other Works by the same author, *see* DIOGRAPHICAL, BELLES LETTRES, and LINGUISTIC CATALOGUES).

Archbishop Trench is well known as a writer who has the happy faculty of being able to take with discrimination the results of the highest criticism and scholarship, and present them in such a shape as will be not only valuable to scholars, but interesting, intelligible, and of the greatest use even to the ordinary reader. It is generally acknowledged that few men have been more successful in bringing out the less obvious meanings of the New Testament, or done more for the popular yet scholarly exposition of the Bible generally.

NOTES ON THE PARABLES OF OUR LORD.
Eleventh Edition. 8vo. 12s.

This work has taken its place as a standard exposition and interpretation of Christ's Parables. The book is prefaced by an Introductory Essay in four chapters:—I. On the definition of the Parable. II. On Teaching by Parables. III. On the Interpretation of the Parables. IV. On other Parables besides those in the Scriptures. The author then proceeds to take up the Parables one by one, and by the aid of philology, history, antiquities, and the researches of travellers, shew forth the significance, beauty, and applicability of each, concluding with what he deems its true moral interpretation. In the numerous Notes are many valuable references, illustrative quotations, critical and philological annotations, etc., and appended to the volume is a classified list of fifty-six works on the Parables.

NOTES ON THE MIRACLES OF OUR LORD.
Ninth Edition. 8vo. 12s.

In the 'Preliminary Essay' to this work, all the momentous and interesting questions that have been raised in connection with

Trench—*continued.*

Miracles, are discussed with considerable fulness, and the author's usual candour and learning. The Essay consists of six chapters: —I. On the Names of Miracles, i. e. the Greek words by which they are designated in the New Testament. II. The Miracles and Nature—What is the difference between a Miracle and any event in the ordinary course of Nature? III. The Authority of Miracles—Is the Miracle to command absolute obedience? IV. The Evangelical, compared with the other cycles of Miracles. V. The Assaults on the Miracles—1. The Jewish. 2. The Heathen (Celsus etc.). 3. The Pantheistic (Spinosa etc.). 4. The Sceptical (Hume). 5. The Miracles only relatively miraculous (Schleiermacher). 6. The Rationalistic (Paulus). 7. The Historico-Critical (Woolston, Strauss). VI. The Apologetic Worth of the Miracles. The author then treats the separate Miracles as he does the Parables.

SYNONYMS OF THE NEW TESTAMENT. New Edition, enlarged. 8vo. cloth. 12s.

The study of synonyms in any language is valuable as a discipline for training the mind to close and accurate habits of thought; more especially is this the case in Greek—"a language spoken by a people of the finest and subtlest intellect; who saw distinctions where others saw none; who divided out to different words what others often were content to huddle confusedly under a common term.... Where is it so desirable that we should miss nothing, that we should lose no finer intention of the writer, as in those words which are the vehicles of the very mind of God Himself?" This work is recognised as a valuable companion to every student of the New Testament in the original. This, the Seventh Edition, has been carefully revised, and a considerable number of new synonyms added. Appended is an Index to the Synonyms, and an Index to many other words alluded to or explained throughout the work. "He is," the Athenæum says, "a guide in this department of knowledge to whom his readers may intrust themselves with confidence. His sober judgment and sound sense are barriers against the misleading influence of arbitrary hypotheses."

Trench—*continued.*

ON THE AUTHORIZED VERSION OF THE NEW TESTAMENT. Second Edition. 8vo. 7*s.*

Archbishop Trench's familiarity with the New Testament makes him peculiarly fitted to estimate the value of the present translation, and to give directions as to how a new one should be proceeded with. After some Introductory Remarks, in which the propriety of a revision is briefly discussed, the whole question of the merits of the present version is gone into in detail, in eleven chapters. Appended is a chronological list of works bearing on the subject, an Index of the principal Texts considered, an Index of Greek Words, and an Index of other Words referred to throughout the book.

STUDIES IN THE GOSPELS. Second Edition. 8vo. 10*s.* 6*d.*

This book is published under the conviction that the assertion often made is untrue,—viz. that the Gospels are in the main plain and easy, and that all the chief difficulties of the New Testament are to be found in the Epistles. These "Studies," sixteen in number, are the fruit of a much larger scheme, and each Study deals with some important episode mentioned in the Gospels, in a critical, philosophical, and practical manner. Many learned references and quotations are added to the Notes. Among the subjects treated are:—The Temptation; Christ and the Samaritan Woman; The Three Aspirants; The Transfiguration; Zacchæus; The True Vine; The Penitent Malefactor; Christ and the Two Disciples on the way to Emmaus.

COMMENTARY ON THE EPISTLES to the SEVEN CHURCHES IN ASIA. Third Edition, revised. 8vo. 8*s.* 6*d.*

Bengel was wont above all things to recommend the study of these Epistles to youthful ministers of Christ's Word and Sacraments; and, as the author says in his Preface, the number of aspects in which they present themselves to us as full of interest, is extraordinary. They are full of interest to the student of ecclesiastical history; possess a strong attraction for those who occupy them-

Trench—*continued.*

> *selves with questions of pure exegesis, from the fact of their con-*
> *taining so many unsolved problems of interpretation; their purely*
> *theological interest is great; their practical interest in their*
> *bearing on the whole pastoral and ministerial work is extreme;*
> *and finally, there is about these Epistles a striking originality,*
> *an entire unlikeness, in some points at least, to anything else in*
> *Scripture. The present work consists of an Introduction, being*
> *a commentary on Rev. i. 4—20, a detailed examination of each of*
> *the Seven Epistles, in all its bearings, and an Excursus on the*
> *Historico-Prophetical Interpretation of the Epistles.*

THE SERMON ON THE MOUNT. An Exposition
drawn from the writings of St. Augustine, with an Essay on his
merits as an Interpreter of Holy Scripture. Third Edition, enlarged. 8vo. 10s. 6d.

> *The first half of the present work consists of a dissertation in eight*
> *chapters on "Augustine as an Interpreter of Scripture," the titles*
> *of the several chapters being as follow:—I. Augustine's General*
> *Views of Scripture and its Interpretation. II. The External*
> *Helps for the Interpretation of Scripture possessed by Augustine.*
> *III. Augustine's Principles and Canons of Interpretation. IV.*
> *Augustine's Allegorical Interpretation of Scripture. V. Illustra-*
> *tions of Augustine's Skill as an Interpreter of Scripture. VI.*
> *Augustine on John the Baptist and on St. Stephen. VII. Au-*
> *gustine on the Epistle to the Romans. VIII. Miscellaneous Ex-*
> *amples of Augustine's Interpretation of Scripture. The latter half*
> *of the work consists of Augustine's Exposition of the Sermon on*
> *the Mount, not however a mere series of quotations from Augustine,*
> *but a connected account of his sentiments on the various passages of*
> *that Sermon, interspersed with criticisms by Archbishop Trench.*

SERMONS PREACHED in WESTMINSTER ABBEY.
Second Edition. 8vo. 10s. 6d.

> *These Sermons embrace a wide variety of topics, and are thoroughly*
> *practical, earnest, and evangelical, and simple in style. The*
> *following are a few of the subjects:—" Tercentenary Celebration*

Trench—*continued.*

of Queen Elizabeth's Accession;" "Conviction and Conversion;"
"The Incredulity of Thomas;" "The Angels' Hymn;" "Counting the Cost;" "The Holy Trinity in Relation to our Prayers;"
"On the Death of General Havelock;" "Christ Weeping over
Jerusalem;" "Walking with Christ in White."

SHIPWRECKS OF FAITH. Three Sermons preached
before the University of Cambridge in May, 1867. Fcap. 8vo.
2s. 6d.

*These Sermons are especially addressed to young men. The subjects
are "Balaam," "Saul," and "Judas Iscariot," three of the
mournfullest lives recorded in Scripture, "for the greatness of
their vocation, and their disastrous falling short of the same,
for the utter defeat of their lives, for the shipwreck of everything
which they made." These lives are set forth as beacon-lights,
"to warn us off from perilous reefs and quicksands, which have
been the destruction of many, and which might only too easily be
ours." The* John Bull *says, " they are, like all he writes, affectionate
and earnest discourses."*

Tudor.—The DECALOGUE VIEWED as the CHRIST-
IAN'S LAW. With Special Reference to the Questions and
Wants of the Times. By the Rev. RICH. TUDOR, B.A. Crown
8vo. 10s. 6d.

*The author's aim is to bring out the Christian sense of the Decalogue
in its application to existing needs and questions. The work will
be found to occupy ground which no other single work has hitherto
filled. It is divided into Two Parts, the First Part consisting of
three lectures on "Duty," and the Second Part of twelve lectures
on the Ten Commandments. The* Guardian *says of it, "His volume
throughout is an outspoken and sound exposition of Christian
morality, based deeply upon true foundations, set forth systematically, and forcibly and plainly expressed—as good a specimen of
what pulpit lectures ought to be as is often to be found." The*
Westminster Review *says, " There is an earnestness in his
purpose and evidently a sincere endeavour to apply the words of
Scripture to present needs."*

Tulloch.—THE CHRIST OF THE GOSPELS AND
THE CHRIST OF MODERN CRITICISM. Lectures on
M. RENAN'S "Vie de Jésus." By JOHN TULLOCH, D.D.,
Principal of the College of St. Mary, in the University of St.
Andrew's. Extra fcap. 8vo. 4s. 6d.

> *While Dr. Tulloch does not hesitate to grapple boldly with the
> statements and theories of Renan, he does so in a spirit of perfect
> fairness and courtesy, eschewing all personalities and sinister in-
> sinuations as to motives and sincerity. The work will be found
> to be a fair and full statement, in Dr. Tulloch's eloquent style,
> of the case as it stands against Renan's theory. "Amongst direct
> answers," says the Reader, " to M. Renan, this volume will not
> be easily surpassed. . . The style is animated, pointed, and scholarly;
> the tone fair and appreciative; the philosophy intelligent and
> cautious; the Christianity liberal, reverent, and hearty."*

Vaughan.—Works by CHARLES J. VAUGHAN, D.D., Master
of the Temple :—

> *Dr. Vaughan's genuine sympathy with the difficulties, sorrows and
> struggles of all classes of his fellow-men, his thorough disinterested-
> ness, and his high views of life have been acknowledged by critics of
> all creeds. No sermons can be more applicable to the ever-
> recurring ills, bodily, mental, and spiritual, that flesh is heir to.
> His commentaries and expository lectures are those of a faithful
> evangelical, but at the same time liberal-minded interpreter of
> what he believes to be the Word of God.*

CHRIST SATISFYING THE INSTINCTS OF HU-
MANITY. Eight Lectures delivered in the Temple Church.
Extra fcp. 8vo. 3s. 6d.

> *The object of these Sermons is to exhibit the spiritual wants of human
> nature, and to prove that all of them receive full satisfaction in
> Christ. The various instincts which He is shewn to meet are those
> of Truth, Reverence, Perfection, Liberty, Courage, Sympathy,
> Sacrifice, and Unity. "We are convinced that there are congrega-
> tions, in number unmistakeably increasing, to whom such Essays
> as these, full of thought and learning, are infinitely more beneficial,
> for they are more acceptable, than the recognised type of sermons."*
> —John Bull.

Vaughan (Dr. C. J.)—*continued.*

MEMORIALS OF HARROW SUNDAYS.   A Selection
of Sermons preached in Harrow School Chapel.   With a View
of the Chapel.   Fourth Edition.   Crown 8vo.   10s. 6d.

*While these Sermons deal with subjects that in a peculiar way concern
the young, and in a manner that cannot fail to attract their attention and influence their conduct, they are in every respect applicable
to people of all ages.   "Discussing," says the* John Bull, *" those
forms of evil and impediments to duty which peculiarly beset the
young, Dr. Vaughan has, with singular tact, blended deep thought
and analytical investigation of principles with interesting earnestness and eloquent simplicity."   The* Nonconformist *says " the
volume is a precious one for family reading, and for the hand
of the thoughtful boy or young man entering life."*

THE BOOK AND THE LIFE, and other Sermons,
preached before the University of Cambridge.   New Edition.
Fcap. 8vo.   4s. 6d.

*These Sermons are all of a thoroughly practical nature, and some of
them are especially adapted to those who are in a state of anxious
doubt.   " They meet," the* Freeman *says, " in what appears to us
to be the one true method, the scepticism and indifference to religious
truth which are almost sure to trouble young men who read and
think.   In short, we know no book more likely to do the young and
inquiring good, or to help them to gain that tone of mind wanting
which they may doubt and ask for ever, because always doubting
and asking in vain."*

TWELVE DISCOURSES on SUBJECTS CONNECTED
WITH THE LITURGY and WORSHIP of the CHURCH
OF ENGLAND.   Fcap. 8vo.   6s.

*Four of these discourses were published in 1860, in a work entitled
Revision of the Liturgy; four others have appeared in the form
of separate sermons, delivered on various occasions, and published
at the time by request; and four are new.   All will be found to*

Vaughan (Dr. C. J.)—*continued.*

fall strictly under the present title, reviewing the chief matters suggested by the Church Liturgy. The Appendix contains two articles,—one on "Subscription and Scruples," the other on the "Rubric and the Burial Service." The Press characterises the volume as "eminently wise and temperate."

LESSONS OF LIFE AND GODLINESS. A Selection
of Sermons preached in the Parish Church of Doncaster. Fourth and Cheaper Edition. Fcap. 8vo. 3s. 6d.

This volume consists of Nineteen Sermons, mostly on subjects connected with the every-day walk and conversation of Christians. They bear such titles as "The Talebearer," "Features of Charity," "The Danger of Relapse," "The Secret Life and the Outward," "Family Prayer," "Zeal without Consistency," "The Gospel an Incentive to Industry in Business," "Use and Abuse of the World." The Spectator *styles them "earnest and human. They are adapted to every class and order in the social system, and will be read with wakeful interest by all who seek to amend whatever may be amiss in their natural disposition or in their acquired habits."*

WORDS FROM THE GOSPELS. A Second Selection
of Sermons preached in the Parish Church of Doncaster. Second Edition. Fcap. 8vo. 4s. 6d.

In this volume are Twenty-two Sermons on subjects taken from one or other of the four Gospels. The Nonconformist *characterises these Sermons as "of practical earnestness, of a thoughtfulness that penetrates the common conditions and experiences of life, and brings the truths and examples of Scripture to bear on them with singular force, and of a style that owes its real elegance to the simplicity and directness which have fine culture for their roots. . . . A book than which few could give more holy pleasantness and solemn purpose to their Sabbath evenings at home."*

Vaughan (Dr. C. J.)—*continued.*

LESSONS OF THE CROSS AND PASSION. Six Lectures delivered in Hereford Cathedral during the Week before Easter, 1869. Fcap. 8vo. 2s. 6d.

This volume contains Six Sermons on subjects mainly connected with the death and passion of Christ. The titles of the Sermons are:— 1. "Too Late" (Matt. xxvi. 45). II. "The Divine Sacrifice and the Human Priesthood." III. "Love not the World." IV. "The Moral Glory of Christ." V. "Christ made perfect through Suffering." VI. "Death the Remedy of Christ's Loneliness." "This little volume," the Nonconformist *says, "exhibits all his best characteristics. Elevated, calm, and clear, the Sermons owe much to their force, and yet they seem literally to owe nothing to it. They are studied, but their grace is the grace of perfect simplicity."*

LIFE'S WORK AND GOD'S DISCIPLINE. Three Sermons. Fcap. 8vo. cloth. 2s. 6d.

The Three Sermons contained in this volume have a oneness of aim indicated by the title, and are on the following subjects:—I. "The Work burned and the Workmen saved." II. "The Individual Hiring." III. "The Remedial Discipline of Disease and Death."

THE WHOLESOME WORDS OF JESUS CHRIST. Four Sermons preached before the University of Cambridge in November 1866. Second Edition. Fcap. 8vo. cloth. 3s. 6d.

Dr. Vaughan uses the word "Wholesome" here in its literal and original sense, the sense in which St. Paul uses it, as meaning healthy, sound, conducing to right living; and in these Sermons he points out and illustrates several of the "wholesome" characteristics of the Gospel,—the Words of Christ. The subjects of these Sermons are as follow:—I. "Naturalness and Spirituality of Revelation—Grandeur and Self-Control—Truthfulness and Tenderness." II. "Universality and Individuality of Christ's Gospel." III. "Oblivions and Ambitions of the Life of Grace." IV. "Regrets and Preparations of Human Life." The John Bull *says this volume is "replete with all the author's well-known vigour of thought and richness of expression."*

Vaughan (Dr. C. J.)—*continued.*

FOES OF FAITH. Sermons preached before the University of Cambridge in November 1868. Fcap. 8vo. 3s. 6d.

> *The "Foes of Faith" preached against in these Four Sermons are:— I. "Unreality." II. "Indolence." III. "Irreverence." IV. "Inconsistency,"—" Foes," says the author, "which must be manfully fought against by all who would be finally admitted into that holy communion and fellowship which is, for time and eternity, the blessed company of all faithful people." "They are written," the* London Review *says, "with culture and elegance, and exhibit the thoughtful earnestness, piety, and good sense of their author."*

LECTURES ON THE EPISTLE to the PHILIPPIANS. Second Edition. Crown 8vo. 7s. 6d.

> *Each Lecture is prefaced by a literal translation from the Greek of the paragraph which forms its subject, contains first a minute explanation of the passage on which it is based, and then a practical application of the verse or clause selected as its text. The* Press *speaks of these Lectures thus:—"Replete with good sense and practical religious advice... The language of the Apostle assumes a practical significance, which it seldom wears in the eyes of any ordinary reader, and Dr. Vaughan's listeners would feel themselves placed in the position of men receiving inspired instruction on the ordinary business of life. We can scarcely praise this plan too highly."*

LECTURES ON THE REVELATION OF ST. JOHN. Third and Cheaper Edition. Two Vols. Extra fcap. 8vo. 9s.

> *In this the Third Edition of these Lectures, the literal translations of the passages expounded will be found interwoven in the body of the Lectures themselves. In attempting to expound this most-hard-to-understand Book, Dr. Vaughan, while taking from others what assistance he required, has not adhered to any particular school of interpretation, but has endeavoured to shew forth the significance of this Revelation by the help of his strong common*

Vaughan (Dr. C. J.)—*continued.*

sense, critical acumen, scholarship, and reverent spirit. "*Dr. Vaughan's Sermons,*" *the* Spectator *says,* "*are the most practical discourses on the Apocalypse with which we are acquainted.*" *Prefixed is a Synopsis of the Book of Revelation, and appended is an Index of passages illustrating the language of the Book.*

EPIPHANY, LENT, AND EASTER. A Selection of Expository Sermons. Third Edition. Crown 8vo. 10s. 6d.

The first eighteen of these Sermons were preached during the seasons of 1860, indicated in the title, and are practical expositions of passages taken from the lessons of the days on which they were delivered. The last eight Sermons were added to the Second Edition. As in the case of the Lectures on Philippians, each Lecture is prefaced with a careful and literal rendering of the original of the passage of which the Lecture is an exposition. The Nonconformist *says that* "*in simplicity, dignity, close adherence to the words of Scripture, insight into 'the mind of the Spirit,' and practical thoughtfulness, they are models of that species of pulpit instruction to which they belong.*"

THE EPISTLES OF ST. PAUL. For English Readers. PART I., containing the FIRST EPISTLE TO THE THESSALONIANS. Second Edition. 8vo. 1s. 6d. Each Epistle will be published separately in its chronological order.

It is the object of this work to enable English readers, unacquainted with Greek, to enter with intelligence into the meaning, connection, and phraseology of the writings of the great Apostle. (1) *Each Epistle will be prefaced by an Introduction containing information as to the circumstances, design, and order of its composition.* (2) *The Authorised English Version occupies the foremost place in each page.* (3) *Beside it, in smaller type, is a literal English Version, made from the original Greek.* (4) *A free paraphrase stands below, in which it is attempted to express the sense and connection of the Epistle.* (5) *The Notes include both doctrinal explanation and verbal illustration; occasionally a brief word of application has been introduced.*

Vaughan (Dr. C. J.)—*continued.*

ST. PAUL'S EPISTLE TO THE ROMANS. The Greek
Text, with English Notes. Third Edition, greatly enlarged.
Crown 8vo. 7s. 6d.

*This volume contains the Greek Text of the Epistle to the Romans as
settled by the Rev. B. F. Westcott, D.D., for his complete recension
of the Text of the New Testament. Appended to the text are copious
critical and exegetical Notes, the result, of almost eighteen years'
study on the part of the author. The "Index of Words illustrated
or explained in the Notes" will be found, in some considerable
degree, an Index to the Epistles as a whole. "I have desired,"
the author says, "to catch and to represent the meaning of each
passage and of the whole, without deriving it from any secondary
source. One of my principal endeavours has been, to trace through
the New Testament the uses of the more remarkable words or phrases
which occur in the Epistle, arranging them, where the case required
it, under their various modifications of sense." Prefixed to the
volume is a discourse on "St. Paul's Conversion and Doctrine,"
suggested by some recent publications on St. Paul's theological
standing. In the Preface to the Third Edition, which has
been almost entirely rewritten, among other things, is a Synopsis of
the contents of the Epistle. The Guardian says of the work,—
"For educated young men his commentary seems to fill a gap
hitherto unfilled... As a whole, Dr. Vaughan appears to us to
have given to the world a valuable book of original and careful and
earnest thought bestowed on the accomplishment of a work which
will be of much service and which is much needed."*

THE CHURCH OF THE FIRST DAYS.

Series I. The Church of Jerusalem. Second Edition.
" II. The Church of the Gentiles. Second Edition.
" III. The Church of the World. Second Edition.
Fcap. 8vo. cloth. 4s. 6d. each.

*The work is in three volumes:—I. "The Church of Jerusalem,"
extending from the 1st to the 8th chapter (inclusive) of the Acts.
II. "The Church of the Gentiles," from the 9th to the 16th chapter.
III. "The Church of the World," from the 17th to the 28th
chapter. Where necessary, the Authorized Version has been*

Vaughan (Dr. C. J.)—*continued.*

departed from, and a new literal translation taken as the basis of exposition. All possible topographical and historical light has been brought to bear on the subject; and while thoroughly practical in their aim, these Lectures will be found to afford a fair notion of the history and condition of the Primitive Church. The British Quarterly *says,—" These Sermons are worthy of all praise, and are models of pulpit teaching."*

COUNSELS for YOUNG STUDENTS. Three Sermons preached before the University of Cambridge at the Opening of the Academical Year 1870-71. Fcap. 8vo. 2*s.* 6*d.*

The titles of the Three Sermons contained in this volume are:—I. "The Great Decision." II. "The House and the Builder." III. "The Prayer and the Counter-Prayer." They all bear pointedly, earnestly, and sympathisingly upon the conduct and pursuits of young students and young men generally, to counsel whom, Dr. Vaughan's qualifications and aptitude are well known.

NOTES FOR LECTURES ON CONFIRMATION, with suitable Prayers. Eighth Edition. Fcap. 8vo. 1*s.* 6*d.*

In preparation for the Confirmation held in Harrow School Chapel, Dr. Vaughan was in the habit of printing week by week, and distributing among the Candidates, somewhat full notes of the Lecture he purposed to deliver to them, together with a form of Prayer adapted to the particular subject. He has collected these weekly Notes and Prayers into this little volume, in the hope that it may assist the labours of those who are engaged in preparing Candidates for Confirmation, and who find it difficult to lay their hand upon any one book of suitable instruction. The Press *says the work "commends itself at once by its simplicity and by its logical arrangement. . . . While points of doctrine, as they arise, are not lost sight of, the principal stress is laid on the preparation of the heart rather than the head."*

THE TWO GREAT TEMPTATIONS. The Temptation of Man, and the Temptation of Christ. Lectures delivered in the Temple Church, Lent 1872. Extra fcap. 8vo. 3*s.* 6*d.*

Vaughan.—Works by DAVID J. VAUGHAN, M.A., Vicar of St. Martin's, Leicester :—

SERMONS PREACHED IN ST. JOHN'S CHURCH, LEICESTER, during the Years 1855 and 1856. Crown 8vo. 5s. 6d.

These Twenty-five Sermons embrace a great variety of topics, all of the highest interest, are thoroughly practical in their nature, and calculated to give a hopeful view of life as seen in the light shed upon it by Christianity.

SERMONS on the RESURRECTION. With a Preface. Fcap. 8vo. 3s.

In the Preface to this work, the author expounds and endeavours to justify his view of the Atonement, shewing it to be more reasonable and scriptural than the ordinary doctrine. There are Seven Sermons in all, bearing the following titles :—I. "The Fellowship of Christ's Sufferings." II. "Christ the Resurrection and the Life." III. "Christ our Passover." IV. "Christ the Shepherd." V. "The True Light which lighteth every man." VI. "The City of God, and the Light thereof." VII. "Christ going to the Father, and the Way to the Father."

CHRISTIAN EVIDENCES AND THE BIBLE. New Edition, revised and enlarged. Fcap. 8vo. cloth. 5s. 6d.

The main object of this series of Twelve Sermons is to shew, that, quite irrespective of any theory as to the nature of the Bible and the special inspiration of its authors, there is good and sufficient reason for believing that Jesus Christ is the Son of God, who reveals and reconciles men to the Father. The author thinks that the true and solid rock, upon which the Church really stands and ought consciously to stand, is simply the confession that "Jesus is the Christ, the Son of the living God." The Preface to this, the Second Edition, consists of an "Analysis of the Nature of Scientific Truth,"—the nature of the evidence which is universally held to be sound and conclusive. In the Sermons themselves the Internal and External Evidences of Christianity and cognate subjects are

Vaughan (D. J.)—*continued.*

discussed, and throughout the volume are several long notes on points occurring in the text. Appended is a short Essay on " The Nature and Sphere of Law."—" This little volume," the Spectator *says, "is a model of that honest and reverent criticism of the Bible which is not only right, but the duty of English clergymen in such times as these to put forth from the pulpit."*

Venn.—ON SOME OF THE CHARACTERISTICS OF BELIEF, Scientific and Religious. Being the Hulsean Lectures for 1869. By the Rev. J. VENN, M.A. 8vo. 6s. 6d.

These discourses are intended to illustrate, explain, and work out into some of their consequences, certain characteristics by which the attainment of religious belief is prominently distinguished from the attainment of belief upon most other subjects. The first Lecture is an attempt to explain what is the nature of the logical foothold for differences of opinion among men ; to shew what there is in the constitution of the evidence which makes it possible for these differences to commence and persist. The second meets the question, What is the criterion of truth ? How are we to decide which of the varying but honest judgments on the same subject is right and which wrong ? The third and fourth Lectures are devoted to working out into several of their consequences the characteristics of evidence on religious subjects which were explained and illustrated in the first.

Warington.—THE WEEK OF CREATION ; OR, THE COSMOGONY OF GENESIS CONSIDERED IN ITS RELATION TO MODERN SCIENCE. By GEORGE WARINGTON, Author of "The Historic Character of the Pentateuch Vindicated." Crown 8vo. 4s. 6d.

*The greater part of this work is taken up with the teaching of the Cosmogony. Its purpose is also investigated, and a chapter is devoted to the consideration of the passage in which the difficulties occur. "A very able vindication of the Mosaic Cosmogony by a writer who unites the advantages of a critical knowledge of the Hebrew text and of distinguished scientific attainments."—*Spectator.

Westcott.—Works by BROOKE FOSS WESTCOTT, D.D.,
Regius Professor of Divinity in the University of Cambridge ;
Canon of Peterborough :—

The London Quarterly, *speaking of Mr. Westcott, says,—"To a
learning and accuracy which command respect and confidence, he
unites what are not always to be found in union with these qualities,
the no less valuable faculties of lucid arrangement and graceful and
facile expression."*

AN INTRODUCTION TO THE STUDY OF THE
GOSPELS. Fourth Edition. Crown 8vo. 10s. 6d.

*The author's chief object in this work has been to shew that there is
a true mean between the idea of a formal harmonization of the
Gospels and the abandonment of their absolute truth. After an
Introduction on the General Effects of the course of Modern Philosophy on the popular views of Christianity, he proceeds to
determine in what way the principles therein indicated may be
applied to the study of the Gospels. The treatise is divided into
eight Chapters:—I. The Preparation for the Gospel. II. The
Jewish Doctrine of the Messiah. III. The Origin of the Gospels.
IV. The Characteristics of the Gospels. V. The Gospel of St.
John. VI. and VII. The Differences in detail and of arrangement in the Synoptic Evangelists. VIII. The Difficulties of
the Gospels. The Appendices contain much valuable subsidiary
matter.*

A GENERAL SURVEY OF THE HISTORY OF THE
CANON OF THE NEW TESTAMENT DURING THE
FIRST FOUR CENTURIES. Third Edition, revised. Crown
8vo. 10s. 6d.

*The object of this treatise is to deal with the New Testament as a
whole, and that on purely historical grounds. The separate books
of which it is composed are considered not individually, but as
claiming to be parts of the apostolic heritage of Christians. The
Author has thus endeavoured to connect the history of the New
Testament Canon with the growth and consolidation of the Catholic*

Westcott (Dr. B. F.)—*continued.*

Church, and to point out the relation existing between the amount of evidence for the authenticity of its component parts and the whole mass of Christian literature. "The treatise," says the British Quarterly, "is a scholarly performance, learned, dispassionate, discriminating, worthy of his subject and of the present state of Christian literature in relation to it."

THE BIBLE IN THE CHURCH. A Popular Account of the Collection and Reception of the Holy Scriptures in the Christian Churches. Third Edition. 18mo. 4s. 6d.

The present volume has been written under the impression that a History of the whole Bible, and not of the New Testament only, would be required, if those unfamiliar with the subject were to be enabled to learn in what manner and with what consent the collection of Holy Scriptures was first made and then enlarged and finally closed by the Church. Though the work is intended to be simple and popular in its method, the author, for that very reason, has aimed at the strictest accuracy. The History of the Bible is brought down to the 16th century, and the Appendix contains two articles,—I. "On the History of the Canon of the Old Testament before the Christian Era." II. "On the Contents of the most ancient MSS. of the Christian Bible." The Literary Churchman says, "Mr. Westcott's account of the 'Canon' is true history in the very highest sense."

A GENERAL VIEW OF THE HISTORY OF THE ENGLISH BIBLE. Crown 8vo. 10s. 6d.

In the Introduction the author notices briefly the earliest vernacular versions of the Bible, especially those in Anglo-Saxon. Chapter I. is occupied with an account of the Manuscript English Bible from the 14th century downwards; and in Chapter II. is narrated, with many interesting personal and other details, the External History of the Printed Bible. In Chapter III. is set forth the Internal History of the English Bible, shewing to what extent the various English Translations were independent, and to what

Westcott (Dr. B. F.)—*continued.*

extent the translators were indebted to earlier English and foreign versions. In the Appendices, among other interesting and valuable matter, will be found "Specimens of the Earlier and Later Wycliffite Versions;" "Chronological List of Bibles;" "An Examination of Mr. Froude's History of the English Bible." The Pall Mall Gazette calls the work "A brief, scholarly, and, to a great extent, an original contribution to theological literature."

THE CHRISTIAN LIFE, MANIFOLD AND ONE.
Six Sermons preached in Peterborough Cathedral. Crown 8vo. 2s. 6d.

The Six Sermons contained in this volume are the first preached by the author as a Canon of Peterborough Cathedral. The subjects are:—I. "Life consecrated by the Ascension." II. "Many Gifts, One Spirit." III. "The Gospel of the Resurrection." IV. "Sufficiency of God." V. "Action the Test of Faith." VI. "Progress from the Confession of God." The Nonconformist calls them "Beautiful discourses, singularly devout and tender."

THE GOSPEL OF THE RESURRECTION. Thoughts
on its Relation to Reason and History. New Edition. Fcap. 8vo. 4s. 6d.

The present Essay is an endeavour to consider some of the elementary truths of Christianity, as a miraculous Revelation, from the side of History and Reason. The author endeavours to shew that a devout belief in the Life of Christ is quite compatible with a broad view of the course of human progress and a frank trust in the laws of our own minds. After a "Statement of the Question," and an Introduction on "Ideas of God, Nature, Miracles," Chapter I. treats of "The Resurrection and History;" Chapter II. "The Resurrection and Man;" Chapter III. "The Resurrection and the Church."—" We owe," the Patriot says, "Mr. Westcott a very great debt of gratitude for his very able little treatise, so faithful to the great truths which are so precious to us, so catholic and spiritual in its conceptions of these truths, and, moreover, so philosophical in analysis, organism, and presentation."

Wilkins.—THE LIGHT OF THE WORLD. An Essay, by A. S. WILKINS, M.A., Professor of Latin in Owens College, Manchester. Second Edition. Crown 8vo. 3s. 6d.

This is the Hulsean Prize Essay for 1869. The subject proposed by the Trustees was, "The Distinctive Features of Christian as compared with Pagan Ethics." This the author treats in six chapters:—I. "The Object and Scope of the Discussion." II. and III. "Pagan Ethics—their Historical Development," and their Greatest Perfection." IV. V. and VI. "Christian Ethics —their Method," their Perfection," and their Power." The author has tried to show that the Christian ethics so far transcend the ethics of any or all of the Pagan systems in method, in purity and in power, as to compel us to assume for them an origin, differing in kind from the origin of any purely human system. "It would be difficult to praise too highly the spirit, the burden, the conclusions, or the scholarly finish of this beautiful Essay."—British Quarterly Review.

Wilson.—RELIGIO CHEMICI. With a Vignette beautifully engraved after a Design by Sir NOEL PATON. By GEORGE WILSON, M.D. Crown 8vo. 8s. 6d.

"George Wilson," says the Preface to this volume, "had it in his heart for many years to write a book corresponding to the Religio Medici *of Sir Thomas Browne, with the title* Religio Chemici. *Several of the Essays in this volume were intended to form chapters of it, but the health and leisure necessary to carry out his plans were never attainable, and thus fragments only of the designed work exist. These fragments, however, being in most cases like finished gems waiting to be set, some of them are now given in a collected form to his friends and the public." The Contents of the volume are:—"Chemistry and Natural Theology." "The Chemistry of the Stars; an Argument touching the Stars and their Inhabitants." "Chemical Final Causes; as illustrated by the presence of Phosphorus, Nitrogen, and Iron in the Higher Sentient Organisms." "Robert Boyle." "Wollaston." "Life and Discoveries of Dalton." "Thoughts on the Resurrection; an Address to Medical Students."—"A more fascinating volume," the* Spectator *says, "has seldom fallen into our hands."*

Wilson.—THE BIBLE STUDENT'S GUIDE TO THE MORE CORRECT UNDERSTANDING of the ENGLISH TRANSLATION OF THE OLD TESTAMENT, BY REFERENCE TO THE ORIGINAL HEBREW. By WILLIAM WILSON, D.D., Canon of Winchester. Second Edition, carefully revised. 4to. 25s.

" *The author believes that the present work is the nearest approach to a complete Concordance of every word in the original that has yet been made: and as a Concordance, it may be found of great use to the Bible student, while at the same time it serves the important object of furnishing the means of comparing synonymous words, and of eliciting their precise and distinctive meaning. The knowledge of the Hebrew language is not absolutely necessary to the profitable use of the work; and it is believed that many devout and accurate students of the Bible, entirely unacquainted with it, will derive great advantage from frequent reference to these pages." Introductory to the body of the work, the author gives a sketch of the Construction of Hebrew. The plan of the work is simple: every word occurring in the English Version is arranged alphabetically, and under it is given the Hebrew word or words, with a full explanation of their meaning, of which it is meant to be a translation, and a complete list of the passages where it occurs. Following the general work is a complete Hebrew and English Index, which is, in effect, a Hebrew-English Dictionary. Appended are copious examples of the Figure* Paronomasia, *which occurs so frequently in the Bible.*

Worship (The) of God and Fellowship among Men. Sermons on Public Worship. By Professor MAURICE, and others. Fcap. 8vo. 3s. 6d.

This volume consists of Six Sermons preached by various clergymen, and although not addressed specially to any class, were suggested by recent efforts to bring the members of the Working Class to our Churches. The preachers were—Professor Maurice, I. "Preaching, a Call to Worship." II. "The Bible, a Revelation of the Beginning and End of Worship." Rev. T. J. Rowsell, "Common Prayer, the Method of Worship." Rev. J. Ll. Davies,

I. "Baptism, an Admission to the Privilege of Worship." II. "The Sabbath Day, the Refreshment of Worship." Rev. D. J. Vaughan, "The Lord's Supper, the most Sacred Bond of Worship." "They are very suggestive to those who may have to prepare sermons, and well calculated to be lent amongst the more thoughtful parishioners."—Literary Churchman.

Yonge (Charlotte M.)—SCRIPTURE READINGS for SCHOOLS AND FAMILIES. By CHARLOTTE M. YONGE, Author of "The Heir of Redclyffe." Globe 8vo. 1s. 6d. With Comments. 3s. 6d.

A SECOND SERIES. From Joshua to Solomon. Extra fcap. 8vo. 1s. 6d. With Comments. 3s. 6d.

Actual need has led the author to endeavour to prepare a reading book convenient for study with children, containing the very words of the Bible, with only a few expedient omissions, and arranged in Lessons of such length as by experience she has found to suit with children's ordinary power of accurate attentive interest. The verse form has been retained because of its convenience for children reading in class, and as more resembling their Bibles; but the poetical portions have been given in their lines. When Psalms or portions from the Prophets illustrate or fall in with the narrative, they are given in their chronological sequence. The Scripture portion, with a very few notes explanatory of mere words, is bound up apart to be used by children, while the same is also supplied with a brief comment, the purpose of which is either to assist the teacher in explaining the lesson, or to be used by more advanced young people to whom it may not be possible to give access to the authorities whence it has been taken. Professor Huxley at a meeting of the London School-board, particularly mentioned the Selection made by Miss Yonge, as an example of how selections might be made for School reading. "Her Comments are models of their kind."—Literary Churchman.

In crown 8vo. cloth extra, Illustrated, price 4*s.* 6*d.* each Volume ; also kept in morocco and calf bindings at moderate prices, and in Ornamental Boxes containing Four Vols., 21*s.* each.

MACMILLAN'S SUNDAY LIBRARY.

A Series of Original Works by Eminent Authors.

The projectors of the Sunday Library *feel that there is a want of books of a kind that will be welcome in many Households for reading on Sundays, and will be in accordance with earnest convictions as to the nature of the "Sabbath Day."*

Sunday should contain the theory, the collective view, of our work-day lives; and these work-days should be the Sunday in action.   Our Sunday Books, therefore, ought to do more than afford abstract subjects of meditation; they should exercise a living power, by bringing us into direct contact with all that is true and noble in human nature and human life, and by shewing us the life of Christ as the central truth of humanity.

For Sunday reading, therefore, we need not only history, but history in its relation to Christianity; not only biography, but the lives of men who have consciously promoted the Christian religion—Christian heroes in art, in science, in divinity, and in social action.   The history of Christianity, permanent and progressive, is also the history of civilization, and from the growth of the latter we may be strengthened in the faith that the former will ultimately prevail throughout the whole world.

The Publishers have secured the co-operation of very eminent writers, a list of whom, with the works they undertake, is herewith given.

The Pupils of St. John the Divine.—By CHARLOTTE M. YONGE, Author of "The Heir of Redclyffe."

The author first gives a full sketch of the life and work of the Apostle himself, drawing the material from all the most trustworthy authorities, sacred and profane; then follow the lives of his immediate disciples, Ignatius, Quadratus, Polycarp, and others; which are succeeded by the lives of many of their pupils. The author then proceeds to sketch from their foundation the history of the many churches planted or superintended by St. John and his pupils, both in the East and West. In the last chapter is given an account of the present aspect of the Churches of St. John,—the Seven Churches of Asia mentioned in Revelations; also those of Athens, of Nîmes, of Lyons, and others in the West. Throughout the volume, much of early Church History is necessarily introduced, and details are given of the many persecutions to which Christianity was subjected during its struggling infancy. "Young and old will be equally refreshed and taught by these pages, in which nothing is dull, and nothing is far-fetched."—Churchman.

The Hermits.—By CANON KINGSLEY.

In the Introduction to this volume, Mr. Kingsley shews that early hermit-life was a natural outcome of the corrupt condition of Roman society, "which was no place for honest men,"— "where but to think was to be full of sorrow and leaden-eyed despair." The hermits "were a school of philosophers who altered the whole current of human thought; their influence is being felt around us in many a puzzle—educational, social, and political;" these lives afford a "key to many a lock, which just now refuses to be tampered with or burst open." The volume contains the lives of some of the most remarkable early Egyptian, Syrian, Persian, and Western hermits. The lives are mostly translations from the original biographies; "the reader will thus be able to see the men as wholes, to judge of their merits and defects."—"It is from first to last a production full of interest, written with a liberal appreciation of what is

6

memorable for good in the lives of the Hermits, and with a wise forbearance towards legends which may be due to the ignorance, and, no doubt, also to the strong faith of the early chroniclers."—London Review.

Seekers after God.—By the Rev. F. W. FARRAR, M.A., F.R.S., Head Master of Marlborough College.

In this volume the author seeks to record the lives, and gives copious samples of the almost Christ-like utterances of, with perhaps the exception of Socrates, "the best and holiest characters presented to us in the records of antiquity." They are Seneca, Epictetus, and Marcus Aurelius, most appropriately called "Seekers after God," seeing that "amid infinite difficulties and surrounded by a corrupt society, they devoted themselves to the earnest search after those truths which might best make their lives 'beautiful before God.'" The reader will learn from this volume in what kind of atmosphere the influences of Christianity were forced to work. Many details are also given which afford an insight into Roman life and manners, the kind of education bestowed on Roman youth, and the characteristics of the chief systems of ancient philosophy. The volume contains portraits of Aurelius, Seneca, and Antoninus Pius. "We can heartily recommend it as healthy in tone, instructive, interesting, mentally and spiritually stimulating and nutritious."—Nonconformist.

England's Antiphon.—By GEORGE MACDONALD.

This volume deals chiefly with the lyric or song-form of English religious poetry, other kinds, however, being not infrequently introduced. The author has sought to trace the course of our religious poetry from the 13th to the 19th centuries, from before Chaucer to Tennyson. He endeavours to accomplish his object by selecting the men who have produced the finest religious poetry, setting forth the circumstances in which they were placed, characterising the men themselves, critically estimating their productions, and giving ample specimens of their best religious lyrics, and quotations from larger poems, illustrating the religious feeling of the poets or their times. Thus the volume, besides providing a concert of the sweetest and purest music, will be found to exhibit the beliefs held and aspirations cherished by many of the noblest, purest, and most richly endowed minds during the last 600 years. —"Dr. Macdonald has very successfully endeavoured to bring together in his little book a whole series of the sweet singers of England, and makes them raise, one after the other, their voices in praise of God."—Guardian.

Great Christians of France : ST. LOUIS and CALVIN. By M. GUIZOT.

From among French Catholics, M. Guizot has, in this volume, selected Louis, King of France in the 13th century, and among Protestants, Calvin the Reformer in the 16th century, "as two earnest and illustrious representatives of the Christian faith and life, as well as of the loftiest thought and purest morality of their country and generation." In setting forth with considerable fulness the lives of these prominent and representative Christian men, M. Guizot necessarily introduces much of the political and religious history of the periods during which they lived. "A very interesting book," says the Guardian.

Christian Singers of Germany. — By CATHERINE WINKWORTH.

In this volume the authoress gives an account of the principal hymn-writers of Germany from the 9th to the 19th century, introducing ample (altogether about 120 translations) specimens from their best productions. In the translations, while the English is perfectly idiomatic and harmonious, the characteristic differences of the poems have been carefully imitated, and the general style and metre retained. The book is divided into chapters, the writers noticed and the hymns quoted in each chapter, being representative of an epoch in the religious life of Germany. In thus tracing the course of German hymnology, the authoress is necessarily "*brought into contact with those great movements which have stirred the life of the people.*"—"*Miss Winkworth's volume of this series is, according to our view, the choicest production of her pen.*" —British Quarterly Review.

Apostles of Mediæval Europe.—By the Rev. G. F. MACLEAR, D.D., Head Master of King's College School, London.

In two Introductory Chapters the author notices some of the chief characteristics of the mediæval period itself; gives a graphic sketch of the devastated state of Europe at the beginning of that period, and an interesting account of the religions of the three great groups of vigorous barbarians—the Celts, the Teutons, and the Sclaves—who had, wave after wave, overflowed its surface. He then proceeds to sketch the lives and work of the chief of the courageous men who devoted themselves to the stupendous task of their conversion and civilization, during a period extending from the 5th to the 13th century; such as St. Patrick, St. Columba, St. Columbanus, St. Augustine of Canterbury, St. Boniface, St. Olaf, St. Cyril, Raymond Sull, and others. In narrating the lives of these men, many glimpses are given into the political, social, and religious life of Europe during the Middle Ages, and many interesting and instructive incidents are introduced. "Mr. Maclear will have done a great work if his admirable little volume shall help to break up the dense ignorance which is still prevailing among people at large."—Literary Churchman.

Alfred the Great.—By THOMAS HUGHES, M.P., Author of "Tom Brown's School Days."

"*The time is come when we English can no longer stand by as interested spectators only, but in which every one of our institutions will be sifted with rigour, and will have to shew cause for its existence. . . . As a help in this search, this life of the typical English King is here offered." After two Introductory Chapters, one on Kings and Kingship, and another depicting the condition of Wessex when Alfred became its ruler, the author proceeds to set forth the life and work of this great prince, shewing how he*

conducted himself in all the relations of life. In the last
chapter the author shews the bearing which Christianity has on the
kingship and government of the nations and people of the world in
which we live. Besides other illustrations in the volume, a Map of
England is prefixed, shewing its divisions about 1000 A.D., as well
as at the present time. "Mr. Hughes has indeed written a good
book, bright and readable we need hardly say, and of a very considerable historical value."—Spectator.

Nations Around.—By Miss A. KEARY.

*This volume contains many details concerning the social and political
life, the religion, the superstitions, the literature, the architecture,
the commerce, the industry, of the Nations around Palestine, an
acquaintance with which is necessary in order to a clear and full
understanding of the history of the Hebrew people. The authoress
has brought to her aid all the most recent investigations into the
early history of these nations, referring frequently to the fruitful
excavations which have brought to light the ruins and hieroglyphic
writings of many of their buried cities. "Miss Keary has skil-
fully availed herself of the opportunity to write a pleasing and instructive book."—Guardian. "A valuable and interesting volume."*
—Illustrated Times.

St. Anselm.—By the Very Rev. R. W. CHURCH, M.A., Dean
of St. Paul's.

*In this biography of St. Anselm, while the story of his life as a
man, a Christian, a clergyman, and a politician, is told impartially and fully, much light is shed on the ecclesiastical and
political history of the time during which he lived, and on the
internal economy of the monastic establishments of the period.
Of the worthiness of St. Anselm to have his life recorded, Mr.
Church says, " It would not be easy to find one who so joined the
largeness and daring of a powerful and inquiring intellect, with
the graces and sweetness and unselfishness of the most loveable of
friends, and with the fortitude, clear-sightedness, and dauntless*

9 783742 815897